SOCIOLOGICAL REVIEW MONOGRAPH 30

Urban Social Research:
Problems and Prospects

Sociological Review

Managing Editors: John Eggleston, Ronald Frankenberg,
                    Gordon Fyfe, Gabriel Newfield
University of Keele

Editorial Board

J. A. Banks
University of Leicester

G. Fyfe
University of Keele

L. Baric
University of Salford

M. Harrison (Chairman)
University of Keele

P. Bourdieu
Centre de Sociologie Européenne,
Paris

M. Jeffreys
Bedford College, London

S. Cohen
Hebrew University, Jerusalem

J. G. H. Newfield
Hatfield Polytechnic

S. J. Eggleston
University of Keele

W. M. Williams
University College, Swansea

SOCIOLOGICAL REVIEW MONOGRAPH 30

Urban Social Research: Problems and Prospects

Edited by Valdo Pons and Ray Francis

Routledge & Kegan Paul
London, Boston, Melbourne and Henley

First published in 1983
by Routledge & Kegan Paul plc
39 Store Street, London WC1E 7DD,
9 Park Street, Boston, Mass. 02108, USA,
296 Beaconsfield Parade, Middle Park,
Melbourne 3206, Australia, and
Broadway House, Newtown Road,
Henley-on-Thames, Oxon RG9 1EN
Printed in Great Britain by
Billing & Sons, Worcester
© The Sociological Review 1983
Library of Congress Cataloging in Publication Data
Main entry under title:
Urban social research
  (Sociological review monograph: 30)
  1. Municipal research—Great Britain—Addresses, essays, lectures.
  2. Sociology, Urban—Research—Addresses, essays, lectures.
  I. Pons, Valdo   II. Francis, Ray.   III. Series.
  HM15.S545   no. 30   [HT110]   301s   [307.7'64'072]   83-9459
  ISBN 0-7100-9471-X (US)

Contents

Contributors

Andrew Cox
Department of Politics, University of Hull

Ray Francis
Department of Sociology and Social Anthropology, University of Hull

David T. Herbert
Department of Geography, University College of Swansea

Elizabeth Lebas
School of Architecture, The Architectural Association, London

J. R. Mellor
Department of Sociology, University of Manchester

Valdo Pons
Department of Sociology and Social Anthropology, University of Hull

Ian Proctor
Department of Sociology, University of Warwick

E. J. Reade
Department of Town and Country Planning, University of Manchester

Preface

Six of the seven essays in this volume were first read at a conference held in the Department of Sociology and Social Anthropology at Hull University in 1979. Two of the six papers—by Elizabeth Lebas and Ray Francis—were extensively rewritten following discussion at the conference. We wish to thank all who participated in the conference. We are also especially indebted to David Herbert who later wrote the seventh paper on request to complement the conference papers for publication and we gratefully acknowledge the support of the editorial board of the *Sociological Review* in the preparation of this publication.

Valdo Pons
Ray Francis

Editors' introduction

Valdo Pons and Ray Francis

This collection of essays aims to clarify and explore some of the implications and consequences for specifically sociological research of the considerable volume of writing by both sociologists and non-sociologists in the broad field of 'urban studies' over the past decade. The nature and scope of 'urban sociology' in Britain is, and has been, the subject of repeated self-criticism by its practitioners. [1] As a recent example, we may cite Ray Pahl's complaint that much of the work conducted in the 1970s is 'curiously disembodied' in character, an assessment which, he suggests, may be accounted for partly by the paucity of 'detailed, empirical work which would show the interconnections between "public issues and private troubles" in the phrase of C. Wright Mills', and partly by 'the lack of any clear methodology which would link macro and micro analysis'. [2] We agree with the general line of Pahl's comments, but we would stress, as Francis does in his paper in this volume, that the malaise felt by 'urban sociologists' about the definition of their field, as well as about their uncertain position in the ranks of scholars interested in urban problems, has a long history stretching back to well before the 1970s. This kind of malaise is endemic and its source needs to be understood if we are to stimulate more relevant debate and research in the 1980s. It is difficult to see, for example, how some of the indisputably important developments that have occurred in British urban studies can be adequately developed without a great deal of contingent research. [3] But we rather doubt that such work will be undertaken unless the present intellectual and political context of 'urban sociology' changes.

We certainly endorse Pahl's view that there has been too little concern to develop empirical projects that might demonstrate the connections between different levels of social organization and differing perceptions of social, economic, and political problems. In general, there is a serious dearth of sound, detailed, and sophisticated

1

empirical studies. In particular, we would argue for the need for more purposeful community and ethnographic studies, and we see no reason why these should be characterized—in the way that some writers do—as 'anthropological' in style, content, and relevance. But how and why did this position arise? The short answer is simply that in the current climate of sociology—including 'urban sociology'—the relevance and status of observation, description, and analysis has been played down in favour of so-called theoretical discourse. As a result, postgraduate students and other young researchers have not been sufficiently stimulated or encouraged to conduct thorough and sensitive empirical work. If the present intellectual climate continues, it is in our view unlikely that urban sociologists will produce analyses of the kind and quality which are taken as a matter of course in sister disciplines such as social anthropology and geography.

To the extent that we are correct in this view, and it does seem to be widely shared, the question as to why there is comparatively little significant empirical research in our field can to a large extent be answered by pointing to the key debates which have preoccupied general sociology in Britain in the recent past. While a short list drawn up by two sociologists is of course likely to be challenged in some particulars by others, there would probably be a good measure of agreement that the mainstream of British sociological thought over the past decade has developed around the following set of interrelated problems and areas: (a) epistemology and method, (b) the nineteenth-century origins of sociology, (c) the analysis of social development and transformation, (d) the status of social science as critique,[4] and (e) the institutional unity and coherence of sociology itself.[5]

The problems of British 'urban sociology' are thus not simply that its recent work is 'curiously disembodied', as Pahl puts it, or that there is a paucity of empirical research, but also that those who *are* inclined to pursue such work have to struggle in a sociological milieu in which the theoretical and conceptual relevance of their work is not immediately or readily apparent. In looking at much contemporary 'urban sociology', we are reminded of Sorokin's 'fads and foibles effect' of 'rejection by reversal', that is, of the tendency for those who are in hectic pursuit of new ideas and alternative perspectives to ignore what was relevant in earlier work and to posit too radical a break with the past.[6] It seems to us that some critics overplay the backwardness, the isolation and the fragmentary nature of 'urban sociology', and that they perhaps do this partly in an effort to meet inherited problems and ambiguities and partly to combat their own sense of marginality.

We, for our part, are much less concerned to establish a definitive subject matter for 'urban sociology' as an independent and legitimate field of study in its own right than to locate the central concerns of sociology within the development of 'urban studies' and the social sciences in general. We thus hope that this collection of essays may serve to stress the *appreciation* of past and present work, rather than necessarily to correct or redefine it. We are concerned to argue for the *diversity* required in 'urban sociological' research, rather than to press for particular types and forms of research. And we wish to remind colleagues of the *complexity* of our field of study while at the same time stressing the problems inherent in simplifying knowledge and the objects of that knowledge.

There is much to admire and welcome in contemporary British urban studies. Instead of simply regretting the relative absence of certain topics and types of empirical work, we should devote attention to the nature of the work that is done and make suggestions for its integration and development. This, essentially, is what we hope the papers in this collection may help to do. We believe that, individually and collectively, the papers can be used to forge links both within 'urban sociology' itself and between various disciplines concerned with urbanization and urban problems. These essays constitute a plea and a set of suggestions for wide-ranging and more sophisticated research activity. They look both backwards and forwards, and they all move in varying degrees from overview and review to problems and prospects.

While each paper warrants attention in its own right, much can be gained by exploring the points of convergence and divergence among them. Thus, for example, the issues raised by Elizabeth Lebas in the first paper reverberate throughout the discussions of Cox, Mellor, Proctor, Francis, and Herbert. In this paper, Lebas provides a timely and cogent assessment of the development of French Marxist urban research and its reception in Britain. The question, 'Why is a theory of the state important for understanding capitalist urban development?' is used (a) to trace the intellectual origins and political context of French Marxist urban research over the last decade, and (b) to outline some of the problems associated with the utility for urban research of the conception of the state embedded in the State Monopoly Capitalist thesis. Of particular interest is the way the work of Jean Lojkine is singled out as worthy of much closer attention than it has hitherto received. As Lebas sees it, British urban research workers have accepted the relevance of the question, but have not yet come to grips with it in the context of their own intellectual and political interests.

The contribution from Andrew Cox focuses on the role of the state and of bureaucratic agencies in urban policy-making, in shaping urban form, and in the allocation of resources. An overview of the debate on the role of the state in urban change provides his foundation for a critique of both structuralist and instrumentalist approaches. The discussion is developed around an assessment of Castells's explanation of the origins of the New Towns policy in Britain [7] and of instrumentalist Marxist accounts of Britain's inner city policy reappraisals of the 1970s. Cox's conclusions relate quite directly to the issues raised by Lebas, while the conflicts of the summer of 1981 and their aftermath give added importance to the issues, debates, and problems which he discusses.

Rosemary Mellor's paper is concerned to re-emphasize and substantiate the theoretical, methodological, and empirical relevance of regional questions for the study of urbanization. The paper provides a critical evaluation of the most prominent theories of spatially uneven development—'colonialism', 'dependency', 'underdevelopment', 'imperialist overdevelopment', 'capitalist concentration', and 'central place theory'. All assume that the metropolis is a unique environment for social transactions and social control, but without ever establishing the content of this centrality. Mellor stresses that the study of regionalism is important because it requires, and calls for, analyses to explain the pull of urban centres as well as the vitality of local identification in the modern state.

Ian Proctor sets out to develop a framework for the analysis of the urbanization of British society under capitalist industrialism. He argues that much of the work on this problem displays a lack of appreciation of the different levels of spatial structuring of social institutions and of the complexity of their interrelationships. One consequence has been that various levels have been reified, e.g. 'the community', 'the city', 'the national polity-economy'. The central argument of Proctor's paper is that we need to focus on the historically specific organization of social institutions in space in terms of factors which operate within the various units ('horizontal') and between different levels ('vertical') taken for urban analysis.

The paper by Ray Francis was prompted by an original interest in urban imagery and symbolism, but his central concern is to stress the need for studies on that rather narrow and highly specialized front to be informed by, and incorporated into, a much wider set of issues and perspectives. He queries the value of studies of imagery and symbolism that are not related to the overall problem of the study of social and cultural organization. He is thus led to raise major issues about the study of urban society in general.

The main topic of Eric Reade's paper is the curious separation of 'urban sociology' and town planning in Britain. The origins, nature, and extent of this gulf are traced and discussed. Reade is concerned to outline the epistemological, methodological, and institutional precon-ditions for a more fruitful, rational, and relevant collaboration between these two fields in the future. He concludes his paper with some pithy comments on the notion of relevant research—past, present and future—in both 'urban sociology' and town planning. The issues and problems raised here are of special significance in the current economic situation and political climate.

David Herbert's contribution traces the major theoretical, metho-dological, and substantive changes that have taken place in British urban geography since the early 1960s. The paper highlights important points of convergence and divergence between geographers on the one hand, and sociologists, economists, psychologists, and political scientists on the other. The section entitled 'A new framework for urban geographical study' merits close attention and careful development. The relevance of David Harvey's call for a 'geographical imagination' to complement a 'sociological imagination' is very clearly and amply demonstrated. [8]

At the conference which was the source of this collection of papers we did not attempt to direct the attention of authors along particular lines or to cover the whole varied field of 'urban sociology'. Our primary aim was to provide a forum for the exploration and discussion of some general themes and problems which pervade urban studies, sociological or otherwise. Thus the present collection of papers is clearly not a comprehensive stock-taking of 'British urban sociology today'. It may, therefore, be helpful to students using this volume as a text to draw attention to a few recent works which cover topics that are either not touched upon, or are insufficiently dealt with, here. The main areas of study from this point of view can be referred to under the crude labels of 'urban politics', 'inner city problems', 'policy and planning', and 'race relations'.

Acting as a corrective to many years of relative neglect, and as a response to recent theoretical developments, the study of urban politics has recently become a central focus. Saunders [9] and Dunleavy [10] take up themes and issues which closely parallel several discussed in this collection and both merit a place on any list of compulsory readings. Among the more stimulating and interesting collections of papers in this area are those edited by Young [11] and Newton. [12]

The issues, problems, and conflicts that beset Britain's inner city areas have taken on pressing relevance. Among the many publications on these special problems, we would direct the reader's attention to the collections edited by Jones, and by Loney and Allen, as well as to the thorough discussion provided by Lawless. [13] Of particular relevance, too, is the final report of the Social Science Research Council's Inner City Working Party, edited by Hall. [14] The concluding chapter of this report is in our view likely to form the basis of research on inner city problems for some years to come.

The issues specifically related to policy-making and planning have only been dealt with tangentially in this collection, but they constitute a basic and continuing area of concern, debate, and research. The collection of papers edited by Stewart [15] remains essential reading here. Among more recent publications, those by Kirk, [16] Donnison, [17] and especially Ashford, [18] merit special attention.

It is quite impossible to divorce 'race studies' from 'urban studies' in the intellectual and political growth and context of British sociology. The points of intersection and convergence are manifold. The publications in this area are multiplying rapidly, but Rex and Tomlinson [19] and Pryce [20] are of special relevance, the latter being one of the most stimulating and interesting ethnographic studies of recent years. Also worthy of close attention is the final report of the Policy Studies Institute, [21] undertaken for the Home Office Research Unit, which focuses on the local implementation of central government policies relating to racial disadvantage.

Finally, we would refer to three recent edited collections of essays which should prove particularly helpful in placing the papers in this volume in an appropriate overall perspective. Taken together, these three publications give a fairly representative profile of contemporary British urban studies. The first is an important collection edited by Michael Harloe under the title *New Perspectives in Urban Change and Conflict*; [22] the second, edited by Michael Harloe and Elizabeth Lebas is, as its title of *City, Class and Conflict* [23] suggests, primarily concerned with recent developments in the political economy of cities and regions; and the third, edited by Andrew Blowers *et al.* under the title *Urban Change and Conflict: An Interdisciplinary Reader*, [24] is a very comprehensive collection of papers covering a wide range of issues and perspectives.

The above references are selected from a much larger body of recent work, for there is at the present time a veritable efflorescence of writings on British urbanization and 'urban problems'. To our minds, however, a careful reading of this burgeoning literature serves to reinforce, rather than to answer, the kinds of problems to which the papers in this volume address themselves. The field is far from static and it does not reside securely in any one discipline. The impact of the developments and the shifts to which we have drawn attention cannot yet be seen with full clarity. We hope that the following essays may help anyone trying to grapple with the recent literature and its consequences for British urban studies and 'urban sociology' in particular.

Notes

1 We use inverted commas in referring to the field of study known as 'urban sociology', because its boundaries are porous and the label itself has often been the topic of heated debate.
2 R. E. Pahl, 'Employment, work and the domestic division of labour', *International Journal of Urban and Regional Research*, vol. 4, no. 1, 1980, p. 1.
3 See, for example, the basic research called for if we want to pursue topics discussed in the following: C. G. Pickvance, 'On the study of urban social movements', in C. G. Pickvance (ed.), *Urban Sociology: Critical Essays*, Tavistock, London, 1976; C. G. Pickvance, 'Theories of the state and theories of urban crisis', *Current Perspectives in Social Theory*, vol. X, 1980, pp. 31-54; and P. Dunleavy, *Urban Political Analysis*, Macmillan, London, 1980.
4 A. Giddens, 'Introduction: Some issues in the social sciences today', in A. Giddens, *Studies in Social and Political Theory*, Hutchinson, London, 1977.
5 J. Urry, 'Sociology as parasite: Some vices and virtues', in P. Abrams, R. Deem, J. Finch and P. Rock (eds), *Practice and Progress: British Sociology 1950-1980*, Allen & Unwin, London, 1981.
6 P. Sorokin, *Fads and Foibles in Modern Sociology*, Regneys, New York, 1956.
7 Manuel Castells, *The Urban Question: A Marxist Approach*, Edward Arnold, London, 1977.
8 David Harvey, *Social Justice and the City*, Edward Arnold, London, 1973, p. 24.
9 P. Saunders, *Urban Politics: A Sociological Interpretation*, Hutchinson, London, 1979.
10 P. Dunleavy, *Urban Political Analysis*, Macmillan, London, 1980.
11 K. Young (ed.), *Essays on the Study of Urban Politics*, Macmillan, London, 1975.
12 K. Newton (ed.), *Urban Political Economy*, Frances Pinter, London, 1981.
13 C. Jones (ed.), *Urban Deprivation and the Inner City*, Croom Helm, London, 1979; M. Loney and M. Allen (eds), *The Crisis of the Inner City*, Macmillan, London, 1979; P. Lawless, *Britain's Inner Cities:*

Problems and Policies, Harper & Row, London, 1981.

14 P. Hall (ed.), *The Inner City in Context*, Heinemann, London, 1981.

15 M. Stewart (ed.), *The City: Problems of Planning*, Penguin, Harmondsworth, 1972.

16 G. Kirk, *Urban Planning in a Capitalist Society*, Croom Helm, London, 1980.

17 D. Donnison, *The Good City*, Heinemann, London, 1980.

18 D. E. Ashford, *British Dogmatism and French Pragmatism: Central-Local Policymaking in the Welfare State*, Allen & Unwin, London, 1982.

19 J. Rex and S. Tomlinson, *Colonial Immigrants in a British City: A Class Analysis*, Routledge & Kegan Paul, London, 1979.

20 K. Pryce, *Endless Pressure*, Penguin, Harmondsworth, 1979.

21 K. Young and N. Connelly, *Policy and Practice in the Multi-Racial City*, Policy Studies Institute No. 598, London, 1981.

22 M. Harloe (ed.), *New Perspectives in Urban Change and Conflict*, Heinemann, London, 1981.

23 M. Harloe and E. Lebas (eds), *City, Class and Conflict*, Edward Arnold, London, 1981.

24 A. Blowers, C. Brook, P. Dunleavy and L. Mc Dowell (eds), *Urban Change and Conflict: An Interdisciplinary Reader*, Harper & Row, London, 1982.

The state in British and French urban research, or the crisis of the urban question

Elizabeth Lebas

It is now almost a truism that a class conception of the state is integral to an understanding of capitalist urban development. In France, following a period of reorganisation and de-Stalinisation within the French Communist Party, such a conception, embodied in the State Monopoly Capital thesis, came after 1968 to dominate a whole body of urban research.[1] In Britain, a critical evaluation of Weberian approaches,[2] synchronised with the introduction of examples of French Marxist studies,[3] and confirmed by the observation of profound changes in the Welfare State, has given rise to urban writings which allude to and illustrate the role of a capitalist state based on a distinct form of exploitation and class divisions. For example, there are studies on forms of administrative corporatism,[4] local state shareholding,[5] landed property,[6] the class impact of urban renewal,[7] the privatisation of public housing,[8] as well as a rich literature arising out of researches by the Community Development Projects (CDPs).

Recognition, even application, are, however, not sufficient, either here or in France and we can, with the hindsight of a decade, observe some serious problems in the use of a Marxist theory of the state to order or influence urban research. We note that in France there has been an observable decline in references to a theory of the state as a means of explanation.[9] This, we shall see, relates not only to the internal limitations of a particular theory, but also to the relationship of a school of research to the state itself. In Britain, it would seem that problems are also structural, but that their intellectual and political origins are different.

British urban research has been both endowed and hampered by a long tradition of empiricism. In the early 1950s, one of its distinguished practitioners was to remark with some acerbity that its empiricism had failed to sustain the sense of social commitment which had characterised early urban research. [10] This sense of commitment was restored with the CDP studies, yet the introduction of a Marxist approach to the study of the capitalist state has failed to establish a set of problematics on the nature of urban development under British capitalism.

This absence may in part be explained by aspects of more properly theoretical Marxist writings on the state in Britain. One can sense a certain lack of conviction about the purpose of a *political* theory of the state. This has been expressed either in terms of the primacy of theoretical and epistemological purity, [11] or in terms of an academicism which has confounded theoretical reflection on the subject with the erection of self-enclosed typologies. [12] The influence of the capital logic school, while able to exercise some analyses of fiscal accountability, has not been very successful in explaining the *politics* of restructuration. [13] Civil society is reduced to a protracted saga between capitalists and workers; the subtleties of traditional tales having been conveniently omitted.

Moreover, these features are reflected in the limited availability and treatment of Marxist theoretical writings on the state. Notably, there are few original and indigenous contributions. The tradition set by Harold Laski and Ralph Miliband has, quite surprisingly, apart from promising critiques in the early 1970s, been left undeveloped. [14] We have relied on imports, few as they have been. The publication of essays from the German School [15] has been noteworthy, and in urban research, the work of Claus Offe has enjoyed some reflection. [16] But in what concerns us here—French state theory and its concrete application—we argue that the imports have been narrowly and apolitically appropriated. This, we think, is symptomatic of present difficulties in urban research in Britain. These difficulties have been compounded by a concerted attack by the state on social research in general and urban research in particular, and they have become more urgent by the present dismantling of the Welfare State.

The aim of this essay is an attempt to evaluate how a Marxist conception of the state has so far fared in British urban sociological research, and to compare its reception here with some of the reasons for its waning influence in French urban studies. We hope to overcome a simple and negative criticism and to address ourselves to the underlying question, 'Why is a theory of the state important for understanding capitalist urban development?' This question is not as redundant as it may appear for we know that the reproductive aspects of state intervention can be abstracted from a class theory of the state; moreover, it is possible that an understanding of the state in itself is not sufficient for an understanding of capitalism as a generalised historical relation. [17]

Two approaches are possible and, ideally, complementary. The first concerns the structure, and the condition of production, of research, as well as the distribution of research findings. Not long ago, researchers used to complain of exhortations to 'applicability' and 'policy relevance'; now, the very means of their livelihood is at stake. This approach, while essential, goes beyond the scope of this paper. We can only allude to it within a second approach whose focus here is extremely circumscribed. In this approach we lay ourselves open to well-founded criticisms of 'bookishness' for its own sake, and logically, of irrelevance. For what we hope to accomplish is little more than to illustrate the reception of French urban state theory in *some* British writings, and in turn, to examine the origins of this theory and its evolution in *some* French writings. It is not possible here to attempt a full retrospective review of both literatures.

None the less, we hope that our illustrations and comments will serve to point to gains and losses and to certain promising directions. It may be useful to keep in mind the admirable words of a now unfashionable writer, Harold Laski, writing in 1937: 'No theory of the state is ever intelligible, save in the context of its time. What men think of the state is the outcome always of the experiences in which they are immersed.' [18]

The French influence

The appearance in translation of French Marxist urban writings in the early 1970s followed a period of theoretical reconstruction in France from the mid-1960s. These essays reached Britain at a time when Althusserian structuralism was receiving much attention and when British urbanists were confronted by a method of thinking and a style of writing which was far removed from their Weberianism. Despite some reticence, there was a ready recognition that these essays and the questions they raised could not be ignored. [19] There duly followed a period of appropriation and criticism of these ideas.

We can detect three types of influence brought to bear on British urban studies by the French literature. The first simply led some authors to take sides: *against* vulgar Weberianism and relentless empiricism, and *for* political involvement and the *right* to hold a Marxist perspective; the second was towards the incorporation into general analyses of selected constructs; and the third found expression in didactic and theoretical statements which included the comparative assessment of certain urban problematics and their implications for a concept of 'urban' specificity.

A recent study of council housing policies in Birmingham by Lambert, Paris and Blackaby [20] illustrates the first type of influence. The introductory chapter of this book is devoted to a rejection of Weberianism as it is found in British urban research in preference for a Marxist approach, especially as developed by Miliband and Castells. What follows, however, is a descriptive account of the effects of Birmingham Council's housing policies between 1971 and 1974 in four inner city areas, and this account remains largely within the tradition of urban research from which the authors are apparently seeking emancipation. Their conclusions, valid as they may be, remain wholly evidential and do not help to answer the questions which the authors themselves raise: Why is a housing shortage accepted as inevitable by council and clients alike? What structures these shortages? And why are such questions as these never articulated and debated? The authors' awareness of the political import of their approach (the notion of 'research action') is essentially moral ('taking the predatory aspect out of research') and they pay little attention to any Marxist theory and epistemology with political meaning.

The second type of influence stemming from French writings may be seen in the incorporation of constructs from the general problematic of 'urban social movements' elaborated by Castells. [21] The works of Dunleavy, [22] Pickvance, [23] and Lloyd [24] come to mind. But although criticisms of the problematic are pointed (its 'undirectionality', its inability to account for quiescence or right-wing mobilisation, its neglect of the role of the state in the management of urban social movements), the authors tend to take the problematic set by Castells at face value, and they do not consider its consequences for an overall class theory of political action. The criticisms do not discuss or challenge a salient aspect of Castells's problematic, namely, that 'urban social movements' are essentially empirical and political confirmations of the problematic of the 'urban' based on the distinction between production and consumption. Yet, if we review the evolution of this problematic in France, we can observe its decline on empirical, theoretical, and political grounds.

As stated above, Castells's conception of 'urban social movements' was integral to an epistemological distinction between the realms of production and consumption. But it also related to a Poulantzian conception of political processes. The political ('le politique') referred in Poulantzas to institutionalised and legal forms of political expression, while politics ('la politique') also has a legitimate use and could be taken to include more punctuated and uninstitutionalised struggles. Urban social movements were struggles lacking recognised legitimate institutional avenues and expressed in and around issues related to aspects of consumption in extended social reproduction.

Castells's contribution in politicising the entire analysis of capitalist urbanisation is vital and cannot be underestimated. Moreover, his problematic introduced the very important idea that modes of uninstitutionalised protest can reveal the underlying structures and ideological paraphernalia from effects emerging out of new developments in capital accumulation. His analysis of ecological movements, while preliminary, is such an example. [25] Yet his overall problematic encountered difficulties.

There are evidential problems in his work. Urban social movements are difficult to detect and classify. [26] Their popular basis and their absence of integration within recognised political ideologies and institutions is problematic. [27] Theoretically, the study of this phenomenon reveals the fundamental question of social needs. If urban social movements are movements expressing unfulfilled needs, what are these needs? How do they relate to the development of the social formation as a whole? What political, as opposed to economic, logic lies behind the state's provision or witholding of these needs? How does state action in this domain relate to complex institutions such as that of landed property? Finally, why are these needs often either privately satisfied or simply unexpressed? [28]

There are also problems with political implications. For example, Lojkine has argued that Castells's separation of consumption from production tends to reduce the urban crisis to a secondary contradiction within the circuit of capital. [29] Simply expressed, this contradiction is one between the demand for the socialisation of the means of consumption and the non-profitability of their provision under capitalism. This forced Castells to place the concept of urban social movements within a problematic defined wholly in consumption and urban terms, with the result that the working classes can no longer be seen as being in direct confrontation with capital, but are instead merged into an ensemble of popular classes. In his 1977 article in *La Pensée*, Lojkine declared with uncharacteristic acrimony that Castells's conceptualisation of urban social movements leads to a *'pluriclassiste'* notion of class alliance—'the same as that which is maintained by the Socialist Party's notion of "front de classe".' [30] While this attack could be attributed to a certain 'conjunctural' political nervousness, elsewhere Lojkine had also pointed out how Castells's notion of social change was akin to one of 'disturbance' arising from dissatisfaction with state policies of reproduction. [31] And in later works Lojkine went on to demonstrate the existence and specificity of a long and politically expressed tradition of working-class associations. It is, then, in this direction, namely of the study of working-class and also middle-class associations, that French research has developed.

In Britain, the problematic of urban social movements has not developed beyond a few discursive essays. To our knowledge, there have been no serious research projects in this field and there are no extensive published accounts of any urban social movements. [32] Yet the essays referred to represent virtually the only attempt to appropriate for active analysis concepts borrowed directly from the French urban literature. The study of Croydon politics by Saunders [33] is a post factum analysis which cannot be classified as neatly falling into the same category of work. Although the interest of the book lies in its tensions between empirical description and theoretical analysis, and between Weberianism and Marxism, there is only a faint recognition that theories of the state have precise and conjunctural contexts. Once generally located, the state remains neutral in its specificity. As we will point out when considering the third type of influence, there has in didactic British presentations of French work been all too little discussion of the theoretical origins and political meaning of the theory of the state, namely the state monopoly capital (SMC) thesis.

The third type of French influence is of particular interest because it, too, has attempted to convey an imported theoretical information. But in doing so, it has given only the most fleeting attention to the SMC thesis. An obvious reason is that this has been the thesis of a political party (Partie Communiste de France), whose British counterpart has not enjoyed the same membership and relevance among academics as in France. The neglect of the SMC thesis may be symptomatic of the difficulty in understanding the nature of Marxist theory and, as such, the difficulties of a Marxist comparative analysis. At a more immediate level which we only refer to in passing here, it has led to a basic confusion. This may have arisen, paradoxically, out of an attempt to clarify, although in this case classification may have been confused with clarification.

In the first part of his article entitled 'Marxist approaches to the study of urban politics: divergences among some recent French works', [34] Pickvance reviews a debate which engaged Lojkine and Poulantzas between 1972 and 1974. [35] We do not argue with Pickvance's outline of the debate, but we do criticise simplification, and his neglect to account for the thesis on the economic role of the state which is at the base of the differences in interpretation of its political role. The SMC thesis is referred to in a single sentence: 'The PCF view, embodied in the theory of the state monopoly capitalism, sees the state and the monopolies as fused in a single mechanism' (p. 224).

Pickvance does draw attention to the similarity of Poulantzas's and Lojkine's description of French capitalism, but he does not develop his observations into a questioning of why this is so, given the differences between them in explaining the political nature of state intervention. A brief description of the SMC thesis, outlining its conception of stages of economic maturation and its interpretation of the importance of the tendency of the rate of profit to fall, would have led to a discussion of some insights which are available in an article which Poulantzas wrote in the Spring issue of *Dialectiques*, 1976.[36] The differences which Pickvance does not elaborate in his typology are in part epistemological, but they are also based on a critical but common position.

It was over the concept of periodisation and the tendency for the rate of profit to fall that Poulantzas disagreed with the SMC thesis in *Dialectiques*. In the SMC thesis, periodisation is not only a means of distinguishing advanced capitalism from nineteenth-century competitive capitalism, but also a way of relating economic maturation with the development of consciousness. Poulantzas rejected the notion of periodisation on the basis of historicism: history is a process without a subject and there is no necessary connection between the development of productive forces and the consciousness of class agents. The tendency for the rate of profit to fall (TRPF) is central to the SMC thesis, because it is on this notion that explanations of state intervention rest. Simply, the state must intervene to counteract this ineluctable process. Now Poulantzas argued first that the TRPF could not be related *directly* to the *extraction* of surplus value (exploitation). It could only be *indirectly* related via the *distribution* of surplus value (profits) and, as such, was symptomatic of profound changes within relations of production and division of labour. In other words, the TRPF was an object of the class struggle, and state intervention in the form of a devalorisation of constant capital (which the SMC thesis advocated as its central role) could not counter the TRPF since the devalorisation of constant capital into public capital in no way 'neutralised' it or removed it from the enlarged reproduction of social capital. Not only did public capital continue to produce surplus value (i.e. continue to exploit), but it also continued to relate to the economic property of the capitalist class.

15

While the political consequences of Poulantzas's criticisms are clearly a rejection of the hope of nationalisation as preliminary to the overthrow of the state, he does not in the article reject the SMC thesis; and he is at pains to point out agreements on the nature of monopoly capital and the fact that the state is compelled to devalorise certain less profitable capital in its interest. Hence, one can deduce how Poulantzas and Lojkine arrive at a common *description* of capitalism in France. This degree of agreement, which belies Pickvance's simple classification, is also observable in *Monopolville*, where the authors concurrently use the SMC thesis to explain the behaviour of large firms 'implanting' in Dunkirk and Poulantzas's conception of class fraction and relative autonomy of the state to explain institutionalised political reactions to the impact of 'implantation'. [37]

In an article entitled 'Marxism, the state and the urban question: critical notes on two recent French theories', [38] Harloe compares the paradigms developed by Castells and Lojkine. Here again we do not question the usefulness of such an exercise, but we must point out that it fails to discuss the SMC thesis and that this leads to an important oversight. The SMC thesis is only mentioned in terms of its analogy to Baran and Sweezy's conception of the dominance of monopoly capital. [39]

The analogy is unfortunate because it confuses appearance for essence, and as such ignores a central distinction between much of American Marxist urban research and its French counterpart. Both Baran and Sweezy and the SMC thesis emphasise the importance of the processes of accumulation and overaccumulation to explain the TRPF. However, while Baran and Sweezy stress the profit *motives* and what they term 'the tendency of surplus to *rise*', [40] the SMC thesis dwells on the tendency of the rate of profit to *fall*; the first locates the control of overaccumulation in the realms of consumption and circulation, the latter in the devalorisation of capital and the development of productive forces. Both theories attribute importance to the necessity of innovation, but for Baran and Sweezy this is generated through the 'sales effort' and the market penetration of needs, while in the SMC thesis it is encompassed by the technological development of productive forces and the non-marketing of certain needs. In the latter, these needs refer to the reproduction of labour as variable capital, and state intervention in this domain is a form of devalorisation.

These differences have implications for urban sociological research. For Baran and Sweezy, state intervention consists of fostering private consumption and containing socialised consumption. This has implications for the treatment of the unemployed or unemployable sections of the population. It is not their labour power which is vital, but their buying power. As O'Connor points out in *The Fiscal Crisis of the State*, one contributing aspect of the crisis is the cost of maintaining this buying power in the form of welfare payments. [41] The SMC thesis on the other hand, because it emphasises the development of productive forces, sees increasing exploitation, and thus employment, as the central means of counteracting the TRPF. In this sense, it has difficulty in developing a problematic of unemployment, and French urban (and regional) research has thus far given little attention to this issue.

The foregoing would suggest that there is a case for examining a little more closely the SMC thesis, particularly in view of the way its critique and its changing political status have had repercussions in the evolution of French urban research. We will have to limit ourselves to a brief discussion of the work of Paul Boccara and to using the writings of Jean Lojkine by way of illustration.

Notes on the state monopoly capital thesis

Before approaching the main elements of the SMC thesis, a few points must be stressed. Firstly, as expressed in the writings of Boccara, [42] the thesis has evolved continuously and critically within the PCF since his first series of articles in *Economie et Politique* in 1961. However, its most direct precursor was much earlier, dating from Eugene Varga's 1934 text entitled *The Economic, Social and Political Crisis*. The defeat of the PCF in the 1978 elections has seriously undermined the thesis. Secondly, Boccara only states the thesis in bare outline; its main relevance can be seen in its application by Lojkine, J.-P. Delilez, P. Herzog, F. Hincker, [43] and others. Thirdly, it is not a political theory of the state but an economic theory of state intervention under advanced capitalism.

This last point explains why an interpretation of the relation between state and capital is subsumed under other more important elements of the thesis. These include, first and foremost, a conception of overaccumulation in relation to devalorisation, as well as a conception of long-cycle fluctuations in relation to what is termed 'technical transformation'. The concept of the periodisation of capitalist modes of production acts as a kind of epistemological and political umbrella to account for major changes in the behaviour of capital and in the consciousness of the proletariat.

The most important theoretical source for Boccara's work is the analysis of absolute and relative overaccumulation which appears in Chapter XV, Volume III of Marx's *Collected Works*. Sections II and III are particularly important for Boccara, as it is in Marx's discussion of the expansion of capital and the production of surplus value that the problem of 'excess capital and excess population' is approached in terms of capitalism needing to arrive at 'modes of settlement' which will enable the redistribution of the production of surplus value. This problem, identified but not developed by Marx, becomes the first facet of Boccara's theory of devalorisation. The theory is developed in terms of what can best be understood as the second stage of Marx's explanation for the tendency of the rate of profit to fall. The second part of Marx's explanation emphasises how the increase of accumulation of capital as *mass* is related to a fall in the rate of profit which not only eliminates the plethora of small capitalists, but also prevents the formation of new independent capital, in turn, leading to overproduction and surplus capital. [44] This overaccumulation is defined in relational terms, as an extreme condition, *absolute* overaccumulation to which a relative condition, *relative* accumulation refers.

Absolute accumulation is defined thus: [45]

> There would be absolute over-production of capital as soon as additional capital for purposes of capitalist production $= 0$.... As soon as capital would therefore have grown in such a ratio to the labouring population that neither the absolute working-time supplied by the population, nor the relative surplus working-time could be expanded any further....

But, in actual fact, overaccumulation is relative in that [46]

> it would appear that a portion of capital would lie completely or partially idle (because it would have to crowd out some of the active capital before it could expand its own value), and the other portion would produce values at a lower rate of profit, owing to the pressure of unemployment or partly employed capital.

Relative overaccumulation necessarily involves conflict between 'portions of' capital struggling to counter the TRPF. This can be partially resolved through competition and the export of capital, but the substitution of new for old capital lying idle must involve a 'mode of settlement'. This settlement can, moreover, only bring about a temporary resolution, for in the long run the absolute development of productive forces continually comes into conflict with the conditions of production. [47]

The theme of 'mode of settlement' characterising the competitive stage is picked up by Boccara and reinterpreted as state intervention under advanced capitalism. He *hypothesises* that one form of intervention is the 'de-capitalisation' or devalorisation (mainly via public financing) of certain productive capital which, while unprofitable, is essential to the maintenance or growth of other fractions of total social capital. This devalorisation necessarily means that only the strongest capital (monopoly capital) determines, with the assistance of the state, the public programme. It is this public programme which constitutes the descriptive outline of SMC, and it includes the following measures:

the public financing of accumulation and private production;

the public financing of certain means of consumption and services, these being separated into two types of expenditures:

i) parasitical and 'domination' expenditure (e.g. army and police);

ii) expenses for the development of productive forces (e.g. housing) in the interest of capital, but as a result of popular pressures;

state appropriation of revenues and increased intervention in financial circuits;

elaboration of plans and a general 'public programming' denoting the co-ordination of state intervention;

increased state support of capital and commodity exports.

These features outlining the state's relation to large and/or essential capital make up the essence of the thesis. It is immediately apparent that this opens up a very wide arena for interpretations of the relations not only of monopoly capital to the state, but also of this to other capital, its agents, and the masses of the population owning no capital.

Two things are surprising and must be referred to. The first is how the crudity of this outline appealed to urban researchers despite the fact that in the field they continually encountered exceptions to this instrumental and rational view of state intervention. At one point, the thesis did cease to appeal. Yet, and this is the second surprise, the unidirectionality of intervention ('the state never withdraws once committed') has attracted very little reflection and discussion. [48]

It could be argued that what has continued to influence researchers in France, partly because it can be integrated with other paradigms, is Boccara's understanding or highlighting of the relationship between long-cycle fluctuations and technical change. At the heart of the relation between long-cycle fluctuations and technical change, lies a contradiction which is central to capitalism. This is the contradiction between the development of productive forces and the relations of production. Each crisis leads to a further concentration of productive forces which entails technological innovations. In turn, these innovations imply a transformation of the conditions of production into general and social conditions which are increasingly common. But the generalisation of conditions of production also produces their polarisation—between skills, between intellectual and manual labour, between the employed and the unemployed. For Boccara, this generalisation of conditions of production not only means the increasing proletarianisation of non-capital owning classes and the appearance of social needs which 'outstrip' the capital relation, but also a socialisation of the work force whose costs grow disproportionately in relation to the profits that can be derived from the continuous application of innovative methods of management and technology.

Despite highlighting this particular and fundamental issue, Boccara still saw 'technicism' as a central means of emancipation from capitalist relations of production in the transition to socialism. But it was not this optimistic conception of technology which influenced researchers such as Bleitrach and Chenu. [49] What Boccara may have done was to remind them of the importance of the technical composition of capital for understanding the relations not only abstractly, between accumulation and technical division of labour, but concretely, between the technical divisions of labour embodied in the labour process, and their relations to a discipline of daily life.

These few notes on the SMC thesis may be useful for understanding its effect on French urban research. They can be reduced simply to this: on the one hand, the thesis, with its notion of a 'single mechanism between state and monopoly capital', could not provide a political theory of the state; on the other hand, it ensured that a political understanding of the state, and through it urban development, was ultimately to rest on either an allusion to, or even an analysis of, capitalist relations of production.

The place of the state monopoly capital thesis: an example in French urban research

The SMC thesis as a theory of the state in its relations to advanced capital, as opposed to either the exclusive study of capital, or a theory of the state in itself, as apparatus, not only ordered French research, but also gave it much of its political identity. This identity was also shared with the identity the state itself gave to it.

On the one hand, it arose from the relationship between researchers as social scientists and researchers as Party members. Marxist approaches in urban and regional sociology in France are not, even today, majority approaches; nor are all Marxist researchers Party members. Yet, the SMC thesis as a thesis and as the strategy of a political party came to dominate Marxist urban research. In a sense, it came to represent a particular 'distancing' from urban policies; policies which placed demands on this research. On the other hand, the state itself, through its urban and regional policies, and through its research regime, also gave identity to the research. The highly centralised and formalised planning policies of the 1960s could easily illustrate empirically the value of the SMC thesis. Their formalism and instrumentalism have no equivalent either in Britain or the USA. A certain absence of sectarianism (which had its own effects on the political neutralisation of concepts) was also accompanied by the omission of an historical and comparative reflection on the contemporary state. The state in France, as it then was, *was* the state of advanced capitalism, and there are extremely few accounts of the historical evolution of urban policies in France. [50] This can in part be attributed to the research regime imposed by the state which also gave priority to 'policy relevance' and rapid turnover. It also for a time provided significant funds. [51]

To illustrate textually the evolution of the SMC thesis in urban research, we can briefly turn to the writings of Jean Lojkine. His work expresses a major strand in the literature, in that, from its beginnings, it stood against Althusserian structuralism and maintained the primacy of explanations based on a more direct reference to relations of production and the economic instrumentality of the state. We cannot summarise each individual article and study, but we can attempt a broad profile.

Unlike that of Castells, Lojkine's theory of urbanisation was not constructed 'in one piece', but followed a sort of contrapunctual evolution whereby theoretical articles have alternated with specifically empirical studies. The first article, on urban rent, [52] was followed in 1972 by two major articles [53] which attempted on the one hand a clarification of his position on the question of class alliances *vis-à-vis* Poulantzas, and on the other, expressed the beginnings of a theory of urbanisation. These two articles coincided with the publication of his study on Paris which was soon followed by a similar study of property development in Lyon. [54] This work culminated in a state doctoral dissertation, and the reflections of his work were summarised in *Le marxisme, l'Etat, et la question urbaine.* [55] Since this book, Lojkine has been pursuing, in conjunction with colleagues working on Fos-sur-Mer, a study of political associations in the Socialist town of Lille, [56] and has written articles in *La Pensée*, as well as a position paper on the state for a CERM [57] conference held in January 1979 specifically to debate the question of a thesis of the state.

It is important to remember that, for Lojkine, neither 'state' nor 'urban' are central concepts. They must be subsumed under a labour theory of value, for urban restructuration by state and capital are always actions to ensure accumulation and the maintenance of capitalist relations of production. The urban is not the privileged place for the reproduction of human and material forces for, as he argues, the moment productive forces are no longer limited to the physical unit of the plant (because of the socialisation of productive forces and the interrelations of markets), one can no longer distinguish between the concentration of men and machines, the location of their reproduction and capital accumulation. In this sense, the advanced capitalist city cannot be defined 'in itself', but only in terms of its purposes and the institutional relations which ensure them. The capitalist city enables the control of markets and the spatial distribution of the means of production, thus contributing to the reduction of production costs and the speeding-up of capital rotation. Urban institutions ensure these mechanisms and reflect their class divisions. It is only in later work, as in the study of Lille, that Lojkine begins to consider the question of urban autonomy in terms of the specificity and of the historical and ideological roles of local institutions. This model contrasts with that of Castells, for whom the city is not an instrument of accumulation, but a counter to it. The notion of 'urban crisis' is therefore very different for each author; for Lojkine it relates directly to a crisis of accumulation, while for Castells it is mediated by a crisis of the state in providing for the means of collective consumption which are a drain on capital accumulation.

Within this paradigm of the urban as an instrument of accumulation, the state plays three essential and self-limiting roles which are controlled by the movements of capital accumulation and the private ownership of land:

(a) the control of urban space and spatially segregated functions which are subject to the 'obstacle of land', i.e. the contradiction between the private ownership of landed property and the generalisation of conditions of production;

(b) the financing of means of consumption which are understood simply as urban expenditures which are costs incurred by 'the social power of capital'. Their financing is subject to the fluctuations of the economic cycle and is integral to the development of the material means (including labour) which produce them. That is, the provision and financing of means of consumption reflect the general level of development of the society;

(c)   the control over the social division of labour. (This aspect relates to Boccara's thesis on 'technical transformation'.)

Taking up Boccara's notion that the most profound contradiction in advanced capitalism is that between the socialisation of productive forces and technological development, Lojkine attempts to develop it by positing that a major role of state intervention is to create new urban referents for changes in the social division of labour which are incurred by technological development. In other words, the state intervenes through new forms of spatial divisions and segregations, through new timetables, to promote an adaptive socialisation of labour to new technological changes.

Up to the period of Lojkine's *Le Marxisme, l'Etat et la question urbaine* (1977), the SMC thesis remained central to his conceptualisation of advanced capitalist urbanisation. At this point, he began to question some of Boccara's assumptions regarding accumulation (what economic processes might actually rupture its logic?) and the nature of the socialist transformation. Technical transformation may indeed lead to further class polarisation, but why would this necessarily lead to the formation of antimonopolist alliances? Moreover, if the socialist transformation did take place and the Left found itself in power, what would guarantee that it would not become isolated from the masses and that capitalism could not survive within an accommodation to socialist political domination? The questioning of the thesis is in the first instance a political questioning rather than a theoretical one. It was soon to coincide with a theoretical questioning.

The notion of a 'unique and single mechanism' between state and monopoly capital raised two important questions: How could it explain the survival of institutions which, if not in fact then at least ideologically and politically, countered it; and how were these in turn managed by the central state? These institutions survived mostly at the local level and were close to the 'grass roots'. Yet again, the problem of state autonomy and its relation to civil society was posed.

Before abandoning the SMC thesis altogether, Lojkine proposed an interesting solution to these questions. [58] It consisted, briefly, in splitting up the notion of 'unique mechanism'. Political and economic logics of central state policies do not exist autonomously from each other, but are 'active reflections' of each other. Via very flexible policies, which follow the movements of capital, central state policies can effectively regulate economic contradictions, at least in the short term. These policies, which are essentially fiscal, need to operate in close conjunction with capital. However, they are also hampered by an institution of legitimation which rests on a form of representation which is not only individualistic, but which is also territorially and administratively constituted. These institutions, which are strongly localised, are necessary to co-ordinate and legitimise the various domains of intervention; yet they also tend to develop their own autonomies which are based on local conditions of exploitation.

Lojkine argued that in order to continue to attend to the demands of large capital, while veiling its policies from the growing class conflicts created by monopolisation, the state had to evolve a style of intervention which could deal locally with these conflicts and which could revert them to local institutions. Therefore, one could no longer speak of a state power, but of regional, municipal, sectoral powers which could be segregated from each other. This fragmentation of state power *vis-à-vis* civil society could dilute the politicisation of conflicts both in immediate production and in reproduction, while its concentration at central level could answer more directly the demands of the monopolistic classes.

From this dual model Lojkine evolved an interest in the re-examination of local political institutions as well as informal associations. His current interest lies in the reasons for their survival and their relations to the central state. The SMC thesis has become redundant for it cannot explain this phenomenon. It has of course led to the exploration of other models: Gramsci's conception of hegemony and civil society, Bourdieu's concept of 'class habitus',[59] and Foucault's work on 'normalisation',[60] as well as a new interest in Weber. These models in effect consider an entire realm of experience which policy analysis had hitherto failed to recognise, namely, the relations between modes of thinking and living, crystallised in institutions, and the evolution of a capitalist economy.

This trend away from the use of the SMC thesis towards interest in the 'texture' of everyday experience, its control and expression by institutions, including the capitalist productive enterprise itself,[61] is noticeable in other studies. Lojkine as a researcher most explicitly expressed this movement because he was also the most explicit in using and then rejecting the SMC thesis.

Comparing notes: a crisis in the urban question?

When Castells coined the term 'the urban question',[62] he meant it in two ways: the displacement of the study of capitalist contradictions on to an ideologically laden 'urban' realm; and, in turn, the role of a study of capitalist urbanisation in understanding advanced capitalism. The term 'urban question' may have been borrowed from state urban ideologies, but it also came to symbolise Marxist perspectives. When we speak of the 'crisis' of the urban question, we refer to the former meaning, although the latter is obviously the more important. Its discussion falls beyond the limited scope of this paper. The problem we are posing is whether a crisis has occurred in Marxist urban sociology, and beyond that, whether it may be related to approaches to the state which have been operative. The dilemma apparent in this paper is that this problem cannot be contemplated without going outside an abstracted discussion of the place and explanatory consequences of theory. This is what we meant at the beginning when we proposed that two approaches were necessary to understand why a theory of the state was important for understanding capitalist urban development. The first approach lay in a necessary contemplation and questioning of the structure and conditions of production of research. Only in this way could we see how urban studies reverberate the conditions of their existence and development.

With hindsight, we can see that in France the decline of the SMC thesis coincided not only with the rejection, ultimately, of a precise definition of 'the urban' (on the grounds that it was overdetermined by a consumption perspective, that, empirically, it was undefinable, and that it was in part constructed by the state itself),[63] but also with the decline of the state's interest in urban policies and urban research as such. French urban problematics were clearly based on an interventionist notion of the state and consequently experienced difficulties in operating explanations for non-intervention (beyond a paradigm of profitability) and state withdrawal. These central problematics appear to have been abandoned in favour of various theories and epistemologies which contemplate issues related to everyday culture and ideologies; these have been subsumed under the now ubiquitous term of 'les modes de vies'.[64] These central problematics were also based on the assumption of a visible state. The study of urban policies could, in a sense, unveil the true character of the state and make it visible. It was their integrated character, supported by empirical evidence—and also funding—which gave them authority. The question is whether the fragmentation of urban problematics and research signals a new maturity, the final emancipation from an ideological conception of the urban, or whether it is symptomatic of a loss of institutional and political power. Urban research was part and parcel of state intervention in collective consumption; it was its critical study. The withdrawal of he state also meant the withdrawal of its visibility in sociological explanation.

In Britain we cannot observe the presence of an integrated and cogent theory of the state in urban research, although, as mentioned at the very beginning, there is a critical recognition of its role and some description of its actions. Why this is so can only be understood in terms of the relations of its practitioners to the state as researchers, and also as political individuals. Urban research in Britain has mostly consisted of description and evaluation of policies for 'fine tuning'. This has not changed with the introduction of French urban studies; instead, their appearance has revealed how very deep the habits of empiricism and idealism are. What this paper has tried to do is to draw attention to these habits and to remind colleagues that even in academic discourse Marxists concepts are not neutral, and that their translation from one society to another necessitates some political and contextual foresight. Without such foresight true comparability, as an attempt to identify the very broad dynamics of capitalism and the visible and invisible state therein, is not possible.

Notes

1 E. Lebas, 'Some comments on a decade of Marxist urban and regional research in France—and accompanying annotated bibliography', in preparation.

2 P. Norman, 'Managerialism—a review of recent work', Centre for Environmental Studies, Conference on Urban Change and Conflict, 1975.

3 C. G. Pickvance (ed.), *Urban Sociology: Critical Essays*, Tavistock, London, 1976.

4 C. Cockburn, *The Local State: Management of Cities and People*, Pluto Press, London, 1977.

5 R. Minns and J. Thornley, *State Shareholding*, Macmillan, London, 1978.

6 D. Massey and A. Catalano, *Capital and Land: Landownership by Capital in Britain*, Edward Arnold, London, 1978.

7 C. Paris and B. Blackaby, *Not Much Improvement: Housing Improvement Policy in Birmingham*, Heinemann, London, 1979.

8 P. Mugnaioini, 'London: metropolitan government, housing policy and democratic transformation', Housing Workshop of the Conference of Socialist Economists, January 1979.

9 *Société Française de Sociologie*, 'Crise et avenir des sociologies spécialisées: le cas de la sociologie urbaine', Université de Bordeaux, June 1979. Not one of the papers presented at this conference made an explicit reference to a concept of the capitalist state. The discussion centred

around the purposes of urban studies and the value of a concept of the urban.

10 R. Glass, 'Urban sociology in Great Britain', *Current Sociology*, vol. IV, no. 4, 1955, pp. 5-19.

11 M. Ball, D. Massey and J. Taylor, review article of A. Cutler, B. Hindess, P. Hirst and A. Hussein (1977/78), 'Marx's Capital and capitalism today', in *Capital and Class*, no. 7, 1979.

12 B. Jessop, 'Recent theories of the capitalist state', *Cambridge Journal of Economics*, vol. 1, no. 4, 1977, pp. 353-73.

13 CSE State Group, *Struggle over the State: Cuts and Restructuring in Contemporary Britain*, CSE Books, London, 1980. Analogies between elements of the State Monopoly Capital thesis and the views held by authors such as S. Clarke, and B. Fine and L. Harris would be worthy of investigation as these perspectives display similar insights and weaknesses. See S. Clarke, 'Marxism, sociology and Poulantzas' theory of the state', *Capital and Class*, Summer 1977, pp. 3-31; and B. Fine and L. Harris, *Re-reading Capital*, Macmillan, London, 1978.

14 E. Laclau, 'The specificity of the Political: the Miliband-Poulantzas Debate', *Economy and Society*, vol. IV, no. 1, 1975, pp. 87-110.

15 J. Holoway and S. Piciotto (eds), *Capital and State*, Edward Arnold, London, 1978.

16 See, for example, M. Harloe, 'Housing and the state: recent British developments', *International Social Science Journal*, vol. XXX, no. 3, 1978, as well as P. Saunders, *Urban Politics: A Sociological Interpretation*, Hutchinson, London, 1979.

17 The first instance could be expressed for example in terms of a purging of the concept of class struggle from the problematic of collective consumption, with its translation, via empirical redefinitions, into typologies, for a re-worked but none the less passive definition of 'the urban'. The precariousness of Castells's 'means of collective consumption' lends itself to this. The second instance is more difficult to illustrate. It might refer to the idea that capitalist relations have an economic dynamic (accumulation) which, while relating increasingly to the state, remains more than 'relatively independent' from it. This view is of course contrary to the SMC thesis. It might also refer to the existence of cultural and institutional models which, although conducive to capitalist relations, preceded the existence of a truly advanced capitalist state to confirm them. The writings of Weber and Foucault are in many ways attempts to understand this phenomenon. A last illustration might refer to the idea that capitalism as a generalised relation actually creates contradictions and forms of consciousness which can evade the control of the state. On the other hand, the notion of 'repressive tolerance' denies in part this possibility, etc.

18 H. Laski, *A Grammar of Politics*, Allen & Unwin, London, 1966. We refer to the 1937 Introduction.

19 Centre for Environmental Studies, Conference on Urban Change and Conflict, York University, 1975.

20 J. Lambert, C. Paris and B. Blackaby, *Housing Policy and the State: Allocation, Access and Control*, Macmillan, London, 1978.

21 M. Castells, 'Theoretical propositions for an experimental study of

urban social movements' , in C. G. Pickvance (ed.), op. cit., 1976.

22   P. Dunleavy, 'Protest and quiescence in urban politics: a critique of some pluralist and structuralist myths', *International Journal of Urban and Regional Research*, vol. 1, no. 2, 1977, pp. 193-218.

23   C. G. Pickvance, 'On the study of urban social movements', *The Sociological Review*, vol. 23, no. 1, new series, 1975, pp. 29-49.

24   J. Lloyd, 'Immigrants in Britain: new "occupational communities" or "urban social movements"?', *Papers in Urban and Regional Studies*, no. 1, February 1977, pp. 1-15.

25   M. Castells, 'Ideological mystification and social issues: the Ecological Action Movement in the United States', in *City, Class and Power*, Macmillan, London, 1978.

26   M. Castells, 'The social prerequisites for the upheaval of urban social movements: an exploratory study of the Paris metropolitan area, 1968-1973', in *City, Class and Power*, op. cit., 1978.

27   E. Cherki and D. Mehl, *Les Nouveaux Embarras de Paris: de la révolte des usagers des transports aux mouvements de défense de l'environnement*, Maspéro, Paris, 1979.

28   These issues are raised in, for example, F. Godard, 'Classes sociales et modes de consommation', *La Pensée*, no. 180, mars-avril 1975, pp. 140-63; and in F. Godard and J.-R. Pendariès, *Les Modes de Vies dans le discours de la représentation: Institutions locales et production politique des besoins*, Université de Nice, Laboratoire de Sociologie, research report, 1978.

29   J. Lojkine, 'Crise de l'état et crise du capitalisme monopoliste d'état', *La Pensée*, no. 193, juin 1977, pp. 113-26.

30   Ibid., p. 121.

31   J. Lojkine, *Le Marxisme, l'Etat et la question urbaine*, Presses Universitaires de France, Paris, 1977.

32   C. Cockburn, op. cit., is a partial exception, but although she does refer to this problematic, it is not operative in her account of struggles in Lambeth.

33   P. Saunders, *Urban Politics: A Sociological Interpretation*, Hutchinson, London, 1979.

34   C. G. Pickvance, 'Marxist approaches to the study of urban politics: divergences among some recent French work', *International Journal of Urban and Regional Research*, vol. 1, no. 2, 1977, pp. 219-55.

35   J. Lojkine, 'Pouvoir politique et lutte des classes à l'époque du capitalisme monopoliste d'état', *La Pensée*, no. 166, décembre 1972; N. Poulantzas, *Classes in Contemporary Capitalism*, New Left Books, London, 1975.

36   N. Poulantzas, 'Problèmes actuels de la recherche marxiste sur l'Etat', *Dialectiques*, printemps 1976, pp. 30-43.

37   M. Castells and F. Godard, *Monopolville: l'entreprise, l'Etat, l'urbain*, Mouton, Paris and The Hague, 1974.

38   M. Harloe, 'Marxism, the state and the urban question: critical notes on two recent French theories', in C. Crouch (ed.), *British Political Sociology Yearbook*, Croom Helm, London, 1978.

39   P. Baran and P. Sweezy, *Monopoly Capital*, Pelican, London, 1966.

40   Ibid., chapter 3, 'The Tendency of Surplus to Rise'.

41 J. O'Connor, *The Fiscal Crisis of the State*, St Martin's Press, New York, 1973.

42 P. Boccara, *Etudes sur le capitalisme monopoliste d'Etat—sa crise et son issue*, Editions Sociales, Paris, 1974; 'Crise du capitalisme, crise de la société, crise de l'Etat: un débat (with C. Buci-Glucksmann, M. Castells, F. Hincker, N. Poulantzas), *La Nouvelle Critique*, no. 101, février 1977; *La Mise en mouvement du 'Capital'*, Editions Sociales, Paris, 1979.

43 For a fuller account of the SMC thesis and its uses by these and other authors, see J. Fairley, 'State Monopoly Capitalism theory and its critics', unpublished paper, 1978.

44 K. Marx, *Collected Works vol. III*, Lawrence & Wishart, London, 1971, p. 249.

45 Ibid., p. 249.

46 Ibid., p. 252.

47 Ibid., p. 253.

48 E. Preteceille, 'Collective consumption, the state and the crisis of capitalist society', in M. Harloe and E. Lebas (eds), *City, Class and Conflict*, Edward Arnold, London, 1981. It is so far only in this essay that there appears an incidental query and comment on the problems posed by the withdrawal of the state from the provision of 'means of collective consumption'.

49 D. Bleitrach and A. Chenu, *L'Usine et la Vie: luttes régionales: Marseille et Fos*, Maspéro, Paris, 1979; and M. Harloe and E. Lebas (eds), op. cit., 1981.

50 One exception may be cited, namely M. Dagnaud, *Le Mythe de la qualité de la politique urbaine en France*, Mouton, Paris and The Hague, 1977.

51 M. Conan and L. Floch, *Urban Research in France: Trends and Results*, Centre de Documentation sur l'Urbanisme, Paris, 1975.

52 J. Lojkine, 'Y a-t-il une rente foncière urbaine?', *Espaces et Sociétés*, mars 1971, no. 2, pp. 89-94.

53 J. Lojkine, *La Pensée*, no. 166, 1972; J. Lojkine: 'Contribution à une théorie marxiste de l'urbanisation capitaliste', *Cahiers Internationaux de Sociologie*, vol. 50, no. 2, 1972, pp. 123-46.

54 J. Lojkine, *La politique urbaine dans la région parisienne, 1945-1972*, Mouton, Paris and The Hague, 1972; J. Lojkine, *La politique urbaine dans la région Lyonnaise, 1945-1972*, Mouton, Paris and The Hague, 1974.

55 J. Lojkine, *Le Marxisme, l'Etat et la question urbaine*, Presses Universitaires de France, Paris, 1977.

56 J. Lojkine et al., *Politique urbaine et pouvoir local dans l'agglomération Lilloise*, CRAPS/CEMS Research Report, 1978; and M. Harloe and E. Lebas (eds), op. cit., 1981.

57 J. Lojkine, 'L'Etat capitaliste aujourd'hui', Centre d'Etude et de Recherches Marxistes (CERM), mimeo, 1979.

58 J. Lojkine, 'L'Etat et l'urbain: contribution à une analyse matérialiste des politiques urbaines dans les pays capitalistes développés', *International Journal of Urban and Regional Research*, vol. 1, no. 2, 1977.

59 P. Bourdieu, *Outline for a Theory of Practice*, Cambridge University Press, Cambridge, 1978.

60 M. Foucault et al., *Les Equipements du pouvoir: Villes, territoires et équipements collectifs*, numéro spécial, *Recherches*, no. 13, 1973.

61 D. Bleitrach and A. Chenu, op. cit., 1979; and in M. Harloe and E. Lebas (eds), op. cit., 1981.

62 M. Castells, *The Urban Question*, Edward Arnold, London, 1977.

63 Société Française de Sociologie, op. cit., 1979.

64 It would be difficult to describe what is meant by 'les modes de vies'. Not only is the term very loosely used to mean everyday practices and culture, but its conceptual justifications range very widely—from H. Lefèbvre's 'la vie quotidienne' to the problematics developed by P. Grevet, E. Preteceille and others on the notion of need, via influences from Foucault's concept of 'normalisation' and Gramsci's conception of the Fordian Worker.

On the role of the state in urban policy-making: the case of inner-city and dispersal policies in Britain

Andrew Cox

The question of the role of the state government and bureaucratic agencies in urban policy-making is a relatively new concern for students of urban problems and forms. Although Park and Wirth, who were the major proponents of the ecological approach to urban sociology, did look at the role of governments, [1] their main concern was with the *effects* of urban living on social and psychological phenomena, rather than with the mechanisms by which urban resources are allocated.

If urban sociologists largely ignored these latter issues, so did political scientists. Students of government have traditionally looked at the role of local and central government and other bureaucratic agencies in terms of intra-governmental relationships—the access to political resources, the nature of political goals and ideologies, and party political organisations—without ever asking whether or not government and other bureaucratic agencies actually play an autonomous, or significant, role in shaping urban forms and resource allocation. The position has tended to be one in which it was taken as axiomatic that if constitutional theory postulated a central role for the government then this could be taken as the starting point for analysis. Thus by analysing what governments decide, and how, it has been assumed that we can explain how spatial forms develop and who gets what in urban areas.

Clearly, these two main approaches to the analysis of urban resource allocation are dichotomous, but, in recent years, there has been a desire to bring the two disciplinary approaches together. This desire has been occasioned mainly by the growing interest of Marxist writers in urban resource allocation, after the seminal influence of the works of Rex and Moore and R. E. Pahl in questioning the traditional ecological approach to urban problems. Rex and Moore, as well as Pahl, argued in the 1960s that traditional sociological approaches ignored political phenomena.[2] From this reinterpretation there developed a Marxist critique of Pahl's explanation of the role of the state in urban change, which has resulted in a major controversy over whether the state is 'autonomous' or merely 'relatively autonomous' in urban resource allocation.[3]

This paper has four goals. Firstly, it is intended that an overview of the development of the theoretical debate over the role of the state in urban change will be presented—concluding with a discussion of the instrumentalist and structuralist Marxist explanations of the state's role. Secondly, from this, a critique of the structuralist and instrumentalist approaches will be developed on a theoretical level, and thirdly, this will then illuminated by two case studies: critique of Manuel Castells's explanation of the gestation of the New Towns policy in Britain in 1946,[4] and a critical appraisal of the recent instrumentalist Marxist explanations of Britain's inner city policy reappraisal in the 1970s.[5] Finally, the paper will attempt to draw some theoretical conclusions for the analysis of the role of the state from these critiques.

The theoretical debate over the role of the state in urban policy

It can be argued that there are at least four views or explanations of the role of the state as it impinges on urban policy-making.[6] These four approaches can be categorised as the *pluralist/neutral, managerialist/elitist, instrumental Marxist* and *structural Marxist* theories.

Traditionally, as we saw, sociologists concerned with urban problems concentrated on the effects of urban living on individuals: the emphasis was on the development of alienation and anomie in individuals due to the break-up of the traditional rural community. This approach tended to underplay the political and economic forces shaping urban change, and to emphasise the problems of urban living rather than the role of government and bureaucratic agencies in exacerbating these problems. At the same time there were sociologists who were concerned with bureaucratic and political phenomena; but their interests were at first not confined to urban power structures. This school of sociological enquiry was associated with C. W. Mills at the national level and with Floyd Hunter and his disciples at the local level.[7] These theorists were mainly concerned with the analysis of decision-making. They argued that the state and its agencies were not neutral but were controlled by elites. For C. W. Mills a 'power elite' controlled national politics in America, and for Hunter 'economic notables' determined the most important decisions in the local community.

Surprisingly, the view that the state is influenced by elites, who could therefore shape urban forms, did not generate much serious reappraisal of the ecological analysis of urban problems. On the contrary, the major criticism of this approach came from political scientists like R. A. Dahl and his associates at Yale University. [8] At the end of the 1950s and at the beginning of the 1960s, Dahl began to question the elite analysis of community power after conducting a major research project in New Haven, Connecticut. In a seminal book, *Who Governs?*, he argued that the state was neutral in policy-making and that a pluralistic policy process existed in which no one elite dominated. [9] Dahl was arguing, therefore, that although elites did make decisions in government no one elite was able to dominate in all issues, and that all interests and groups had relatively equal access to political decision-makers and political resources. This explanation of power came to be known as 'the law of dispersed inequalities'. It held that the state was neutral and merely referred struggles between different elites, or interests, in society. [10]

This *pluralist/neutral* view of the role of the state was, of course, seriously questioned by elite theorists—in particular by Bachrach and Baratz. [11] Dahl, according to Bachrach and Baratz, seriously limited his analysis of power by failing to analyse the concept of agenda setting and also in failing to understand that elites were only interested in certain key issues; on issues that were not of central importance to 'economic notables' a relatively pluralistic process was allowed to operate. [12] Thus elite theories, while recognising that there was scope for some pluralism, refused to accept that the state was ultimately neutral or relatively autonomous of elite determination on 'key' issues. Another response from pluralist writers was to deny the methodological objectivity of the elite critique and to argue that elite theorists wanted to analyse how the political system *ought* to function, rather than describing how it did function in practice. [13] Unfortunately, as Lukes has since argued, this debate did not lead to any theoretical or methodological synthesis and both sides to the debate continued to 'talk past one another': elite theorists concentrated on trying to discover who were the members of the elite; pluralist writers continued to describe only the visible manifestations of power in the actual policy process. [14] It was only with the innovatory work of Rex and Moore in the mid-1960s that this theoretical impasse was broached—although only in the field of urban studies and not in relation to the analysis of power relations as a whole.

In their study of Sparkbrook, Birmingham in the early 1960s, Rex and Moore centrally questioned the ecological bias of much of

Andrew Cox

traditional urban sociology.[15] They indicated clearly that many of the problems experienced by immigrant groups in this 'twilight' area arose not from the exigencies of living in urban areas, but from an inadequate access to social and political resources. It was from this realisation of the inadequacy of much of the traditional work in urban sociology that Pahl was to develop his view of the role of the state at the end of the 1960s. Pahl developed a theory of *managerialism* to explain what determined urban resource allocation. Rejecting the lack of social and political insight in the ecological approach, and drawing on the Weberian tradition in sociology, Pahl tried to fuse the insights of political science and sociological-elite theories. According to Pahl, councillors and officials in cities had an independent effect on urban resource allocation; they acted as the 'city managers' who had their own view of the way in which the city should develop.[16] Clearly, this approach, while having strong Weberian overtones through its view of an independent bureaucratic elite, drew on the pluralist view of the centrality of political decision-makers in the policy process, as well as on the elite theories of power current in sociology at the time. In so bringing together elite and pluralist approaches, Pahl was however also rejecting the pluralist view of the state. For Pahl the state was not neutral, but potentially an autonomous actor, independent of groups and external interests in the society, and with its own goals and interests. This view, initially confined to the local state level, was later to be elaborated at the national level. Thus in 1974 Pahl and Winkler were to argue that the central state in Britain was becoming increasingly corporatist.[17] In other words, the state was conceived as independent of society with goals of its own—order, nationalism, unity and success—which, when followed to their logical conclusions, would result in public control of a mainly privately owned economy and society ('fascism with a human face').

Pahl's work has had a seminal impact on urban studies, and in particular for sociological approaches, because it occasioned a reappraisal of the ecological schema and promoted the study of political and social, as well as spatial phenomena. Despite this Pahl's work was seriously questioned in the early 1970s by both instrumentalist and structuralist Marxist approaches. These approaches share a number of factors in their rejection of the managerialist thesis, as well as having important points of disagreement between their views of how urban change and the role of the state should be analysed and explained. In particular, both these Marxist approaches criticised Pahl for failing to ask the question, 'Who manages the managers?'[18] Marxist approaches have generally, therefore, rejected any theory that argues that the state can be an independent actor in society, although the reasons for this vary depending on the approach that is adopted.

Instrumentalist Marxist approaches to the role of the state are most closely associated in Britain with the writings of Miliband and Aaronovitch. [19] Although Miliband's analysis of the state is by far the more sophisticated, he shares with others the general view that the state operates to defend the interests and hegemony of the 'ruling class' (the owners of the means of production). For Miliband, even though elites and groups may develop with interests antithetical to those of the capitalist mode of production, in the long term these interests are co-opted within the state and inculcated with the mores and goals of the 'ruling class'. Thus, while Miliband rejects the view posited by Aaronovitch (and others) that the state is peopled by the individual members of the ruling class, he accepts that through the use of ideology and socialisation the state must be an instrument in the hands of the ruling class due to the inequality of competition between different ideologies in society. [20] This view has been important outside the general theoretical debate about the state and power; not only does it question Pahl's approach, but it has been used as the framework for analysis by a number of British Marxists attempting to explain urban change and the role of the state in urban policy-making, especially, as in the work of Cockburn and Paris, and in the Community Development Projects. [21]

The major difficulty with this view of the state is that, whereas it does attempt to explain why the state accepts certain policies without assuming a neutral or independent stance, it fails to explain adequately why the state pursues policies antithetical to the interests of the 'ruling class'. The main weakness of this approach is therefore the fact that in conceiving of the state as a monolithic instrument the theory has difficulty in explaining the eclectic and polycentric nature of policy-making in the decision-making process. The problem then becomes therefore one of explaining the determinism of the needs of the capitalist mode of production in all cases. It is in response to these problems that the *structuralist Marxist* approach, associated with the writings of Althusser, Poulantzas, Castells, Lojkine, Lamarche and Preteceille has been formulated. [22]

Although there are a number of important differences between these theorists they do share certain common assumptions about the nature of urban change and the role of the state in this. [23] Firstly, structural Marxists reject both the managerial and instrumentalist views of the state. Within this approach, therefore, the state cannot be seen as an object with independence or autonomy because it does not exist as such. For structuralists the state is either a 'legal subject' with certain rights, or it is a relation expressing the nature of class conflict in the society. This means that the state can only be said to exist as an entity in the legal sense—for example, when a local authority compulsorily purchases property to fulfil a specific 'community' function, such as road construction or redevelopment. At other times the state is 'a field of political struggle' in which different class fractions and interests are in perpetual competition for state power. Ultimately, however, although this political struggle may generate the opportunity for the working class or bureaucratic agencies to pursue policies antithetical to the best interests of the capitalist 'ruling class', this autonomy can only be limited. In other words, the state has 'relative autonomy' from the requirements of the capitalist mode of production, and not true autonomy, because in the final analysis it must act as a repressive tool of the bourgeoisie against the working class. This is a crucial point because, for structuralists, the state in a capitalist society must always return to the defence of capitalism in the last instance. This insight leads therefore to the conclusion that because state actions can only be relatively autonomous of the capitalist base of society such actions can only be reformist and can never question the capitalist mode of production. For structuralists the opportunity for qualitative change can only come from urban social movements (radicalised working- and middle-class groups politicised by the contradictions and uneven developments of capitalism) which either force concessions from the state or work to smash it.

Clearly, this explanation of the state's role and functions overcomes most of the reductionist difficulties inherent in the managerialist and instrumentalist approaches: it can explain the eclectic/pluralistic policy process in the short term and the determinism of the capitalist mode of production in the last instance. Indeed it is within this approach that a more detailed analysis of the role of the state in generating and promoting urban change has been formulated. This approach is most closely associated with the writings of Poulantzas, Castells and Lojkine.[24]

Structuralists argue that the state fulfils four main roles for the maintenance and perpetuation of the capitalist mode of production. Firstly, the state provides 'collective consumption' to ensure a high effective demand for the products of the capitalist enterprise and also to ensure the 'reproduction of labour power'. By this structuralists mean that the expansion of the state's role in welfare provisions—education, social services, housing, and transport facilities—not only ensures social stability, but also provides a healthy and proficient labour force and the maintenance of a high level of demand in the economy. This indirect defence of capitalism is also, it is contended, supported directly by the state's provision of 'infrastructure' as a subsidy to the costs of production. Thus, the provision of water and sewerage services, the construction of roads, and the public installation of utilities are examples of the state subsidising the costs of the private firm and thereby reducing overheads and ensuring competitiveness in markets. More importantly, since the circulation of capital is necessary for the accumulation of surplus value, and because this process is speeded by the close proximity of different fractions of capital—financial, commercial and productive—with the consumer, the agglomeration of cities is regarded as functional for capitalism. The state, however, acts to speed and rationalise this process of agglomeration by becoming involved in land-use planning and the zoning of areas for different types of development. In this way the state acts functionally to assist capital accumulation because powers for land-use planning allow the capitalist enterprise to overcome the problems of multiplicity of landowners inherent in traditional land-ownership patterns. By this means the capitalist enterprise is able to overcome the potential power and limitation of its own role rooted in the ownership of land by interests not concerned primarily with profit maximisation.[25] Finally, the 'relatively autonomous' state also acts as a safety valve for political discontent. Since the state's role is ultimately repressive and because capitalism and its urban expression are contradictory and exploitative of the working class, by allowing for short-term compromises and reforms the state allows for the dissipation of any radical action against the capitalist mode.

It is argued, however, that this role and function are inherently contradictory. Since the expanded state role in urban and welfare functions can only be provided by taxation on incomes or corporate profit, which both result in imposts on the capitalist enterprise and its generation of surplus value, a contradiction exists in which a structural gap develops between the state's ability to raise revenue and the expanding requirement for expenditure inherent in the state's interventions to defend capitalism. This is known as the 'fiscal crisis of the state', and it is argued that this is exacerbated by the tendency of the rate of profit to decline within capitalism which imposes a squeeze on profits.[26] This crisis can only be solved by the state acting in a repressive way to cut the level of social expenditure in the welfare state and thereby attacking the living standards of the working class. For structuralists, however, this dilemma is the moment when the possibility for qualitative change is heightened. The state's repressive role, as well as its radicalising interventions into urban areas for clearance and redevelopment which question traditional community structures physically, politicise the urban working and middle classes; from this urban social movements are created which either win qualitative concessions from the state or ultimately lead to its destruction.

Clearly, then, the structuralist explanation of the forces shaping urban development and change is one which, like the instrumentalist approach, sees the requirements of the capitalist mode of production as being the major explanatory variable. The major disagreement occurs over the role of the state in this process. Instrumentalists see the state as a monolith and an instrument of the capitalist class, whereas the structuralists reject both this and Pahl's managerial approach by arguing that the state's role is ultimately repressive, but that in the short-term there is scope for 'relative autonomy'. Although this re-emphasis on the structural economic forces shaping urban change is useful and a necessary corrective to the pluralist and managerialist explanations, it can be argued that in so far as both Marxist approaches deal with the state they are reductionist, because, notwithstanding the sophistication of the structuralist approach, they are merely a reworking of Stalinist economism with its simplistic view of the determinism of the base over the superstructure of political forms. [27] By indicating some of the theoretical weaknesses of the structuralist approach, and then by a detailed critique of a structuralist and instrumentalist explanation of urban policy-making in Britain, it is intended that the limits of these two Marxist approaches will be revealed.

Theoretical problems

First of all, it is important to stress that, despite the fact that this paper takes issue with Marxist explanations of the forces shaping change and the nature and functions of the state in capitalist societies, it does not disagree with the general argument that there is a need to analyse the structural economic forces behind urban forms. Furthermore, as indicated earlier, I would also concur with much of the Marxist critique of Pahl's managerialist approach. However, it is one thing to agree that the notion of a monolithic state—with goals and interests of its own—is fatuous, but it is quite another to accept the alternative view that this is because the state is determined by the needs of the capitalist mode of production and its 'ruling class'. There are yet other explanations of the role and functions of the state that would lead one to doubt Pahl's thesis; and these are not Marxist.

In 1974-5, Norman questioned Pahl's thesis because he felt that central and quasi-governmental bureaucratic agencies were in conflict, rather than harmony, with local authorities. Furthermore, he argued that private interests can shape and influence many issue areas, but without arguing that this was due to the determinism of the needs of the capitalist mode of production in the last instance. [28] This is not a surprising conclusion nor is the view that the state is far from being a monolith, but that it is in fact constituted of a wide number of agencies at different functional and territorial levels with varying goals, routines, aspirations, and interests, which more often than not generate conflict rather than unity of purpose as Pahl argued. This realisation is hardly surprising because most pluralist or political science/public administration research has discovered just such conflicts of interest. Thus, as any number of studies have shown, local councillors and officers are often in conflict and yet sometimes they are not—it depends on the issue. [29] Similarly, even at the local level, the view that the state is unified, as expressed by managerialist (Pahl) and instrumentalist Marxist (Cockburn) theorists, must be doubted as the evidence of intra-departmental conflict over scarce resources indicates. [30] Similarly, local authorities are continually in conflict with central and quasi-governmental agencies as academic and governmental research projects have indicated. [31] Thus, whereas it is obvious that Pahl's view of a managerial state is invalid, the same must also be said of the instrumentalist Marxist thesis which also tends to view the state as simply a monolith determined in its actions and goals by the requirements of the capitalist mode of production—both views suffer from a reductionist explanation of bureaucratic phenomena. It is hardly surprising, therefore, that these criticisms led Pahl, at least, to rework his earlier thesis and to argue in 1975-6 that the state was more nearly an intervening variable between the requirements of modern capitalism and class conflict, and that it had some scope for autonomous actions. [32]

The Marxist answer to these criticisms, based upon the eclectic and polycentric reality of bureaucratic and governmental decision-making, has been the development of the structural variant or thesis. Clearly, the structuralist thesis does not fall into the same reductionist trap as the instrumentalist approach—at least superficially it does not—because Poulantzas, Castells, and others [33] have argued that the evidence of contingent bureaucratic and governmental behaviour indicates only a 'relative autonomy', not a real autonomy for the state. Thus, in the last instance the needs of the capitalist mode of production will determine the role of the state by setting problems or generating crises in which the state must react to defend capitalism. Further, even in those cases when the state does not appear to react in the manner that these theorists would assume that it should, this contrary evidence and behaviour must also be seen as in the best interests of capitalism and its ruling class because, even though the state or the ruling class do not appreciate it, by allowing interests antithetical to the capitalist mode to have some influence, the state is acting as a 'political safety valve'. The argument for a structural Marxist is therefore all-embracing and neat: no action, even if it is antithetical to the requirements of the capitalist mode in the short term, can ultimately question the requirements of the capitalist mode in the long term—unless, of course, it is due to radicalised working-class action aimed, ultimately, at smashing the state.

As all-embracing as this theory of the state is, it must be rejected on a number of grounds. First of all, Saunders has argued that the thesis is epistemologically invalid because it is tautological. [34] Since the theory can explain all activities—even those that appear to contradict the theory—Saunders has correctly contended that this approach is incapable of disproof, and because it does not contain any counter factual statement it is unscientific. Furthermore, since this theory cannot be falsified, it cannot be taken as capable of explanatory utility, unless, of course, one resorts to the Althusserian epistemological heresy of arguing that since the Marxist theory *is* correct and true, then only knowledge gleaned within the Marxist schema is knowledge, and everything else is bourgeois ideology. [35] Such a retreat into theory for theory's sake must be avoided, as E. P. Thompson amongst others has indicated. Yet the tautology and redundancy of this alternative are also to be clearly seen within structuralist writings, and they lead us to doubt the theory on other than epistemological grounds. Despite structuralist affirmations of the sanctity of the Marxist explanation of the state's role and functions we find clear evidence, both in Castells's and Poulantzas's work, of these theorists contradicting themselves and their theory of the state. As shown by Saunders and Harloe, Castells, Poulantzas, and Lojkine have all accepted, notwithstanding their earlier arguments that the state is a relation reflecting the class struggle and not an object, that under certain circumstances and at certain conjunctures the state may have intentions and goals; and, heresy of heresies, that it may be able to act independently of the requirements of capitalism! [36]

Despite these weaknesses and internal inconsistencies, I would contend that this is not the gravest weakness of the approach. With E. P. Thompson, I would argue that the most striking weakness is that it is ahistorical and therefore develops an inadequate categorisation of the structural forces shaping and constraining state behaviour. [37] Despite the structuralist argument that the requirements of the capitalist mode of production must determine the superstructure of social and political forms in the last instance, and that this explanation is derived from the writings of Marx and Engels, it can be argued that this view of the role of the state and change is an inadequate understanding and reading of these two writers. As Thompson has argued, Marx's theory of capitalism was not a true representation of how the capitalist society did function in practice in the real world, but an *idealised* formulation of how a pure system of capitalism might function, or indeed ought to function, if it were to operate optimally. However, as Thompson has further argued, such an optimally functioning capitalist society did not exist at the time Marx and Engels were writing—even in Britain—nor did they expect such a system to exist in practice due to the actions of human agents working against this system; and also due to the historical and 'society-specific' development of the capitalist mode of production in each country or society. [38] This latter point is crucial. It can be argued that rather than attempting to draw all-inclusive explanations of the role of the state under modern capitalism, and assuming that these roles and functions will be the same across all societies in which the capitalist mode of production operates, we should be concerned with elaborating the unique and 'society-specific' developments which were generated socially, politically, and economically as the capitalist mode of production was extended within each nation-state historically. In this way we would, and should, be concerned with understanding the different ways in which the bourgeoisie and working classes—as well as other actors and interests—were able to entrench themselves in any society. One would of course expect these relationships to vary between France, Britain and Germany, and not that there would be a necessary correspondence between the role and nature of the state and class relationships in all of these countries, irrespective of historical, cultural, political and social differences as structuralist writers tend to argue.

This is not to argue—and the point should perhaps be emphasised here—that the Marxist method, with its emphasis on the 'objective' requirements of different fractions of capital and class actors, is redundant. On the contrary, it can be argued that the emphasis on the objective 'stakes' and interests of the representatives of the different fractions of capital and class actors is both necessary and essential. However, it must be made plain here that we cannot assume any necessary correspondence between the development of the capitalist mode of production or the goals, interests (as subjectively defined) and policies of either the bourgeoisie or the working class. Rather, we need to study the ways in which these actors and this mode of production developed historically in each society and thereby arrive at some conclusions about the degree of correspondence between the requirements of the capitalist mode of production, its class representatives' subjectively defined goals, and the actions of bureaucratic and governmental (state) agencies in practice. It is axiomatic that we cannot assume any necessary correspondence between these actors, agencies, policies, and interests simply by theoretical or definitional fiat: we need actually to establish whether or not there was or has been any such correspondence in practice.

Thus, if we take the British case, we can point immediately to any number of historical developments which would lead us to doubt any simplistic instrumentalist or structuralist explanation of the forces shaping urban change or the nature of the state. First of all, it is not true historically at least that the bourgeoisie were able to oust the landed interest in Britain. On the contrary, one of the most notable historical developments in Britain has been the longevity of the landed interest both socially and politically (and to a lesser extent economically), despite the development of the capitalist mode of production. [39] The maintenance of a strong, if declining, landed class in Britain has meant that the full entrenchment within the social and political systems by the owners of the means of capitalist production must be doubted in the British case. If this is so, and from an early date it can be seen in the way in which the landed interest imposed regulatory Factory Acts on the entrepreneurial class in the nineteenth century, then any assumption of necessary correspondence between the goals of the owners of the means of capitalist production and the actions of the state must be doubted. This view is underscored in the urban field when one appreciates that the major post-war intervention by the state into urban problems—through the provision of statutory planning powers for local authorities to regulate all changes in land-use in the 1947 Town and Country Planning Act—was not initiated by the capitalist enterprise or class, but mainly by the representatives of rural and landed interests who were concerned to stop urban sprawl and ribbon development which threatened their rural way of life. [40] One can, of course, seek to argue that this extension of the state's role was due to the needs of firms in overcoming traditional land-owning patterns, but this is hardly the only, or even the major explanation of why the state's role was extended in this period.

If the longevity of the landed interest is one phenomenon which has seriously constrained the unfettered development of the capitalist mode of production in Britain historically, then the creation of ameliorative and welfare-orientated state agencies is another. The development of a welfare role for the state may well have been functional for the needs of capitalism as a system, as Offé has argued, [41] but the creation of bureaucratic agencies is not unproblematic for capitalism or for the owners of the means of production. The development of local, regional, quasi-central, and central agencies of the state may well impose 'bureaucratic costs' on capitalism due to the ability of interests (working-class or landed for instance) antithetical to the goals of capitalism to colonise and influence these institutions. Similarly, the creation of extensive interventionist state agencies is not only problematic due to the possibility of their subversion by antithetical and opposed interests; there is also the problem that organisations take on values, goals, routines and procedures of their own. Thus most organisational theory—associated with the work of Simon and March, Lindblom, Downs, and Self [42] —has shown conclusively that though agencies may be formed at one historical moment to fulfil certain roles, there is no guarantee that, once this requirement is no longer functional for capitalism, they will be swept away. On the contrary, most evidence from organisational research indicates that bureaucratic agencies are able to develop routine practices and to establish goals which are resistant to change. In this way capitalism may be seen to be locked into the bureaucratic interventions of an earlier age: interventions which limit, distort and constrain the dominance of the state by the requirements of the capitalist class in both the short and the long term. This is not, however, to argue with Pahl that these bureaucratic agencies come to constitute a unified elite with goals and interests of their own; in fact, they are more than likely to be in competition for scarce resources than always able to co-operate with one another. [43] However, this insight does lead us to appreciate that state agencies are not tied to the requirements of capitalist production, because such agencies, operating with 'bounded rationality' and 'satisficing' rather than maximising their own vested interests, have scope to misperceive the best interests of capitalism and to pursue policies which are contrary to this mode of production. [44] The distortion of the location of the British motor car industry by successive governments since the

Second World War, which has contributed to its decline, is but one example of the way in which governments have worked against the capitalist enterprise for reasons other than making the car industry stronger in the long term. In this particular case, governments have been responding to the short-term problems of regional unemployment for electoral reasons and also responding to pressures from local and regional authorities faced with mounting unemployment in their areas.

If there are therefore bureaucratic costs for the capitalist mode of production in the forms and types of intervention, it is clear that we cannot assume that capitalism will be unfettered in either the short or long terms. Thus, it may be true that by refusing to understand the crises engendered by not assisting the capitalist mode of production governments may well be contributing to further economic crises, and there is no guarantee that this 'objective' insight will be appreciated either by politicians or civil servants; they all have scope to misperceive the constraints of the 'real' world. Indeed, this argument about the lack of necessary correspondence between the requirements of capitalist production and state practices is also supported by most Marxist writers of a structuralist persuasion. Marx, as well as Lamarche and Poulantzas amongst recent writers, [45] has contended that there is competition within and between fractions of capital that constitute the capitalist mode of production. Thus, although Marx argued that capital accumulation was assisted by the creation of functionally distinct fractions of capital—productive, commercial, and financial—which by concentration and specialisation speeded the process of capital circulation, he also argued that there was scope for conflict between these fractions over the best policies to be pursued by each fraction and also by the state. [46] Of course, it has been assumed by structuralist writers that, because economic crises may well be generated if the needs of the productive sector are not ultimately accepted as of most importance by the state and other fractions of capital, then in the last instance the state must be dictated to by the needs of the productive sector. It is at this point that we see the ahistoricism of the structuralist approach most glaringly. As indicated earlier, Marx may well have been correct to argue that the perfectly functioning capitalist system would require the state and other fractions of capital to obey the dictates of the productive sector in the last instance, but it does not follow from this that any society, even one in which the capitalist mode of production operates, will reveal these 'optimal' relationships. Simply because this should happen in theory does not mean that it will in practice.

On the role of the state in urban policy-making

This conclusion is reinforced if we turn our attention away from largely theoretical discussions to consider the ways in which fractions of capital developed in any country historically. In Britain, while it is true that one can indicate all the fractions of capital—commercial, productive and financial—outlined within theory, it is not true historically that either the financial and commercial sectors were tied to the creation of the productive sectors nor that, in the last instance, the requirements of the productive sector have ultimately determined the goals and policies of the state or other fractions of capital. As Pollard has argued, one of the major problems for the British economy has been the fact that the financial sector (the City) was never fully constrained by the domestic productive sector, with the consequence that the level of investment in the productive sector has been lower than it should have been to ensure technological change and an international competitive edge. [47] The result has been, therefore, the decline of the British economy throughout the twentieth century: a result which one would hardly expect if the productive sector of the economy were able to shape and dictate the long-term policies of the state and other fractions of capital. What this simple example indicates is that in Britain at least there is a debilitating conflict between the productive and financial fractions of capital, which constrains the productive sector and which was always likely to occur here due to the fact that the financial sector developed on world trading relationships well before the creation of the large productive sector in the early nineteenth century. [48] The corollary of this insight might well be further support for the view that there can be no assumption of the necessary correspondence between the needs of the productive sector and the state in either the short or the long term. This conclusion is also reinforced in the British case when one considers the frequent property booms that have been generated since the Second World War when Conservative governments, in an attempt to encourage the productive sector of the economy, have lowered interest rates and reduced imposts on land and property development. By so doing the financial sector has been freed to move into those areas which it believes are the most lucrative; these have not tended to be productive/manufacturing areas but the property market. [49] Simply because governments and industrialists believe that the productive sector should be enhanced does not mean that the financial sector will invest its accumulated resources in this area —especially if there are safer and more lucrative areas of investment elsewhere.

It can be seen therefore that by looking at the practice of actors and interests in society historically the reductionism of much structuralist Marxist theory is revealed. This view finally is reinforced if one considers the structuralist view that qualitative change is only possible through the actions of urban social movements, or radicalised working- or middle-class groups working to smash or wrest fundamental concessions from the state. This argument has been criticised by Pickvance who has argued that although there may well be a base for social movements to develop, without effective organisation such a base may never generate a movement. [50] Pickvance has also argued that qualitative change can be engendered by middle-class and state reformist agencies: change is not therefore limited to working-class or urban social movements. Pickvance's view must be supported, it is argued here, because structural Marxists accept that there has been qualitative change (Castells on British New Towns), and despite the contention that this has been generated by urban social movements. As we shall see in a moment, these changes were in fact often generated by middle-class reformist activities. Also, notwithstanding structuralist theory, urban social movements in Britain are only very weakly developed with few organisational supports and very little influence on political decision-making. This view also receives support from Harvey who has argued that the working class in Britain is divided into industrial and urban/housing fields. In the former, the working class is highly organised and able to defend its interests, but in the urban field the working class is unorganised and ineffective. [51] If this is the case, it is doubtful, as we shall see, that one can explain examples of qualitative change in the British urban field through the actions of social movements. The fact that Castells and other Marxist theorists do adopt this approach, arguing that any other form of change is not change but reformism, indicates their attachment to theory first and objective explanation of real events in the world second.

Before looking at the inadequacies of both structuralist and instrumentalist Marxist explanations of change and state practices through two detailed case studies, I will briefly summarise the four major conclusions in this section. Firstly, it has been argued that the concept of 'relative autonomy' is epistemologically unsound and tautological. Secondly, it is invalid as a result to argue that the actions of the state must always, in the last instance, operate to repress the working class and work in the interests of the capitalist 'ruling class'. Following from this, I contend that to do so leads to ahistoricism and to an inadequate categorisation of the structure of political relationships within any social formation. Finally, the approach assumes that the working class must be repressed, even by reformist policies, and that change is only possible through the actions of urban social movements. My view is however that this is a reductionist explanation of change which derives from theory rather than analysis of urban social movements or other political interactions at the level of state policy-making. These four major conclusions will now be further illuminated by, first, a critique of Castells's explanation of the development of Britain's post-1945 New Towns policy, and then a critique of instrumentalist Marxist explanations of Britain's inner city policies in the 1960s and 1970s.

Manuel Castells and the explanation of Britain's New Towns policy

In *The Urban Question*, Castells follows the kind of structuralist Marxist approach outlined above. In particular, his explanation of the gestation of Britain's New Towns policy in the 1946 New Towns Act is that this was a qualitative change against the requirements and interests of the capitalist mode of production brought about by the actions of the radicalised working class after the Second World War. [52] This departure is however only a 'relative autonomy', because in the long term the intervention is seen as a failure and unable to counter the process of urban conglomeration in Greater London and the south-east. Castells argues that failure was inevitable and that this 'reformism' was largely intended by governments and state agencies, which did not wish to constrain effectively the process of capitalist urban concentration and agglomeration. My examination of the inadequacies of Castells's explanation of the gestation and failure of the New Towns policy is intended to illustrate the theoretical weaknesses of the structuralist approach.

Castells argues that the post-war emphasis on a dispersal policy in Britain can be accounted for through a number of necessary and sufficient factors. First of all a number of necessary conditions had to obtain before state intervention on the side of dispersal could occur. Throughout the 1920s and 1930s there had in fact been evidence of serious inner-city congestion in cities like London, as well as a growing awareness of a regional imbalance in jobs between the prosperous south-east and the west midlands and the declining areas of the north-east, north-west, central Scotland and south Wales. The drift to the south-east, Castells argues, was generated by the requirements of modern monopoly capital developing in an unfettered way. The corollary of this development had been the growth of ameliorative pressure groups and individuals concerned with both the inequities of regional unemployment and inner-city squalor and overcrowding. Thus, as early as the turn of the twentieth century concerned individuals had come together in Britain under the inspiration of Ebenezer Howard to form, first, the Garden Cities Movement and, second, the Town Planning Institute to defend and argue the case for planning of towns and a planning profession.[53] Despite these pressures for planned dispersal to New Towns and the statutory planning of urban areas, and despite the growing realisation that regional unemployment could only be resolved by a national strategy of planning for jobs and population location (see the 1939 Barlow Report), little was achieved until the end of the war. The reason that change occurred in official attitudes was, according to Castells, due to two factors—one was a necessary cause of the change, the other was the sufficient and major explanation of the new policy. The first factor was the amount of war damage to the housing stock of London and other major cities by German bombing, which led, in London, to the 1944 Abercrombie Plan calling for the decanting of jobs and people from London to self-contained New Towns in the Home Counties —in line with many of the earlier recommendations for dispersal in the Barlow Report.

Despite these calls for, and need for, speedy action by the state, for Castells the decisive element was 'the political conjuncture, with the upsurge of working-class political awareness and the electoral triumph of the Labour Party, which reinforced the pressure for change, and required satisfaction on the level of demand, in order not to radicalise the class struggle.'[54] In other words the post-war dispersal policy was a response to working-class demands, and the state was forced to act to minimise class struggle. This action was, however, only a 'relative autonomy' because the Abercrombie Plan was a reformist intervention in the long term, not a radical departure; it largely failed to stop urban congestion in London, and it contributed very little to the curtailment of the drift to the south-east from the declining industrial regions. Castells's explanation of this is that although Abercrombie called for effective control on industrial location in London, the powers to control capital were not very effective: the industrial development certificate system only operated on factory extensions above 5,000 sq. ft. and the subsidies for advance factories and other tax concessions for New Towns were inadequate. Similarly nothing was done to control either office development or the expansion of the service sector because the IDC system operated only on manufacturing industry, which was not the fastest growing sector of the economy in the post-war period. Thus, despite the attempt to control capital and its location by a policy of dispersal, the whole exercise was a reformist intervention which failed. Castells draws heavily on the fact that although the London region expanded by 1.7 million people between 1946 and 1956, the New Towns only took 19 per cent of this growth, and mainly skilled and unskilled labour, to support his view that the plan did not work. [55] Ultimately for Castells, of course, the plan could not have worked because it would have questioned the locational autonomy of capital if it had done so, and by the 1950s a Conservative government was in office, which was closer to an understanding of the needs of the capitalist system.

This explanation of urban change and the role of the state can be questioned on at least two grounds: the motives that Castells argues were behind the dispersal policy, and the inevitability of failure for the dispersal policy due to its questioning of capital's locational decisions.

Taking the argument that the policy was an inevitable failure (and therefore a reformist exercise) first, it can be argued that Castells fails to understand the possibility that human actors can misperceive the reality of forces shaping change, and that this explains the policy's failure rather than the fact that politicians and civil servants had no intention of giving the state effective powers to constrain capital. In other words the plan for dispersal was a failure not because the politicians failed to control capital, but because they failed to appreciate which sectors of capital would need to be controlled if their policies were to be effective. Thus, Hall has shown that the continuation of the drift to the south-east has been due, since 1945, mainly to the rise of the tertiary sector of the economy. [56] It is clear, however, that the post-war dispersal and industrial locational policies of the Labour government, as well as the emphases of the Barlow and Abercrombie Reports, were premised on the need to control manufacturing industry—which Hall *et al.* have indicated the government was relatively successful in controlling. [57] If this is the case, then it would be correct to criticise the government or state for failing to be able to predict the future, but it is altogether another thing to imply, as Castells does, that this policy failure was both inevitable and largely intentional. Thus we can argue that the immediate post-war dispersal policy failed because planners, civil servants and politicians failed to foresee the growth of the tertiary sector, not because, being reformist, they had no intention of controlling capital, or because the policy was simply an exercise in generating quiescence amongst the potentially rebellious working class.

This conclusion is supported by the fact that at no point does Castells attempt to assess or understand the 'reality', or awareness of the problem, as perceived by planners, civil servants and politicians in 1944-5. In other words Castells looks at the New Towns policy in isolation and fails to grasp the way in which it was inextricably entwined with other post-war urban policies. By failing to look at the totality of the Labour government's post-war urban and locational policies Castells makes the mistake of arguing that it had no intention of controlling capital. But, looking at the range of policies implemented between 1945 and 1947 it is possible to see that the Labour government could argue that it provided a general policy for dispersal, job protection and industrial location control. Thus, while the 1946 New Towns Act was intended to solve the problem of congestion in London by dispersal, the 1947 Town and Country Planning Act gave local authorities powers to control both physical and industrial developments in their areas with co-ordination from Whitehall. At the same time these powers were supplemented in the 1945 Distribution of Industry Act with an industrial development certificate system which forbade industrial developments above 5,000 sq. ft. without a Board of Trade certificate. True, these certificates only affected manufacturing industry, but, as seen by the Barlow Report, it was the loss of manufacturing industry from the Depressed Areas and relocation in the south-east and west midlands which were the major problems. Added to these regulative powers, there were provisions for tax concessions and for the construction of advanced factories in the depressed regions. Finally, the Labour government expected, given the Registrar-General's prediction that population growth would be relatively static after the war, that most housing construction would be undertaken by either local authorities or New Towns, with only a limited amount by the private housebuilding sector, especially in view of the 100 per cent development charge imposed on gains made in land and property development under the 1947 Act. [58]

Thus, notwithstanding Castells's single policy emphasis it can be argued that the Labour government believed that it had by 1947 created a planning and development system which could be expected to control all industrial location, to cater for most new homes and do so within a planned local environment, with decongested central cities and regional balance. To argue that they were wrong is one thing; to argue that failure was inevitable because the state cannot allow capital to be controlled in the long term, or that failure was intentional, is to put theory in the place of detailed research and explanation.

This view is further reinforced when we consider that, in fact, the forces which ultimately broke Labour's post-war urban planning and dispersal system had very little to do with capital (and its require- ments) at all. One of the major reasons why the 1947 system was broken was that the Registrar-General's predictions about population growth were totally inadequate: rather than a static population, a 'baby boom' continued into the 1950s and the demand for land and housing far outstripped the expected levels. These demands were felt most acutely in the prosperous south-east and west midlands, although not exclusively, due to the fact that rising living and material standards led to earlier marriages, lower death rates and an immediate increase in household formation, as young people and married couples found it possible to purchase a home of their own much earlier than their parents had been able to. [59] Similarly, as already mentioned, most of the post-war employment growth was in the tertiary sector of the economy, which was less dependent on location to raw materials and thus quite logically located near to markets and the skilled labour force—which happened to be in the south-east and west midlands. These developments could hardly have been foreseen by any government in the mid-1940s. The failure of dispersal and the continuation of suburban growth was also encouraged by an addition- al unforeseen phenomenon—the massive rise in motor car ownership which enabled people to live well away from their place of work. Finally, a factor Castells does not mention at all, there was the fiscal and international monetary crisis which the Labour government faced in 1947. Hall *et al.* have shown that up to 1947 the Labour government was particularly successful in controlling manufacturing industry location and in placing new advance factories in the Depressed Areas. After 1947, with a balance of payments crisis and pressure on sterling, there was an immediate cut back in public expenditure in these areas and in the designation of New Towns. [60] The government was therefore led to give up some of its commit- ments in order to solve problems related to the decline of the British economy internationally. It is false to assume that it could not, or had no intention to, control capital in practice.

Thus, while it is true as Castells argues that the dispersal policy was a failure, there are very different explanations as to why this failure occurred; it was not simply that the state is only 'relatively autonomous' and that the interests of capital must be determinant in the last instance. The weakness of the explanation is also indicated by Castells's contention that the main reason for the development of the policy was the upsurge in working-class militancy which supposedly forced a reformist Labour government to make some concessions to ensure social harmony and quiescence. This in itself shows that Castells does not understand the origins of the policy.

There is no clear evidence that the working classes were demanding New Towns as a solution to their living and unemployment problems in 1945. New Towns were essentially a middle-class establishment solution to social problems. There may well have been some who thought that such a policy might quell the potentially rebellious working class, but there were probably more who were altruistic in their motives. [61] It is also true that there were no really effective urban social movements or organised working-class pressure groups demanding physical solutions to the problems facing the working class. Indeed, the most famous urban social movement—the pre-war Jarrow march—was linked to a demand for jobs in the north-east, rather than to any call for a dispersal of people and jobs away from large cities. In terms of Castells's argument, there was indeed more potential for class struggle and unrest in the periods of high unemployment in the 1930s than in 1944-5. Yet there was no suggestion that the problem could be solved by such a policy in the 1930s. We have to look elsewhere for an explanation of the development of a dispersal policy.

One possible explanation might well be rooted in the displacement effect of the war. [62] It has been argued that one impact of the war, as well as of the Depression in the 1930s, was a radicalising effect on the upper and middle classes in Britain. Elite groups were made aware of the social and economic problems facing the working class, and the belief that planning and controls had been effective in war led to the advocacy of comparable practices in peace time. Politicians thus turned to groups and individuals—like the Town and Country Planning Association and the Town Planning Institute and to planners and civil servants like Barlow and Abercrombie—who had for many years advocated planning and policy solutions to social problems. It is thus possible to agree with Cullingworth that it would have made very little difference whether a Labour or a Conservative government had been elected in 1945 because both parties were committed to some form of welfare state, full employment and land-use planning. [63] This view is further supported by the fact that policy-making is not simply an action-reaction process, but one with a long gestation period. It is thus difficult to accept Castells's suggestion that the Labour government was simply reacting to a potentially rebellious and radicalised working class.

The dispersal policy had a long pedigree stretching from the pre-war Barlow Report, through the wartime Reconstruction Secretariat created by Churchill and the general acceptance in Whitehall of the Reith, Scott, Dower, Hobhouse and Uthwatt Reports which followed the Barlow Report. [64]

Thus we can argue that a great deal of Labour's post-war programme was decided upon well before the new government came into office: the new administration added minor details and embellishments, not the overall structure of post-war urban policy. Interestingly, the evidence also seems to indicate that when there were limitations imposed upon the draconian implications of this legislation they came, not from capital, but from local authorities defending their role from the possibility of New Towns usurping it; from Churchill and the landed interest in the Conservative party resisting full land nationalisation; and from the Treasury and the old Ministry of Health resisting a more interventionist policy for fear of its public expenditure and organisational consequences. [65]

What should be clear from this discussion is that the forces shaping policy-making by the state are far more complex than Castells imagines; indeed working-class demands appear in this interpretation as of minor importance as against the impact of ameliorative reformist interests and the activities of civil servants. And the complexity of forces shaping the New Towns policy was in fact much greater than that presented so far because the landed/rural protectionist interests in Britain were also significant in supporting this policy. Traditional landowners and farmers were and are particularly concerned about the effects of urban sprawl and development in destroying the rural way of life and good agricultural land. [66] Thus it is not surprising that the political representatives of these interests—the National Farmers Union and the Country Landowners Association—have tended to support dispersal policies and land-use planning to stop ribbon development and urban sprawl. The explanation of a dispersal policy in 1945-6 therefore probably owes something to the range of necessary factors which Castells has outlined and the fact that a Labour government was elected may well have speeded up the process, but the true explanation of the gestation of the policy lies not in working-class demands, which were peripheral, but in the coalition of aims between ameliorative middle-class reformers and rural and landed interests. In this sense, then, qualitative change was generated by interests other than the radicalised working class or urban social movements.

Instrumentalist Marxist explanations of Britain's inner-city policies

If the structuralist explanation of change and state behaviour is inadequate, it is nevertheless much more sophisticated in its approach than instrumentalist analyses. The glaring reductionism of the instrumentalist approach will be indicated by a critique of recent explanations of Britain's inner-city policy reappraisal from writers operating within this school.

Since 1968, dispersal policy has been transformed by a growing realisation of the decline of inner-city areas. Starting in 1968, with an urban programme of limited extra financial help to areas with evidence of high crime and poverty rates, a new emphasis was given to urban policy in Britain. This was symbolised by the creation of twelve Community Development Projects in 1969 to act both as research units and action teams on the ground to try and eradicate pockets of deprivation in inner-city areas. [67] Furthermore, although the CDPs were eventually closed after serious conflict with local authorities, this re-emphasis continued with Peter Shore, the Secretary of State for the Environment in the last Labour government, downgrading dispersal and giving additional assistance to inner-city areas with the worst records of deprivation in September 1976. [68] This policy reappraisal has been analysed and explained by some Marxist writers as showing that the state was acting to solve problems of capitalism by cosmetic tactics since effective solutions would require real controls over capital.

Such explanations, associated with the CDPs and a recent article by Paris, are worth examining. While they are Marxist, they are essentially instrumentalist rather than structuralist in their approach. [69] They argue that the state's involvement in the urban programme and in the CDP experiments was merely an attempt to placate potentially rebellious masses in working-class areas, especially racial minorities, who suffer the most from rising unemployment and welfare cuts generated by structural changes in the economic base of modern capitalism. [70] In other words, the policies of the state are diversionary tactics to legitimate the bourgeois state. [71] Limited 'topping-up' of existing programmes within the control of local authorities are seen as a mere 'gilding of the ghetto' rather than tackling the true causes of deprivation: the decline of the manufacturing base of inner-city areas in the face of competition from capital intensive and technologically innovatory industries located elsewhere. The state was seen in the 1960s and 1970s as merely reacting to the potential for unrest by urban social movements, and then as moving into a more repressive role. The subsequent closure of the CDP experiments, the failure to accept the CDP explanation of the problems as one of structural decline, and cuts in public expenditure were all seen as evidence of developing repression. [72] This was taken to indicate, and it was a view expressed in other writings by Cockburn and Bennington, [73] that the state is an instrument of monopoly capital. This is, of course, a very different explanation of the role of the state from that given by structuralist writers.

It can be argued that, while these instrumentalist explanations may well be correct in their specification of the structural economic changes generating inner-city and regional decline, they fail to grasp the complexity of the role of the state and the forces shaping change in urban policy, but they do not have the structuralists' redeeming concept of 'relative autonomy'. The weaknesses of the instrumentalist approach can be seen in the major arguments relating to inner-city policy.

The first, outlined above, is that the state has no real autonomy and that it must function only to placate the working class rather than to solve the problem of inner-city decline. There are, however, other explanations as to why the state intervened in 1968. One is that the loss of the 1968 local government elections led the Labour government to pursue action that might quickly reassure traditional Labour voters in inner urban areas. Given the government's commitments to trade union reform and to public expenditure cuts to make devaluation work in this period, the need to be seen 'to be doing something' may well have been the primary cause for this limited policy package. Here we should note that the Civil Service was taken by surprise by the new policies which only came on to the agenda after Enoch Powell's 'Rivers of Blood' speech to which the Labour government had to respond. [74]

A second suggested explanation of the inner-city reappraisal as cosmetic and largely a failure is that policy-makers actually misperceived the true causes of decline and initiated policy in ignorance of the facts. Thus, some academics and civil servants (particularly Derek Morrell, the civil servant given overall responsibility for the programme in Whitehall) actually did feel that the problem was due to the personal inadequacies of individuals. The argument runs that, since the welfare services provided minimum standards, anyone who fell below these standards did so owing to personality difficulties and inadequacies. In this view, the problem was not structural at all, but was confined to small pockets or 'cankers', whose inhabitants themselves were to blame. Topping up existing programmes by positive discrimination and limited self-help might thus solve the problem. [75] But the experiences of the CDPs, and the follow-up research of the Inner Area Studies, concluded that this was a false assumption and that the problem *was* structural. The CDPs and Paris were therefore correct in arguing that the policies were cosmetic, but one cannot assume from this that the policies were intended to fail, merely that they did so. The explanation that policy-makers actually misperceived the problem would seem, on the available evidence, to have more truth in it than one which stresses machiavellian intent.

There are other arguments which also cast doubt on the view of an instrumental state tied to the needs of capital. While the policy for the inner city clearly failed, it is possible that part of the reason was not just misperception by policy-makers, but the fact that the responsibility for the policy was given to the wrong department. We have noted that the policy was largely a response to Powell's racialist speech and was given to the Home Office as the department responsible for law and order and for immigration. Unfortunately, as it has turned out, the Home Office was out of touch with the problems of urban areas and of industry, issues which have traditionally been the responsibility of the Departments of Environment, Industry, Employment, and Trade. The Home Office was largely out of touch with the problems and there is evidence that the other departments which might have understood the complexities better actually took no real interest in the policy until the mid-1970s. [76] Finally, we cannot discount the financial climate of the times in any attempt to explain the failure of the policy. Due to devaluation and the need to keep public expenditure within bounds, the government simply did not have the revenue to engage in anything but limited aid.

The instrumentalist thesis of the state's role in inner-city policy is therefore an explanation, but it is hardly the only, or the most compelling, one. The same can be said of the argument that in pursuing its inner-city policy the state was merely responding to the threat of a radicalised working class.

Despite being seen as largely cosmetic, the inner-city policy did represent a qualitative change in capitalist society, and it has been argued that this limited reappraisal was generated by the state responding to the rise and influence of squatters, community action groups and ethnic organisations which the state feared might react violently or radically to the crisis of urban redevelopment and inner-city decay in the 1960s and 1970s. [77] This explanation may well fit the theory of how the working class can act to wrest concessions from the capitalist state, but it is not a particularly adequate explanation of the gestation of the inner-city reappraisal. Firstly, there is little evidence that pressure-group or direct action had any influence on government in 1968. The Civil Service was given a brief at short notice and it largely followed the experience of similar experiments already under way in the United States. [78] Secondly, one might also legitimately ask where the potentially rebellious masses were in either the 1960s or the 1970s. Although inner-city poverty may well be a potential breeding ground for unrest, there is very little evidence that any groups were posing a critical problem for the state. [79] Indeed the only active group from these areas was the National Front, and the policies were hardly aimed at placating the interests which it represents. Furthermore, if the policies were aimed at placating racial minorities and the urban poor, then the state was singularly inept, because the CDPs actually radicalised the local inhabitants in many cases and generated conflict with local authorities.

The inner-city reappraisal was clearly generated not by a monolithic state but by civil servants responding to a brief given them by politicians concerned by their poor electoral record. In fulfilling this brief the Whitehall civil servants were constrained by the fiscal conservatism of the Treasury and also by the bureaucratic inertia and conservatism of existing local authorities concerned with using any additional finance available to bolster *existing* policies. It is not surprising that this led to conflict with the CDPs who had a very different conception of the problem, but this was hardly intentional or simply because local authorities defend capital. In practice local authorities are more likely to be concerned with defending their organisational routines and practices than capital or any other interest for that matter.

Such an explanation, rooted in an understanding of the problems of intra-state organisational conflicts and the lack of monolithic goals and interests within bureaucracies, can also help to explain why it is that even in 1976, when the structural problems of decline were even more glaringly apparent, the state failed to do more than move to limited 'partnership' arrangements with some of the worst affected inner-urban local authorities. The limited and cosmetic nature of the post-1976 inner-city policy was therefore due to local authorities defending their existing programmes and policies and using any extra finance to defend past commitments rather than to make any new ones. This can be attributed more to 'bureaucratic inertia' than to attempts to repress or placate the working class. [80] Even Paris and the CDPs would accept that the inner-city policy which followed was not likely to work; and yet if it was a policy that capital required to ensure its permanency and control of the state, one would surely have expected capital to arrive at a policy package through the state that would actually placate the working class, rather than institute a package likely to further alienate the working class and exacerbate the problems of decline. By the very analyses reviewed, therefore, the inner-city policy which followed was hardly evidence of the state acting in the best interests of capital; rather it was evidence of the state pursuing policies which, because they were bound to fail, were antithetical to the interests of capital in the long term. If this is so then instrumentalists are also hoist by their own petard because they inadvertently present evidence of state practices which are not instrumental to the requirements of capital in the long term.

Conclusions

Though this paper has tried to show that there are serious weaknesses with both the structuralist and instrumentalist explanations of the role of the state in urban policy-making, none of the various explanations offered here for the nature of the New Towns policy and the inner-city policies of the 1960s and 1970s falls neatly within either of the other two models of the state outlined at the beginning.

Thus, while we have seen that the state is to some extent pluralistic, in that a range of actors do attempt to shape urban policy, it is not true, as the evidence of Whitehall and local authority bureaucratic involvement in policy-making indicates, that the state and its agencies are neutral. In fact in both inner-city and New Towns policies the state apparatus and agencies were often in conflict internally and prepared to pursue their own separate goals. This conclusion however suggest that the managerialist view of the state must also be invalid because, rather than acting monolithically with definite goals and interests of its own, the state and its agencies at local and central levels are more often in conflict than in co-operation. Nevertheless, one conclusion from the managerialist approach does seem valid, and this is that state agencies can and do exert a considerable influence on policy over and above the dictates of party, pressure group, or capital. This leads us to conclude that the instrumentalist view of the state is simplistic and reductionist; it tends to see the state as a shell to be shaped in whatever manner suits the needs of capital. But in the cases of the New Towns and inner-city policies this was seen to be an inadequate conclusion. Finally, despite its greater subtlety and sophistication the structuralist model must also be doubted mainly because the concept of 'relative autonomy' does not overcome the ultimate reductionism associated with the instrumentalist approach. Eventually the state is tied to the needs of capital in the same manner as before, and yet, in arguing that the state can act autonomously in the short term to accommodate the pluralistic processes of policy-making in practice, the approach carries the seeds of its own rejection. One can legitimately ask: when do the long-term constraints of capital begin and the short-term scope for pluralistic autonomy end? There is no guarantee that contingency in the short term will end quickly and that the needs of capital will be defended whenever short-term policies within the political system threaten capital. If this is so, then, as Poulantzas and Lojkine have argued, the state can and does act autonomously at certain historical conjunctures and the structuralist thesis begins to appear more valid.

Where then does this leave analysts of the role of the state in the process of urban change? If all of the four theoretical models outlined are inadequate in theory and practice, how should we view the state? Saunders has argued that it may well depend on the issues being decided upon by the state, and that in some circumstances the state may be tied to the needs of capital and at other times it may not, depending on whether or not capital has a strong stake in the issue under consideration. [81] This is a useful insight, but it does not resolve the question of the theoretical perspective that must be adopted in viewing state practices, because one may always argue that the state is a capitalist state because it influences those decisions which are important and does not influence those which are not important. Unfortunately this is inadequate because, as we saw in the cases of the New Towns and inner-city policies, capital was not particularly influential and yet, surely, we would not want to argue that dispersal and inner-city policies were not of interest to capital in Britain? If this is the case, and we can find clear examples of capital not being able to influence state policies in either the short or long terms, then Saunders's solution alone cannot be enough, and we require a more flexible approach. I suggest that the beginnings of a more useful approach to the analysis of the state under modern capitalism are located in the writings of Pahl and E. P. Thompson.

Pahl initially viewed the state in a Weberian/elitist way, arguing that it could operate autonomously and ultimately monolithically as an independent actor in society. Since then he has reappraised his approach to argue that the state is not a monolith but an *intervening variable* at the local level between the needs of the central government and private capital where under certain circumstances it may act independently of both these interests. [82] But, while useful, this approach is still limited. If local state agencies can have some intervening effect between central state and private capital, then it follows that the central state must also have an intervening effect between local state and private capital. Furthermore, it is surely possible that private capital may have an intervening effect between local and central state agencies which are also in competition over scarce resources. The value of these views is supported in this discussion by the evidence of central-local state competition and attempts by private capital to shape both local and central state inner-city and dispersal policies. The important point, however, is that in these two policy cases neither of the three factors outlined here dominated either of the two policies all of the time; they were, and are, in competition for policy influence. Furthermore, as indicated in our discussion of the role of the landed interest in New Towns policy and of urban social movements in inner-city policy, the state also intervenes between the goals and interests of political pressure groups and other modes of production within any social formation. Does this mean then that the state is relatively pluralistic? The answer to this must be a qualified no because, whereas the policy-making process is pluralistic, it is not true that all interests have equal access to it, or its resources; and, more importantly, as the discussion has indicated local and central state agencies are not neutral, but have their own goals and values which may conflict with those of other agencies and intervene between the goals of other actors in society.

Having noted the intervening and conflictual nature of the state it is important to take the discussion just one stage further. The central thesis of this paper is that the interrelation of actors seeking to shape state policies is much more complex than any simplistic vision of the working class versus the bourgeoisie in conflict over a relatively instrumental state, in which the capitalist ruling class must dominate in the short term or, if we take the structuralist view, the long term. The state itself is neither an instrument nor a monolithic unity, but this is not the most important point. The central issue is one raised with powerful insight by E. P. Thompson. It concerns the inadequacy of assuming that, because the capitalist mode of production is the major mode of production, its entrenchment at social and political levels (i.e. its ability to control the state) has been as unproblematic as its dominance may have been at the economic level. As Thompson argues, what we really need to know is how the capitalist mode of production developed in Britain historically at social, political and economic levels. In other words, we need to know the 'society-specific' ways in which the capitalist mode of the production developed in every society: asking the questions whether or not it was able to oust the feudal landownership patterns and practices socially, economically, and politically; how it reacted to the extension of working-class political pressures; whether or not it was able to develop a cohesive and conscious unity of purpose at the political level; and, most importantly for our discussion here, whether or not, and if so how far, the capitalist class has been able to ensure the control and direction of the state in its own, as opposed to other interests.

The point here is that we cannot assume, simply because the British state and its agencies, as well as other modes of production and political actors, operate within an international capitalist market economy, that there will therefore be any necessary correspondence between the actions of the state and the domestic or international capitalist class. On the contrary, the benefit of the Marxist method is that it allows us to indicate how an optimally operating capitalist system ought to operate, from which position we may then be able to indicate, due to the lack of necessary correspondence, why it is that some societies are able to function more efficiently and successfully in this international system. The point to be taken from this discussion of state policies for dispersal and the inner city in Britain is not only that the capitalist class is unable to ensure that the state will always pursue its interests, but that this is due, amongst other things, to the persistence of landed interests, the intervening effect of state agencies at local and central levels, with goals and routines of their own, and also the activities of ameliorative middle-class reforms and working-class activists. In this sense, then, one explanation of Britain's poor post-war economic and urban record may well be, in fact, the historic and continuing lack of correspondence between the activities and interests of the state and the capitalist mode of production. The state in Britain is, then, not a capitalist state as such; it is a state, however, which must respond to the contradictions and crises of the capitalist system: crises which an intervening and autonomous state may well help to generate due to the lack of correspondence between its activities and the requirements of British capitalism. The reasons for the development of this non-correspondence in Britain cannot be discovered through theoretical discourse alone. To discover them demands a motivated research exercise rooted in understanding the historical development of the capitalist mode of production and its conflicts with, and defeats by, other traditional modes of production and social and political processes.

Notes

1 For a brief introduction to the views of Park and Wirth see 'Society Today', *New Society*, 15 February 1979.

2 J. Rex and R. Moore, *Race, Community and Conflict*, Oxford University Press, London, 1967, and R. E. Pahl, *Whose City?*, Penguin, Harmondsworth, 1975, pp. 185-306.

3 For an introduction to the debate see Michael Harloe, 'Editor's Introduction', in M. Harloe (ed.), *Proceedings of the Conference on Urban Change and Conflict*, Centre for Environmental Studies, London, 1975.

4 M. Castells, *The Urban Question*, Edward Arnold, London, 1977, pp. 276-83.

5 These approaches are, respectively, The Community Development Projects, *Gilding the Ghetto*, Home Office Central Intelligence Unit, London, 1977; *The Costs of Industrial Change*, London, CDP Inter-project Editorial Team, 1977; and Chris Paris, 'The parallels are striking ... crisis in the inner city? GB 1977', *International Journal of Urban and Regional Research*, vol. 2, no. 1, 1978, pp. 160-70.

6 This discussion draws heavily on Peter Saunders, 'Community power, urban managerialism and the local state', paper presented to the *Centre for Environmental Studies conference on urban change and conflict*, University of Nottingham, 5-8 January 1979.

7 C. W. Mills, *The Power Elite*, Oxford University Press, New York, 1959, and Floyd Hunter, *Community Power Structure*, University of North Carolina Press, Chapel Hill, 1953.

8 Robert A. Dahl, 'Critique of the Ruling Elite model', *American Political Science Review*, vol. 52, June, 1958, pp. 463-9, and *Who Governs?*, Yale University Press, New Haven, 1961.

9 Ibid.

10 Ibid., p. 228.

11 Peter Bachrach and Morton S. Baratz, 'The two faces of power', *American Political Science Review*, vol. 56, 1962, pp. 947-52, and 'Decisions and non-decisions: an analytic framework', *American Political Science Review*, vol. 57, 1963, pp. 641-51.

12 For further elaboration of this point see Frederic W. Frey, 'Comment: on issues and non-issues in the study of power', *American Political Science Review*, vol. 65, 1971, pp. 1081-101.

13 Nelson W. Polsby, *Community Power and Political Theory*, Yale University Press, New Haven, 1963, and, Raymond E. Wolfinger, 'Non-decisions and the study of local politics', *American Political Science Review*, vol. 65, 1971, pp. 1063-80.

14 Steven Lukes, *Power: A Radical View*, Macmillan, London, 1977.

15 Rex and Moore, op. cit., 1967.

16 Pahl, op. cit., 1975, chapters 9 and 10, pp. 185-94.

17 R. E. Pahl and J. T. Winkler, 'The coming corporatism', *New Society*, 19 October 1974.

18 Harloe, op. cit., 1975, pp. 1-3.

19 Sam Aaronovitch, *The Ruling Class; a Study of British Finance Capital*, Lawrence & Wishart, London, 1961, and Ralph Miliband, *The*

State in Capitalist Society, Weidenfeld & Nicolson, London, 1970.

20 Miliband, op. cit., 1970, pp. 179-264.

21 CDPs and Paris, op. cit., 1978, and Cynthia Cockburn, *The Local State*, Pluto Press, London, 1977.

22 For these authors' views see Ernest Laclau, 'The specificity of the political: The Poulantzas-Miliband Debate', *Economy and Society*, vol. 5, 1975, pp. 87-111; F. Lamarche, 'Property development and the economic foundations of the urban question', in *Urban Sociology: Critical Essays*, ed. C. G. Pickvance, Tavistock, London, 1976, pp. 85-118; Castells, op. cit.; C. G. Pickvance, 'Marxist approaches to the study of urban politics: divergences among some recent French studies', *International Journal of Urban and Regional Research*, vol. 1, no. 2, 1977, pp. 219-55; and, Edmond Preteceille, 'Urban planning: the contradictions of capitalist urbanisation', *Antipode*, vol. 8, no. 1, 1976, p. 69.

23 For these differences, related to the state of the political debate in the French Communist Party, see Pickvance, op. cit., and the article by Elizabeth Lebas in this volume.

24 Castells, Poulantzas, and Lojkine, op. cit.

25 For the lack of total clarification of this problematic in the British case, see Doreen Massey, 'The analysis of capitalist landownership: an investigation of the case of Great Britain', *International Journal of Urban and Regional Research*, vol. 1, no. 3, 1977, pp. 404-24.

26 For an overview see J. O'Connor, *The Fiscal Crisis of the State*, St. Martin's Press, New York, 1971, and Andrew Glyn and Bob Sutcliffe, *Workers, British Capitalism and the Profits Squeeze*, Penguin, Harmondsworth, 1972.

27 For an overview of this critique see E. P. Thompson, 'The poverty of theory', in *The Poverty of Theory and Other Essays*, Merlin, London, 1978, pp. 193-406.

28 Peter Norman, 'Managerialism—a review of recent work', in *Proceedings of the Conference on Urban Change and Conflict*, Centre for Environmental Studies, London, 1975, pp. 63-5.

29 For example, Peter Saunders, op.cit., and the discussion in John Dearlove, *The Politics of Policy in Local Government*, Cambridge University Press, London, 1973.

30 On this see Ken Newton, *Second City Politics*, Oxford University Press, London, 1976, and David McKay and Andrew W. Cox, *The Politics of Urban Change*, Croom Helm, London, 1979, pp. 25-68.

31 Andrew Cox, 'Administrative inertia and inner city policy', *Public Administration Bulletin*, no. 29, 1979, and The Central Policy Review Staff, *Relations between Central Government and Local Authorities*, HMSO, London, 1977.

32 Pahl, op. cit., pp. 265-303.

33 For an overview see Rob Flynn, 'The state and planning: a review and critique of some recent Marxist writings', *Public Administration Bulletin*, no. 28, 1978, pp. 4-16.

34 Saunders, op. cit., pp. 2-5.

35 For a critique of the reductionism of this position see Thompson, op. cit., passim.

36 On this point see 'Editor's Introduction', in M. Harloe (ed.), *Captive Cities*, Wiley, London, pp. 27-9.

37 Thompson, op. cit., pp. 334-54.

38 Ibid., pp. 242-62.

39 On this consult Massey, op. cit., and F. M. L. Thompson, 'Land and politics in England in the nineteenth century', *Transactions of the Royal Historical Society*, vol. 15, 1965, pp. 23-44.

40 This conclusion has been forcefully presented in Peter Hall *et al.*, *The Containment of Urban England, Vol. 2*, Allen & Unwin, London, 1973, pp. 390-409.

41 Claus Offé, 'Advanced capitalism and the welfare state', *Politics and Society*, vol. 4, no. 2, 1972, pp. 479-84.

42 On the work of these writers see Herbert Simon and James March, *Organisations*, John Wiley, New York, 1963; C. E. Lindblom, *The Policy-making Process*, Prentice-Hall, New Jersey, 1968; A. Downs, *Inside Bureaucracy*, Little Brown, Boston, 1967; and Peter Self, *Administrative Theories and Politics*, Allen & Unwin, London, 1972.

43 On the internal conflicts within the British central bureaucracy over scarce resources see Hugh Heclo and Arron Wildavsky, *The Private Government of Public Money*, University of California Press, Los Angeles, 1973.

44 For a discussion and practical application of the concepts of 'bounded rationality' and 'satisficing' see G. T. Allison, *Essence of Decision: Explaining the Cuban Missile Crisis*, Little Brown, Boston, 1971, pp. 71-2.

45 Lamarche, op. cit., and Nicos Poulantzas, *Classes in Contemporary Capitalism*, New Left Books, London, 1975, pp. 185-7.

46 On this see 'Historical materialist approaches to urban sociology', in *Urban Sociology: Critical Essays*, ed. C. G. Pickvance, Tavistock, London, 1976, pp. 16-22.

47 Sidney Pollard, *The Development of the British Economy*, Edward Arnold, London, 1973, *passim*.

48 For an introduction to the independence and historical development of 'the City' see Hamish McRae and Frances Caitnerass, *Capital City: London as a Financial Centre*, Methuen, London, 1977; and Richard Spiegelberg, *The City: Power Without Accountability*, Blond & Briggs, London, 1973.

49 Doreen Massey and Alejandrina Catalano, *Capital and Land*, Edward Arnold, London, 1978, pp. 139-66.

50 C. G. Pickvance, 'On the study of urban social movements', in *Urban Sociology: Critical Essays*, op. cit., pp. 198-218.

51 David Harvey, 'Labour, capital and class struggle around the built environment in advanced capitalist societies', *Politics and Society*, vol. 6, no. 3, 1976, pp. 254-68.

52 Most of this critique of Castells is directed at his arguments in *The Urban Question*, op. cit., pp. 277-83.

53 For details of these developments see Gordon E. Cherry, *The Evolution of British Town Planning*, Leonard Hill, Leighton Buzzard, 1974.

54 Castells, op. cit., p. 280.

55 Ibid., p. 283.

56 Peter Hall, *Urban and Regional Planning*, Penguin, Harmondsworth, 1976, pp. 125-54.

57   Hall, *The Containment of Urban England*, op. cit., pp. 102-25.
58   For further details see McKay and Cox, op. cit., pp. 306.
59   Ibid.
60   Hall, *Urban and Regional Planning*, op. cit., pp. 125-39.
61   This is the general conclusion of G. E. Cherry, *The Evolution of British Town Planning*, op. cit., pp. 6-32.
62   This argument has been associated with A. Peacock and J. Wiseman, *The Growth of Public Expenditure in the United Kingdom*, Allen & Unwin, London, 1961.
63   J. B. Cullingworth, *Environmental Planning, Vol. 1*, HMSO, London, 1975, pp. 250-8.
64   For further details see McKay and Cox, *The Politics of Urban Change*, op. cit., pp. 27-36.
65   Ibid., pp. 34-6.
66   Ibid., pp. 92-5.
67   For further elaboration see D. H. McKay and A. W. Cox, 'Confusion and reality in public policy: the case of the British Urban Programme', *Political Studies*, vol. 26, no. 4, December 1978, pp. 491-506.
68   Further details are presented in Cox, 'Administrative inertia and inner city policy', op. cit.
69   CDP, *The Costs of Industrial Change* and *Gilding the Ghetto*, op. cit., and Paris, op. cit.
70   Ibid.
71   This view is particularly associated with the writings of Paris, op. cit.
72   On this view in particular see CDP, *Gilding the Ghetto*, op. cit., pp. 44-63.
73   Cockburn, *The Local State*, op. cit.; and John Bennington, *Local Government Becomes Big Business*, CDP Information and Intelligence Unit, London, 1976.
74   McKay and Cox, 'Confusion and reality ...', op. cit., pp. 493-4.
75   Ibid., pp. 503-5.
76   Ibid., pp. 501-3.
77   In particular see Paris, op. cit., pp. 164-5.
78   McKay and Cox, op. cit., pp. 504-5.
79   Ibid., p. 500.
80   On this see Cox, op. cit.
81   Saunders, op. cit., pp. 14-17.
82   Pahl, *Whose City?*, op. cit., pp. 265-303.

Regionalism and urban theory: the case of Britain

J. R. Mellor

The two immediate questions raised by regionalism are the social costs of development and the nature of political articulation in modern society. The study of regional differences and social and political movements relating to these therefore takes us back to some fundamental problems faced by the founding fathers in sociology in their examination of the making of the modern industrial state. To some extent, these were resolved by them in terms of an urban-based modernisation which bypassed issues of industrialisation and left untouched the formula of national unity. There is still a marked reluctance to deal with regional questions in sociology.

In that respect it is perhaps foolhardy to embark on a field of investigation neglected by both sociologists and Marxists. I wish, however, to claim that:

(i) Regional development raises directly and controversially the nature of state power in a way that the urban question cannot. The 'urban' can be, and is, isolated as a technical problem, interpreted as an issue of consumption, and administered by local authorities that act as mediators in the allocation of resources. In contrast regional developments must concern economic priorities, and the regions have no authoritative mediators of state power. Urban study foreshortens the problems in a way that is impossible with regional analysis.

(ii) Regional development invokes the same methodological, substantive and political issues as the study of towns: that, indeed, their separation is arbitrary. An 'urban' sociology which excludes regional questions is one-sided, a mockery of understanding of why urban places are as they are.

(iii) Unevenness in regional development and urbanisation cannot be taken as detached problems. Urbanisation presupposes inequality in access to resources; the city requires for its support activities which are incompatible with an urban location; there is no way that the assets of agglomeration can be spread over the whole society. Some areas are therefore permanently disadvantaged precisely because they are far from a centre.

(iv) The study of regionalism therefore requires urban social theory to explain the pull of urban centres as well as the vitality of local identification in the modern state.

A regional problem?

In what sense is there a regional problem in modern Britain? To the European observer Britain seems to be a nation retaining a remarkable cohesion. Blondel, for instance, claimed that 'Britain is probably the most homogeneous of all industrial countries',[1] noting its small size, extensive urbanisation, absence of peasant sector, and centralisation. It is true that the grosser internal disparities in development level were being eliminated by the end of the nineteenth century, and current differentials seem quite modest compared with those of France or Italy. Also, there has been no dramatic recent inter-regional shift in population and production comparable with that of the US.[2]

Altogether it is hard to sustain the argument that there is now a critical *regional* economic problem, for several reasons: (1) unemployment is endemic, and moreover, experienced in local labour markets rather than regional ones; (2) while income levels in London and the SE region are higher, if these were related to higher housing and transport costs the differential between these and the rest of the country is greatly diminished; (3) while the old industrial regions have a disproportionate share of some state benefits (e.g. disablement pensions) there is a small share of total welfare expenditure,[3] i.e. the peripheral regions cannot be seen as a major drain on welfare resources. One further argument might be that (4) regional economic policy was not a special policy so much as a forerunner of generalised state intervention in the economy.

The British regional problem, as it is commonly termed, is better related to political history than economic needs. Britain, as the first imperial power, perfected a territorial division of labour deriving from the most intensive use of resources then known. Industrialisation, in the particular conditions of Britain, built up new regions, functioning systems of production with flows of labour and materials signifying global movements of capital, each with a dominant centre on which the productive and distributive components depended.

67

Manchester and the cotton industry is a perfect example. And it is these old productive systems—industrial regions—that constitute the 'regional problem'. They lost their economic rationale with technological innovation and the success of overseas competitors. Not only did 'England's loss of world hegemony lead entire branches of British industry up a blind alley',[4] but also great sections of the country were led into an urban resource hierarchy whose relics foreordain future development. And yet they have no rationale as economic systems, for the divorce of control and production under monopoly capital, and the segmentation of the production process, mean that production space is no longer regionally defined.

For a century, the process of British parliamentary government has depended on the penetration of centrally organised English political parties into these regions.[5] The essential balance between the parties, and the stability of the political system, came to depend on continuity within localities highly vulnerable to changes in processes and markets. It was this regional continuity that was rocked by the Depression, and which regional economic policy was designed to restore. But this same policy facilitated the break-up of local social hierarchies, and modernisation threw up new classes, as in Wales,[6] that found themselves outside traditional party loyalties. There was no choice: the fact of citizenship requires an image of equal access to resources, otherwise there are demonstrable outsiders to the 'people-nation'. In the words of the politician, 'Basically the objectives are to ensure that all our people, wherever they live, enjoy the benefits of national prosperity and of rising national standards.'[7]

There is another political problem presented by these dislocations in regional development, that is, the loss of authority by local government. Interpretations of British political style emphasise 'the authority retained by tradition and the autonomy of local life' (Durkheim)[8] and ascribe political continuity to a system allowing the co-optation of new (regional) elites whose own standing within a locality extended the web of authority to the most humble citizens. The essential fiction was the control over the executive (the expert) by local authority, even the title is revealing. Many of these elites have gone, political bosses have been whittled down, and local democracy loses credibility as it is outfaced by agencies of the central state.

Again, it is difficult to argue that these are specifically regional problems. There is in all the major developed societies a sense of 'crisis of legitimacy' as states expand their powers over all sections of the economy and detail the allocation of resources more closely. Simply, in the old industrial regions there are the greatest dislocations, and the most conspicuous presence of non-local state institutions.[9] There is also the greatest awareness of social distance from the metropolitan core in which the state is centred. In the case of Britain this sense of estrangement is exaggerated by geomorphological history which gave the British Isles industrial resources, and industrial populations, removed from the central axis of trade, financial life and government. There is, nevertheless, a remarkable sensitivity to regional lag, and an unquestioned consensus (from 1940)[10] that this industrial population has the right to remain, and work, in their home locality, which can only be explained in political terms.

The problem of region and regionalism

There is evident a ready use of these terms and a remarkable confusion as to the criteria adopted in their identification. To illustrate the problem consider three sections of the UK: East Anglia, north-east England, and Wales.

The first is one of the oldest settled, historically rich areas of the country which on purely economic criteria (predominance of agricultural interests, low wage rates and poor local services) would seem to have a resource-derived identity. But there is no one centre to the area and increasingly it is subject to the backwash effects of the London region. Politically there is some homogeneity in the pre-eminence of land-owning elites.[11] There are also claims to a cultural tradition. Can it be rejected as a 'region' on the grounds that 'there is no significant and specifically East Anglian social and political force'?[12] That is, does the existence of a region depend on there being a local movement which might be termed regionalism?

North-east England is also generally felt to be economically distinctive (basic industries employing a well-paid skilled labour force) subject to considerable discontinuity in investment and state modernisation. It has a provincial capital, Newcastle, and social and cultural distinctiveness is marked in labour organisation, local government, speech, housing and leisure activities. It also has physical definition in its separation from any other industrial area. But is it a region as many assume? Local people identify with parts of the area—Tyneside, Wearside, Teeside, and districts within these. Even as the area took shape in the nineteenth century it was evident that there were different productive systems with their own momentum, and possibly also their own sources of capital, and their own sub-regional bourgeoisies. And the economic pressures of the twentieth century have created further differentiation. I would treat with great scepticism any claim to this being a region other than its having development area status. Its 'regionalisation' would seem to be the result of state policy. [13]

Turning to Wales, one finds there extreme economic diversity, an absence of social and economic connectedness within the area, no common centre even, a rejection of administrative unity, and a questionable cultural identity. There is a case for Wales as a region on this last criterion: ethnic identity giving low status and exclusion, leading to resentment and organisation on a multi-class basis against the national state as source of despoilation of the homeland. But is this ethnic identification a *regional* identity, something inherent in the common culture of a people sharing a certain environment, or is it an expression of class interests? Khleif argues persuasively that 'the post-1945 new middle class, the new intelligentsia in Wales and elsewhere, has used its ethnicity as a tool for recreating its sense of distinctiveness, as a rallying point for unity amidst competitiveness with other groups.... [It] ... has attempted through an ideology of nationalism to present its interest as general interests and thus influence or mobilise large segments of the population.' [14]

In terms of landscape, history and culture, informed opinion would hold that these areas still have some regional distinction. In terms of economic activity, or political organisation, this regional identity cannot be verified. Nor is it confirmed in the life experience or expressed attitudes of local people whose field of association is very much more restricted than this regional labelling would indicate. It can be argued that, with the possible exception of the underdeveloped periphery to the British Isles, the reality, for choice of job, for social purposes, for marriage and family, is not this region, but the field of association conceptualised as the city region. That is an area in 'functional association with the city' [15] which embraces town and country, crosscuts different productive systems, fluctuates in boundary, but which none the less has an integral quality as a unit because it is the life-space for its residents. The confusion in debate and some at least of the political wrangling about regional policy derives from the conflation of three different usages of the term 'region':

(i) region as an area of functional association with a major central place, as in the term Manchester Region.

(ii) region as expression of a unique symbiosis between man and environment giving rise to distinct landscapes, occupational structures and cultures. The term 'industrial region' belongs to this category.

(iii)   region as a medium of state intervention in problem sectors of the British economy. The term 'the regions' shows the distancing in this categorisation. In Britain over the past forty-five years, state-backed modernisation policies have in a measure created regions, and general regional protest movements which draw their strength from the history and experience signified in these other senses of the term region.

The colonial metaphor

> England's a perfect world: had Indies too: Correct your maps:
> Newcastle is Peru. (1651)[16]

It is only too easy to resort to the colonial metaphor in analysing the experience of the regions. They were all territories taken by force, held through centuries by armed might. Modernisation at the behest and for the market of the dominant metropolitan centre, London; steel and metal-refining succeeded droves of cattle; the regions could be regarded as export enclaves, the coalfields of the north-east and Scotland with their bonded labour being analogous to the plantation. Slaves in Barbados, colliers in Tyneside—it was the same spectacle of uncouth blackened barbarians using primitive machinery, man handling bulky commodities for a distant market, the same transfer of capital from the periphery to the core (Durham coal royalties built Bath crescents). And then further modernisation rescrews the bond of dependency loosened by the initial rush of capital accumulation and, state sponsored, endorses the subordination of a people to an alien elite. The territorial division of labour is also a cultural division of labour in which pride in regional culture is seen as an admission of backwardness:[17]

> The north-east is still its own worst enemy ... it still suffers from a kind of self pity and mistrust of change and modernity on the part of the ordinary man ... people seem reluctant to look beyond their own horizons or to accept to be judged by more advanced standards than their own.... The need is for Britain's poorer regions to recognize their solidarity with the rest of the EEC rather than skulk behind some wall of inverted pride.

Hechter, writing of the so-called Celtic fringe, argues that 'the existence of a culture of low prestige within a peripheral region is justification for the establishment of an internal colony category' (p. 349).[18] On this criterion all the old industrial regions could be termed internal colonies; most certainly Manchester,[19] and probably

Birmingham too. The popular appeal is obvious. It unites all in a given area against the conquistadors of Whitehall, and as evidence there is the obvious wealth of some groups within the core region, the accumulated product of centuries of dominance, continually augmented. And there is too the barely concealed sense of cultural superiority.

And this cannot be ascribed to ethnicity (unless one accepts Toulmin's argument [20]). The cultural divide within England is blatant, whereas that between England and its Celtic fringe is at least tinged with respect for an alternative history (even if this is not how things look from within Wales). Are all these regions, once themselves metropoles in the extortion of resources from the rest of the world, no more than super-exploited colonies of a national metropolis?

In debates such as these, fired by the angry polemic of black Americans, it was tempting for social scientists to feed in writings on development in the Third World. The comparison between Peru and the old coalfields still looked valid; that between north-east Brazil and the Scottish highlands was the basis for a stimulating critique of the policies of the Highlands and Islands Development Board. [21] Dependency and underdevelopment seemed rewarding themes.

Dependency

There is no disagreement that these regions have experienced development since 1945. Analyses of regional policy show that much new plant has been located in the peripheral regions, more recently in the non-industrial fringes. [22] Regional aid has had some effect (quite apart from the accessibility revolution wrought by a motorway system, a rationalised railway network and regional airports). Also, these regions have taken the greater share of investment in urban redevelopment programmes, and replacement housing. Pre-war disparities in living conditions, or access to public services, have greatly diminished with the rate support grant.

Development there has been in no doubt. But of what kind? There has been diffusion of manufacturing industry over the national territory, but this has not necessarily resulted in balanced regional economies. Perhaps the reverse. This accessibility revolution and internationalisation of markets has given a greater freedom of location thereby allowing productive sectors to move to their physically optimal sites. This, in association with the greater scale of production, has meant the concentration of investment say into chemicals, or cars, into a few very large, locally dominant plants in one, or two regions. As smaller plants are scrapped, so local labour forces elsewhere become more reliant on what remains. At the local level there is a revival of that old bogey, the company town; regionally there is development without regional control. The momentum is with the state via the public corporations, and with internationalist companies. Development is therefore seen as creating a new dependency in which 'the result is massive unemployment and the marginalisation of masses of people who engage in low productivity activities',[23] alongside the capital intensive sector around which the industrial economy turns.

We can see in Britain that some areas of the country have a basic role in the productive system, indeed are its very foundation, by reason of physical attributes, which may include their peripheral location as well as such attributes as water, energy (coal, oil, atomic power), basic materials (timber, stone, chemicals, metals). All require massive capital inputs, an intensively worked labour force, and minimal interruption by locals in the exploitation of resources. If, in addition, the economy is 'diversified' by the implantation of 'light' industry, i.e. unthinking assembly line and machine servicing, in one stage of a production process in which profits are taken elsewhere, then there are the elements of dependent industrialisation as modelled by former overseas colonies.

Criticisms of the analysis sketched out here are various:

1. This is after all a secondary rather than a first wave of industrialisation; these are regions with their own internally generated industrial structures, some (Scotland) more than others (Wales).

2. It confers a homogeneity to the regional economic situation, which, while it accords with government data, masks the economic collapse in specific component localities, e.g. Merseyside within the north-west. It drags together so many different 'dependent situations' as to render the term analytically vacuous.

3. The peculiarity of 'dependent development' has to be denied. As Emmanuel stated, 'The mere arrival of foreign capital in a country does not block anything. It enslaves, or develops, the country just as much as any other capital.'[24] If firms in these regions had maintained their previous economic momentum, if they had retained sufficient capital locally to diversify and expand (as indeed did ICI, for one), would it have made any difference to the labour process, the class structure, or the political determination of these sections of the country? Given their physical situation and their natural resources, and the dynamics of the mode of production, could their development path have been any different?

4. The implied comparison with 'independent' economies in the core metropolitan region cannot be sustained. London and its development ring offers, it is argued, the privileged jobs, smartest environment, and greatest opportunity. Would the strap-hanging office hack unable to raise a mortgage within thirty miles of work, or the hospital worker pleading with the local authority for the tenancy of a council flat, agree with that profile? Workers in the corporate glass-towers have never even experienced the sense of liberation of the miners on nationalisation day; they certainly have not the trade-union power wielded so effectively by those workers in 'dependent' economies. The centralisation and state involvement so resented by the local middle classes in the regions has given these groups all the more power.

The thesis of capitalist underdevelopment

There are several excellent commentaries on Frank's statements. [25] I wish to extract selectively. It seems to me that Frank wished to demonstrate that dependency was more than lack of autonomy: 'The satellites remain underdeveloped for lack of access to their own surplus and as a consequence of the same polarisation and exploitative contradictions which the metropolis induces and maintains in the satellite's own domestic structure. That is, as long as the satellite remains capitalist, it will have an internal class structure which will prevent development.' [26] At each step along the chain of exploitation which links global to national to regional centre, there are 'a relatively few capitalists who exercise monopoly power over the many below' [27] but are themselves subordinated. Underdevelopment is not just a natural happening deriving from exhaustion of resources but a structural necessity given the tight locking of metropolitan and satellite economy.

Frank had in mind situations like that of the sugar plantations in north-east Brazil, or the West Indies (including Cuba). Capital and labour were imported, there was no independent agriculture, little production of foodstuffs and an economy wholly orientated to external markets which set the general conditions of production. Copper mining in Chile would be an industrial equivalent. Once this pattern is started, then further economic diversification from within is rendered almost impossible. Further, the previous social structure is broken and the labour force polarised so that the poor are further pauperised despite further economic growth. The possibility is, then, that this is the weak link in the capitalist chain. The analysis points to local struggle by the provincial masses against the capitalist oligarchy.

To a Welshman seeing the Valleys return to forest, or a Tynesider seeing the emptiness down the banks of the river, all this had the ring of relevance: [28]

> What finished them in the end wasn't so much that the coal was running out but a paucity of ideas. Hence that great wilderness the North East, which isn't so much ruination (that's going anyway) as the vacuum left after 300 years of 'Peru'.... The quandary of the city is that, without any reserves and with the paydirt running out, we have to find a new substance to live for, not off. In this respect, of course, Newcastle is Britain, only more so. All the vast granaries below ground have been emptied. Tread softly stranger; for you tread on the bones of empire.

This I take to be the very essence of underdevelopment as attacked by Frank—a regional division of labour which entails a total dedication of the labour force to a few specialised tasks which for a while prove so successful that further change is unnecessary. Current practice therefore becomes customary practice, innovation edged out, the emphasis is on 'a respectable past rather than a promising future'. [29] As profitability is dampened down, the region is 'restabilised', its population comes to expect less and less, and political as well as social life is increasingly parochial. Frank, writing of Brazil, might have been speaking of one of the industrial regions. 'It is in these regions ... in which political life is least ideologically based but instead client-based, and directed to serve immediate local interests ... provincial clientism and opportunism.' [30]

Leaving aside well-founded criticisms of Frank from a Latin American base, [31] there are obvious difficulties in applying this conceptual scheme to a well-developed metropolitan society such as Britain. The first objection must be that the regions which are now labouring under a sense of strangulated development did industrialise, did diversify, did support some of the most powerful industrial systems the world has ever seen. Take the north-east: coal meant glass, chemicals, ships, rope, sails, engines, iron, then railways, then more iron, then steel, then armaments ... and so on. It was a self-directing economic system backed by mineral capital, creating skills, pioneering new technologies. Capitalist, yes, underdeveloped, no. Nairn, in fact, terms these old industrial regions 'over developed' in that they have 'developed more rapidly and successfully than the territory surrounding them'. [32]

Nairn argues that there are two sorts of regional situation resulting from uneven development. The first is that of underdevelopment in the seemingly archaic sectors of the economy, like north-east Scotland, which is often allied with 'ethnic-linguistic exclusion' (p. 72). [33] The second is that of 'relative over-development'. Here he names central Scotland, south Wales and Northern Ireland, along with Catalonia, as dynamic middle-class enclaves struggling to free themselves from a more backward controlling society. But even if one were to accept that these regions had been held back by their ties to the national metropolis, the evidence of reindustrialisation at the instigation of the state would have to be taken into account.

The second objection concerns the involvement of the state in equalising economic and social opportunities across the national territory. Although one might deny the effectiveness of regional policy, none the less planning of resources exists in a way unknown in any of the countries with which Frank was concerned. The industrial regions are not colonies, but integral supports to the bourgeois democratic state. Quasi-feudal they may seem at times, but they are governed by 'barons' whose only source of patronage derives from the state, which in turn depends on the acquiescence of local leaders and the regional population in a centralised political system. Economic planning was a political necessity.

In one interpretation it has also been an economic necessity. Just as Cardoso pointed out that Latin American industrialisation had moved from the export of primary products to industrialisation in which domestic markets were the prime target, so it is argued that the modernisation of the industrial regions is a response to decolonisation (overseas) and the reliance of monopoly capital on the expansion of domestic consumption. Carney and Hudson argued as follows: [34]

> the problems posed by the historical underdevelopment of the NE and of similar regions is this: the basis of British capitalism lies in high real wages and high demand for consumer goods within the domestic market, and on capitalist consumption and state expenditure to prevent realisation crises re-emerging while allowing continued capital accumulation.

Their argument could be extended. The regions are necessary to continued capitalist expansion. Not only their market, but also their resources (minerals, water, space) and their labour. Profit-seeking by monopoly capitalists means a quest for ever cheaper labour, the only means to vary the costs of production as all competitors rationalise production methods/machinery. They are also outlets for capital. It could be argued that the falling rate of profit in existing sectors of production means that there is a constant source for new outlets in currently underdeveloped sectors. Permanent underdevelopment, in the sense of stagnation and neglect, is incompatible with the Marxist analysis of capitalism as a dynamic productive system. Depressed industrial regions, with high rates of unemployment and underemployment, especially of women, represent labour pools, and remarkably few barriers to development. Indeed, they represent almost the reverse—the definite assumption that they must be developed, and will be so in the case of Britain with state funds.

The theory and the accompanying historical analyses, for all their limitations, did have considerable attraction, I suggest for the following reasons:

(i)   They related to a mainstream of economic and political writing in Latin America, the 'dependency school', from which Frank could draw support. The critique of modernisation had good grounding.

(ii) While Marxist in intent, it presented Marxist analyses unorthodoxly in using the concept of the economic surplus, rather than surplus value, and in its emphasis on circulation rather than production. It was also novel within Marxism in the introduction of a spatial component to class analysis. The global chain of expropriation involves two hierarchies, unfortunately conflated by Frank, one of class and the other in space.

(iii) It gave an alternative to the language of colonialism. Dependence that mutilated a local social structure and its economy was not ended by decolonialisation and to break out of these non-imperialist ties required more than bourgeois nationalism. All the same, there was an obvious appeal to sectional identities.

All these might equally be termed weaknesses: [35]

> Though both Fanon and Frank are more sophisticated than their epigones frequently allow for, there is no doubt that in both their cases, their work helped theoretical simplifications and attenuations on the part of philo-Marxists. Key phrases and terms like the 'underdevelopment of development', or 'metropole-satellite' were invoked as a simple master key to unlock the universe without sweat. Such an appeal has often promoted a semantic rather than a substantive solution to the lacunae of sociological theory.

But perhaps the most damaging criticism is that indicated in different respects by Laclau and Cardoso. They argue that Frank, in searching out essential continuities to Latin American history, forgets the very specific articulation of these structural tendencies within and between different modes of production, and further, overlooks the changes in pattern of development consequent on different stages in the expansion of capitalism, in particular monopoly capital. Not only does Frank manage to demonstrate that everything from the days of the neolithic revolution had been capitalist; but it had always been the same kind of capitalism, one that required mercantile oligarchies to effect capital transfers.

The internationalisation of capital

Production is of course the missing element in Frank's model. By contrast it is the requirements of production under conditions of monopoly capital that have been emphasised by many European writers. Castells, for one, put the general assumption quite bluntly: capital accumulation and concentration have enlarged the scale of production so that those locations which offer the easiest access to the widest markets and also the most diversified pool of labour are preferred over all others. [36] The very large urban agglomeration such as the Paris region, and by inference uneven development over the rest of the territory, were therefore inescapable consequences of this system of production. Holland, using evidence from all the major European and American economies, sought to demonstrate similarly the freedom of the international corporation from state-imposed restraints. [37] Given control over international markets the corporation can select the prime location within any national territory, or if baulked, move elsewhere. These prime locations are those which offer the greatest amenity, advantage and accessibility to the corporate managers. He, like Castells, assumes that the major metropolitan regions will be those preferred. Massey's recent paper presents a more careful argument but the basic premise is the same—it is monopoly capital which determines the nature, pace and location of industrial development, and it is these dominant processes of production which define regional differentiations at any point in time. [38]

It is an obvious line of argument, and a strong one. It is wholly reasonable to assume that 'the social and economic structure of any given local area will be a complex result of that area's succession of roles within the series of wider national and international spatial divisions of labour.' [39] But it does not explain the continuities in the national territory that give some localities continuous privilege within this international division of labour. Specifically, there is no explanation of what so shapes corporate decision-making as to steer the industrial giants towards the privileged regions. Two elements are missing—one is a statement of what the metropolitan region has to offer monopoly capital. Is it no more than the 'total social pull of the downtown'[40] attracting the manager and his wife? The other is a statement of the presumed relationship between monopoly capital and the state.

But first a word of caution. The accumulated data from the 1970s offers dubious support for this assumption that industrial production is impelled magnetically towards the major metropolitan regions. In both the UK and the US there would seem to have been a decisive switch from the core regions to the less developed periphery.[41] It would seem arbitrary to dismiss these tendencies as 'exceptional'.[42] Massey is right to point caution here: the salient feature of modern industrial production is the divorce of production and its control, and the segmentation of the production process. Underdeveloped regions within developed societies have their own assets which may draw investment without corresponding control.

Nevertheless there is no dispute that in all these developed economies, the 'intelligent' aspects of industrial production cluster in and around a very few big cities, some, but not all, the seat of government. (In Europe the obvious exceptions are Milan and Dusseldorf.) These places have something to offer monopoly capital other than production space, in conventional terms 'contact' and 'communication'. There is communication with other similar centres, with dependent economies producing and supplying at the behest of these managers of capital; and there is contact with people with information, or influence, or capital. Finance capital, public and private, individual and institutional, must be brought into the equation for the metropolitan magnet. But above all why resort to extra-economic considerations in explanation of this congregation of head-offices? These transactional centres further the process of capital accumulation in speeding up the rotation of capital and ensuring market control.

Secondly, the relationship with the state. Holland opposes the state as the embodiment of the social will of the people to the self-seeking multinational corporation. The interests of capital are against the state, it would seem, as they are against the regions. In Castells's scheme the state weighs in as arbiter of consumption rather than production; Massey makes no statement.

There is of course strong support for Holland from Poulantzas, who points to 'the rapid decline if not the virtual disappearance of national state power ... under the domination of American or international monopoly capital, freed from state fetters'. [43] The multinationalism of capital has pushed not just regions but whole nations into the dependent category, so that the authority and utility of the entire state apparatus, as well as that of local elites, is brought into doubt. But most of the recent Marxist analyses of the national state in capitalist societies see it as implicated in every aspect of capital accumulation. From ensuring law and order, to guaranteeing a fit labour force to ensuring bourgeois hegemony, the state is capital.

Nor is there necessarily any opposition between national state and international capital. If one were to accept Poulantzas's argument, for example, that 'the dis-articulation and heterogeneity of the domestic bourgeoisie' [44] allows the penetration of outside capital, then international monopoly capital can be considered as the dominant fraction in the power bloc whose interests the state apparatus condenses and articulates in policy. The logical corollary of this analysis is that contact, access to the institutions of state power is another element in the equation for the metropolitan magnet. If a major centre is also the seat of government this further differentiates its associated region from the others.

One other dimension is lacking in this economistic interpretation of uneven development, and that is the one emphasised by Frank—exchange, distribution, consumption. One of the oldest symbols for the city is the cross within the circle—the crossroads, market-place, point of contact within a bounded community. [45] The city is the controlling centre for a dependent territory. The opening section of Weber's lecture papers published as *The City* can be interpreted as specification of this view of the city as social form. His definition starts out: 'To constitute a full urban community a settlement must display a relative predominance of trade-commercial relations with the settlement as a whole displaying the following features (i) a fortification, (ii) a market....' [46]

In economic history, as in geography, in writings as diverse as those of Pirenne, the Hammonds, Childe, Mumford, and Christaller and in subsequent locational analysis, the salient characteristic of the urban, of a city, is taken to be its control of a dependent territory (which may not be physically contiguous) through the social institutions predominant in that society. Never, even in Marxist writing, was the city seen as powered by the demands of production, as such. The nineteenth-century towns were indeed the 'barracks of industry' [47] but for that reason they failed as cities. Nor is it altogether evident that they furthered the accumulation of capital. Kiernan's remark provoked in consideration of London, that 'all through history the town has been largely parasitic on the countryside and the metropolis has carried this further by concentrating in itself the parasitism of State and ruling class' [48] indicates their dead-weight effect.

There are several possible lines of reconciliation for this conventional approach and the new emphasis on the organisation of production. They are as follows:

(i)   Industrialisation worked a decisive alteration in the nature of urbanisation, so that this delineation of the city deriving from pre-industrial situations shows a remarkable cultural lag which the Marxist critique has exposed.

(ii) International monopoly capital so overwhelms national state and national ruling class as to nullify their position of control. By implication, the city ceases to be the controlling centre and the source of differentiation within the society. Power is in the hands of monopoly capital which knows no bounds. This is a new situation which invalidates the older theories.

(iii) As the issues of distribution and capital realisation come to the fore, the city in its old guise as a transactional centre whose institutions control the allocation of resources in society is all the more necessary to those who control production. Continuity is imposed on the location of these 'intelligent' aspects of industrial production by the pre-existing structures of urbanisation.

A word of clarification. A city is defined here as a set of institutions of control. In theoretical terms we speak of finance capital, the state, and bourgeois hegemony; in empirical terms we refer to the major financial institutions, government and administration, the press and advertising, as well as the headquarters of the major producing organisations. In locational terms this indicates the central business district but this, like all nodes, has its outliers and threads of connection (linkages) which override a real classification. When I use the term 'centre' these functional extensions are assumed. The term 'metropolis' I suggest could be used to refer to these and other activities which are complementary but not controlling, but which further the pull of resources to the centre. The term 'metropolitan region' should be reserved for the agglomeration of people and activities which make up the body of the urban mass but are not themselves crucial in determining the power within the area to command resources.

Urban social theory

In locational analysis possibly the key concept is that of 'central place'. Points on the earth's surface are considered to have a greater or lesser nodality which economic, social and cultural activities utilise. These central places fall, it is claimed, into a hierarchy derived from accessibility and specialisation of function. Central-place theory lays special weight on circulation and distribution rather than production. An integral component to the theory is the concept of *'city region'*. No central place can be considered in itself; each has a tributary area, which may include a chain of central places of lesser specialisation and rank. There is a vested hierarchy of centres at each level drawing support from a wider area. [49]

This formal locational analysis in effect measures the unevenness of access to resources between different local areas. The provision of services and the availability of commodities depend on a logic of space which gives some central places greater command over resources, and some populations greater access than others. The tax of distance, expressed as time/cost, combined with the threshold levels given by operational costs, stratifies the population on a regional or at least extra-local basis. The metropolitan core/periphery distinction retains its momentum because the metropolis as first-order centre commands the largest market. After all, 'he who dominates is not the biggest producer but the biggest consumer.'[50]

This is the missing element in the theories of 'spatially uneven development' considered here. Neither state centralisation, elite domination, nor concentration of management functions in monopolistic production, are sufficient explanations. Systematic areal differentiation is inherent in the continuing concentration of capital if only to ensure distribution of private and publicly controlled resources, i.e. consumption. Although the chain of central places with dependent regions may appear archaic, it will become of greater importance in a mass consumption economy with some 60 per cent of the known employed male labour force in 'non-productive' activities.

It would seem that in Britain currently the tendencies in location in the productive sector, and those in this non-productive sector, are quite different. In the former there would seem to be a marked freedom in the location of industrial plant, decentralisation from the towns, and also the end of anything approaching regional productive systems. In the latter, there is a relatively constant structure of marketing and administrative regions with an apex in the first-order city, with limited locational outlets for commercial and financial capital. In simple terms, industry may move to Lincolnshire or Shetlands; banking remains in the square mile of the City of London.

Each of the theories of uneven development viewed here—colonialism, dependency, underdevelopment, imperialist overdevelopment, capital concentration and central place theory (and others, e.g. Myrdal's cumulative causation) assume a force to centrality. As Nairn comments: [51]

> one area, one nationality, one well situated urban region, always obtained the upper hand, found its centrality, its powers of domination magically augmented by the new forces of production.

They all take for granted that the metropolis is a unique environment for social transactions and social control, without ever establishing the content to this centrality.

More recent writers who have attempted to elucidate the 'pull of the downtown' have not been sociologists. [52] Very little work on values in locational decisions has been published since Firey's work on Boston. [53] Surprisingly perhaps, writings on urban imagery have not been related to investment decisions despite the agreement of planners that image (expressed as amenity) is of paramount importance in all relocation. [54] And there seems to be little that challenges the utilitarian assumptions of locational science. Writings on regional differentiation resort to macro-structural analyses (meso-economic sector versus state domination) perhaps because there is so little guidance as to 'sentiment' and 'symbolism' in the use of urban space.

To understand the social pull of the metropolis which, despite all technological sophistication still holds the controlling institutions, one has to work into the world of social interaction and manipulation between elites in stock exchange, restaurant and club. To assume simply that there is a 'tendency for human activities to agglomerate to take advantage of scale economies', that 'the organisation of human activity is essentially hierarchical in character' and that 'human occupance is focal in character' [55] is to rationalise the social irrationalities of elite domination which as Weber recognised is communal in character, and as yet focal in definition. The much vaunted empirical tradition in sociology has given us rather more material on attitudes to slum clearance than the uses of centrality to the elites of these institutions. Those at the point of greatest accessibility are precisely those least accessible to social research.

Notes

1 J. Blondel, *Voters, Parties and Leaders*, Penguin, Harmondsworth, 1963, p. 21.
2 B. L. Weinstein and R. E. Firestine, *Regional Growth and Decline in the US*, New York, Praeger, 1978.
3 *Social Trends*, vol. 8, 1977, Table 6.38. The four industrial regions, North, Yorkshire, NW and Wales have 32% population, but 48% disablement, 48% injury and 44% sickness benefits.
4 L. Trotsky, *On Britain* (1925), Monad Press, New York, 1973, p. 33.
5 J. Vincent, *Formation of the Liberal Party 1857-68*, Constable, London, 1966.
6 C. Fletcher, 'Regional community and the era of regional aid', in G. Williams (ed.), *Social and Cultural Change in Contemporary Wales*, Routledge & Kegan Paul, London, 1978, pp. 32-48.
7 C. Chataway, quoted in *The Times*, 21 February 1973.
8 A. H. Halsey, *Change in British Society*, Oxford University Press, London, 1978, p. 141.
9 40% of employment in Wales is in the state sector. And in 1976, the Secretary of State for Wales had 75 nominated bodies in his patronage, with a budget of £2000m. J. Osmond, *Creative Conflict*, Routledge & Kegan Paul, London, 1977, p. 37.
10 The consensus on the need for 'a well-balanced industrial society', to obviate the 'economic waste of enforced idleness', while avoiding the 'social evil' of the excessive concentration of population in London (*Royal Commission on the Distribution of the Industrial Population, Report*, 1940, pp. 208-9), has been taken as a fact of political life, and never, up until 1979, seriously challenged.
11 D. Rose, P. Saunders, H. Newby and C. Bell, 'Ideologies of property: a case study', *Sociological Review*, vol. 24, no. 4, 1976, pp. 699-730.
12 D. Massey, 'Survey: Regionalism, some current issues', *Capital and Class*, no. 6, 1978, p. 110.
13 For a similar argument see J. Cousins, 'Regional problems or problem regions', Rowntree Research Unit, University of Durham, 1974.
14 B. Khleif, 'Ethnic awakening in the First World: the case of Wales', in G. Williams (ed.), op. cit., 1978, pp. 103-4.
15 R. E. Dickinson, *The City Region in Western Europe*, Routledge & Kegan Paul, London, 1967, p. 95.
16 Quoted in J. U. Nef, *The Rise of the British Coal Industry*, vol. 1 (1932) reprinted Frank Cass, 1966, p. 21.
17 J. Ardagh, *The Times*, 21 February 1973.
18 M. Hechter, *Internal Colonialism*, Routledge & Kegan Paul, London, 1975, p. 349.
19 G. Turner, *The North Country*, Eyre & Spottiswood, London, 1967, pp. 67-8 and p. 76 quotes A. J. P. Taylor, 'Manchester ... is irredeemably ugly ... quite as ugly as people say'; *Queen* magazine, 'a compost heap'; Kermode and Cunliffe, 'decay, monotony, mediocrity'.
20 S. Toulmin, 'You Norman, me Saxon', *Encounter*, September 1978.
21 I. Carter, 'The highlands of Scotland as an underdeveloped region',

in E. de Kadt and G. Williams (eds), *Sociology of Development*, Tavistock, London, 1974.

22 D. Keeble, *Industrial Location and Planning in the UK*, Methuen, London, 1976.

23 P. O'Brien, 'A critique of Latin American theories of development', in I. Oxaal *et al.* (eds), *Beyond the Sociology of Development*, Routledge & Kegan Paul, London, 1974.

24 A. Emmanuel, 'Myths of development versus myths of underdevelopment', *New Left Review*, 1974, p. 75.

25 See. D. Booth, 'André Gunder Frank: an appreciation', in I. Oxaal, op. cit., 1974; E. Laclau, 'Feudalism and capitalism in Latin America', *New Left Review*, 1971, p. 67.

26 A. G. Frank, *Capitalism and Underdevelopment in Latin America*, Monthly Review Press, New York, 1967, p. 7.

27 Ibid., p. 8.

28 S. Chaplin, 'The busted empire', in *The Smell of Sunday Dinner*, Frank Graham, Newcastle-upon-Tyne, 1971, p. 124.

29 Ross Mackay, 'The limits to regional policy', *Town and Country Planning*, October 1977, p. 432.

30 A. G. Frank, op. cit., 1967, pp. 166-7.

31 See. F. H. Cardoso, 'Dependency and Development in Latin America', *New Left Review*, 84, 1972; and Laclau, op. cit., 1971.

32 T. Nairn, *The Break up of Britain*, New Left Books, London, 1977, p. 203.

33 Ibid., p. 72.

34 J. Carney and R. Hudson, 'Regional underdevelopment in late capitalism: a study of the north-east of England', *North East Area Studies Working Paper*, no. 9, University of Durham, pp. 12-13.

35 R. Cohen, T. Shanin and B. Sorj, 'Sociology of developing societies: problems of teaching and definition', *Sociological Review*, vol. 25, no. 2, 1977, p. 356.

36 M. Castells, *City, Class and Power*, Macmillan, London, 1978, pp. 38-168.

37 S. Holland, *Capital versus the Regions* and *The Regional Problem*, both Macmillan, London, 1976.

38 D. Massey, 'Survey: Regionalism, some current issues', op. cit., 1978, p. 114.

39 Ibid., p. 116.

40 S. Holland, *The Regional Problem*, op. cit., 1976, p. 48.

41 See D. Keeble and B. Weinstein, op. cit.

42 S. Holland, *Capital Versus the Regions*, op. cit., 1976, p. 159.

43 N. Poulantzas, *Classes in Contemporary Capitalism*, New Left Books, London, 1975, p. 39.

44 Ibid., p. 75.

45 O. Handlin and J. E. Burchard, *The City in History*, MIT Press, Cambridge, Mass., 1963.

46 M. Weber, *The City*, Free Press, New York, 1958, p. 81.

47 J. and B. Hammond, *The Town Labourer* (1917), Longman, Harlow, 1978.

48 V. Kiernan, 'Victorian London', *New Left Review*, no. 76, 1972, pp. 77-8.

49 See R. Chorley and P. Haggett, *Socio-Economic Models in Geography*, Methuen, London, 1968; and H. Carter, *The Study of Urban Geography*, Edward Arnold, London, 1972.

50 A. Emmanuel, op. cit., 1974, p. 72.

51 T. Nairn, op. cit., 1977, p. 318.

52 I can think of J. Jacobs, *The Death and Life of Great American Cities*, Penguin, Harmondsworth, 1964; A. Sampson, *The New Anatomy of Britain*, Hodder & Stoughton, London, 1971, part 5; C. Abrams, 'Decay and renewal', *Journal of American Institute of Planners*, February 1961, pp. 3-9.

53 W. Firey, *Land Use in Central Boston*, Harvard University Press, Cambridge, Mass., 1947.

54 Even in Pons's most perceptive paper, 'Imagery and symbolism in urban society', University of Hull, 1975, there is no more than a hint as to the 'feed-in' of imagery and symbolism into property and investment decisions that govern the development of any urban area.

55 Chorley and Haggett, op. cit., 1968, pp. 304-5.

Urbanization in the framework of the spatial structuring of social institutions: a discussion of concepts with reference to British material [1]

Ian Proctor

I

The object of this paper is to develop a framework for the study of the 'urbanization' of British society under capitalist industrialism. By a framework I mean a relatively simple set of concepts which focus on urbanization in sociological terms. Here the study of British urbanization is faced with a seeming paradox. In contrast to the development of theory in the study of urbanization in areas of peripheral or dependent capitalism, the theoretical analysis of British urbanization, as an aspect of the growth of advanced capitalism, is poorly developed. [2] Yet there has in recent times been a flowering of historical studies of urban life in the nineteenth century.

This calls for explanation and comment. Very few authors have tried to formulate systematic theoretical accounts of British urbanization. In one such attempt, however, Berry claims that there is no single process of urbanization and that one cannot take nineteenth-century European experience as a model for other periods and regions of the world. [3] I agree with him, but in making the claim he gives the impression that the nineteenth-century experience of European urbanization is well understood. Hence he devotes only one chapter, of nine pages, to describing it, and the bulk of this chapter dwells on theories, 'conventional wisdoms', and on how to deal with the consequences of urbanization. Yet what is urbanization? It is significant to note that Berry takes A. F. Weber as his main text. [4] He thus inevitably conceptualizes urbanization mainly in demographic terms. The problem, as he sees it, is the concentration of population in towns, and this is explained mainly as the result of economic change, especially increasing productive efficiency, the developing specialization and division of labour, and the large-scale shift from agriculture to industry. Hence, the structure of the industrial city is analysed within demographic parameters: patterns of migration, age composition, etc.

In the light of much work in recent decades, we can raise two objections to Berry's approach. First, although the demographic aspect of urbanization is undoubtedly important, criticisms of the Chicago School's work has convincingly demolished claims that the social aspects of urbanization can be understood in demographic and ecological terms. [5] Second, in the light of historical work on nineteenth-century cities, to which I refer below, any monolithic and monocausal conception of British urbanization is clearly inadequate. To think of *the* nineteenth-century experience, even within the confines of Britain, implies a similarity between different urban areas which is contradicted by historical research.

There are three main points to be made in relation to historical accounts of British towns and cities. First, in aspect after aspect the *differentiation* of urban life is emphasized. Thus, whether one looks at housing, [6] class conflict, [7] middle-class politics, [8] or studies of old and new cities, [9] one is struck by the variety of social institutions, groupings and movements. But, second, this feature of British urbanization often degenerates into historical particularism, the emphasis upon the unique and the individual. Here Asa Briggs's study of Victorian cities can serve as an example. [10] On the question of differentiation Briggs is quite clear. His statement, 'The first effect of early industrialization was to differentiate English communities rather than standardize them', [11] can serve as a motto for much historical work on British urbanization. Yet there are two rather contrary responses to differentiation in Briggs's book. On the one hand, difference leads to historical particularism, whilst on the other, it signifies the necessity for comparative work to isolate the sources of variety, for some theoretical analysis of difference. For example, he observes, 'Manchester was the shock city of the industrial revolution, but it was not typical. Its real interest lies in its individuality. The comparative history of the economic and social structures and political movements of Manchester and Birmingham shows just how different two individual cities could be.' [12]

In this statement we find both an emphasis on uniqueness and the suggestion of comparative analysis to explain that uniqueness. Unfortunately, from the point of view of this discussion, the dominant response was the former. Briggs's response to Mumford's generic description of 'Coketown' is to state that 'A study of English Victorian cities ... must necessarily be concerned with individual cases.' [13] So his comparisons tend to be *ad hoc* and to taper off from analysis of structural differences to intuitive insights into local idiosyncrasy. On the first point, the comparisons introduced, for example between Leeds and Bradford, are within the context of case studies of individual cities. Second, the comparative framework developed in the Introduction covers economic conditions, property ownership, demography, and political movements, but then immediately turns to 'Other and more complex local differences [which] relate to local "culture" ', a discussion preoccupied with architectural taste. [14] Again, when this framework is put into practice, as in the Leeds-Bradford comparison, it ends once more with architectural symbolism which serves to lead into the case study of the building of Leeds Town Hall. Comparison, then, serves the objective of illuminating the particular rather than isolating the factors which are important in explaining differentiation.

As a third point, attempts by historians themselves to overcome this trend to particularism have not been very successful. For example, a volume edited by Dyos and Wolff contains a massive collection of material on a whole range of life in Victorian cities: nomadic people, pubs, railway and estate development, city literature, disease, prostitution, and religion, to mention but a few. [15] These contributions confirm my first two points. There is ample evidence of differentiation but each study is extremely particularistic. However, one contribution, from Lampard, does attempt a more overall view. [16] Lampard's discussion is unsatisfactory because it is largely confined to a demographic analysis and is premised on a unilinear pattern of demographic/urban development which has recently been subjected to a considerable amount of highly effective criticism. [17] In a later essay by Dyos and Wolff, it is acknowledged that much more work needs to be done, 'especially in regard to the definition and mutations of an urban culture'. [18] Yet their attempt to provide an overview of Victorian cities is firmly based on the idea that such cities constitute a model for some general process of urbanization. Thus, they observe that 'Britain was the first to complete this modern transformation, just as she had been the first to undergo the industrialization of her economy, and represents therefore the prototype of all industrializing, urbanizing, modernizing societies.' [19] They go on to argue that this process of urbanization is not one of an 'acculturation to an urban way of life'. [20] For our purposes, however, the concepts of a unilinear process and of a peculiarly 'urban' way of life are not at all helpful.

We sorely need a theoretical framework for the study of British urbanization to allow us to do two things: to counter excessive historical particularism and to identify just what is sociologically problematic about the growth of an 'urban' society. Such a framework must, however, avoid the well trodden cul-de-sacs of (a) a purely demographic conception of urbanization, (b) a blind adherence to some concept of an urban way of life, and (c) a unilinear pattern of urban development. Such a framework needs to take into account the differences in social structure over space as a central constitutive aspect of urbanization in sociological terms (and not simply as a series of deviations from some generalized process). It is with these requirements in mind that I now examine two recent theoretical discussions of urbanization: that of Castells in Section II and that of Mellor in Section III. Neither seems particularly satisfactory, but each one contains pointers that may be worth following in an attempt to develop a suitable framework.

II

In his approach to urbanization, Castells prefers to think and write of 'the social production of spatial forms',[21] rather than of the development of 'urbanization', and he insists that spatial forms is 'an expression of the social structure'.[22] His concept of social structure is taken directly from Althusserian thought in which a mode of production is a theoretical model of social structure constituted by three interrelated systems: economic, political, and ideological. Different modes of production represent different relationships between the three systems but a particular concrete social formation may incorporate aspects of different modes of production. Each of the three systems is made up of elements, and in the case of the economic system these elements arise out of production, consumption, exchange, and administration. Castells's theoretical point of departure is clearly stated in the form of a hypothesis,[23]

> the hypothesis that the relation between society and space (for that is what urbanization is) is a function of the specific organization of modes of production that coexist historically (with a predominance of one over the others) in a concrete social formation, and of the internal structure of each of these modes of production.

This approach has the advantage of being social structural, and Castells's elaboration of it in effect is being critical of demographic-ecological conceptions and highly sensitive to historical variations in urbanization. However, it is still deficient in relation to the essential requirements I am calling for. The conception of urbanization in Castells's thinking is at best ambiguous and at worst diversionary. His explanatory framework is internally confused and ill-suited to the problem to which I am addressing myself, namely differentiation in patterns of urbanization. The deficiencies are highlighted when we examine Castells's concept of the 'urban system'.

The first weakness lies in the definition of the problem as lying in 'the social production of spatial forms'. The concept of spatial form contains an ambiguity which threads its way through much of what Castells writes. Essentially, one can ask: form of what? Does 'spatial form' refer to the organization of space or the organization of social institutions *in* space? The former refers to the construction and organization of the built environment, which is the manifestation of the structure of social relationships in the physical environment. The latter refers to the articulation of organized social relationships within spatially defined units.

Now if 'spatial form' refers to the organization of space, then the empirical focus is on the production and social logic of the built environment: on the forms of housing and the conditions of variation in housing, on the differentiation of areas of land by function, on transport systems, etc. Castells's analysis of the elements of the urban structure [24] is clear evidence of his concern with the organization of space. When discussing the manifestation of the economic system in spatial form he refers to industrial location under the heading of the production element, to the housing shortage under the consumption element, and to traffic congestion under the exchange element. Turning to the political system, he analyses the segmentation of space into political units, and his discussion of the ideological system focuses on building design and layout as symbolic expressions of social structure. However, if one is concerned with the interrelationships of social institutions in space, then one is not concerned with the distribution of industrial plant, houses or traffic facilities but with the spatial variation of employer-employee relationships, occupational types, labour markets, form of tenancy and household structure; not with the cutting up of space into political units, but with different kinds of political groupings and relationships over space; not with the symbolic significance of churches, schools or historic buildings, but with the spatial incidence of sectarian and established religions or of different forms of education.

It is, of course, self-evident that any institution varies over space, the dispersed economic institutions being an obvious example. What is not self-evident is just how the whole range of institutions interrelate within given spatial units. This seems to me to be an area of real problems, but Castells leads us away from this area in that he is ambiguous as to which conception of social form is problematic for him. This is particularly evident in his review of the urban system. [25]

He outlines various 'ensembles of activities' associated with different elements of the urban system and gives examples of each. The problem is that although each of the elements describes a *social activity*, the examples he gives refer to *environmental artefacts*. Thus the consumption element involves the social activity of the social reproduction of labour power, but the examples Castells gives are housing, minimal pollution, noise, school and social cultural amenities. As examples of the production element, he gives factories, raw materials, industrial environment and offices, and as examples of the exchange element he gives a mixture of examples, including commuting and residential mobility which are social activities or artefacts, and urban transport and historic buildings which are physical artefacts.

My first point is thus that in defining just what is problematical about urbanization Castells equivocates between a concern with the social organization of space and the organization of social institutions in space. On the whole, he diverts our attention to the former at the expense of the latter.

The second difficulty with Castells's theory lies not in his conception of what is at issue in the study of urbanization but in the way he explains the problem of space. His basic notion is that space is the expression of social structure. To be clear about this, we must ask related questions. What specific aspects of social structure are manifested in space? In which spatial units? How, as a particular example, does Castells link the consumption element of social structure and the urban as a spatial unit? To answer questions of this kind, I examine Castells's argument in Chapter 10, where he takes up the issue of the 'theoretical delimitation of the urban' in terms of the elements of social structure. This is an extremely important point, as it is here that he attempts to retrieve the concept of 'urban' after his own criticism of its use as an explanatory category. He himself recognizes this, noting that 'the delimitation of the urban remains ambiguous' and writing of 'the vagueness and the historical relativity of the criteria concerning the urban'. [26] It is therefore essential to examine this section of Castells's book carefully.

Castells begins with the possibility that it is unnecessary to delimit urban space at all. Why not, he asks, 'keep to an analysis of the structure and process of the urbanization of space, whatever their content might be?' [27] But he rejects this possibility on the grounds that it involves an epistemological error; one cannot simply study 'space' without any theoretical framework unless one smuggles in a covert, and thereby possibly ideological, set of theoretical concepts. This is a fair point, but it is misplaced for he has *already* outlined his theoretical framework and has already discussed at length how the Althusserian model of social structure can be employed to conceptualize and analyse a series of problems concerning the organization of space. None of this, however, entails a reference to anything *peculiarly* 'urban'. The problem here is that the general epistemological principle regarding the necessity of conceptualization does not in itself justify any particular concept of 'urban'.

The second step in Castells's argument is to delimit relevant units of space, and this is far more important. Which spatial units—neighbourhoods, districts, cities, regions, states, inter-state systems—are empirically significant? This question is important because although the causal significance of a spatial unit is historically variable it is all too easy to take 'self-evident' boundaries, such as political frontiers, as indicators of 'real' socially organized units. How then does one establish the historically determined efficacity of a certain delimitation of space? [28]

Further, there is the problem of making specific the spatial manifestation of social structural elements. Here, Castells speaks of 'The spatial distribution of each element of the social structure.... Thus there will be an ideological space, an institutional space, a space of production, of exchange, of consumption (reproduction)....'.[29] This seems to involve a shift from a very general formula, that space is the expression of social structure, to a more definite detailing of how space is organized in relation to elements of social structure.

There are, then, two distinct aims: (a) to delimit the relevant spatial units, and (b) to specify how elements of social structure are manifested in space. Castells's argument runs these two aims together, which has the result of providing a resolution to both sets of problems.[30]

> To pose the question of the specificity of a space, and in particular urban space, is equivalent to conceiving of relations between the elements of the social structure within a unit defined in one of the instances of the social structure. In more concrete terms the delimitation 'urban' connotes a unit defined either in the ideological instance, or in the politico-juridical instance, or in the economic instance.

Castells thus proposes that the units of space can be delimited by defining them in terms of the specification of one of the elements of social structure. More particularly, the urban is delimited by reference to the consumption element of the economic instance in the process of reproduction of labour power. An urban system is 'the specific articulation of the instances of a social structure within a (spatial) unit of the reproduction of labour power.'[31]

This is, self-evidently, a major step in Castells's development of his theory; it is the point at which he focuses our attention on cities as social organizations structured to fulfil the function of the reproduction of labour power in the overall social structure; it is the basis for his claim that urbanization in capitalism tends toward the increasing collectivization of consumption and he leads from here to a discussion of urban politics as the politics of consumption. Consequently, we should look carefully at the propositions supporting this argument and its implications.

The first point to consider is the equivalence Castells claims between urban space and consumption. This may mean that wherever one finds processes of consumption one has an 'urban' phenomenon, for example, reservoir systems supplying water are 'urban' even though situated physically in 'rural' areas. This makes some sense, but other aspects of consumption hardly fit the urban description. Village schools, tied agricultural cottages, and rural sports would all count as practices concerned with the reproduction of labour power, yet hardly seem to be part of an 'urban spatial system'. Indeed, Castells would appear to agree, for he notes that 'Urban space thus becomes defined by a section of the labour force, delimited both by a job market and by the (relative) unity of its daily life', adding that 'the map of commuter flows usually serves to delimit an urban area.'[32] Here, Castells is clearly thinking of an urban space circumscribed by a local job market, or a set of services which provide for daily life indicated by the limits of community. So there is no direct equivalence between consumption and the urban, in that consumption practices go on outside what Castells wants to identify as 'urban spatial units'.

If one cannot specify the spatial manifestation of social structure in spatial units such as the city, can one delimit an urban unit in terms of one social structural element? Castells's argument here is not strong. It is largely a negative one.[33] The city cannot be defined in terms of the ideological instance because this leads to the dubious notion of *urban* culture; the city cannot be defined as a political unit because the social relations of the city extend beyond its political frontiers; the city cannot be defined in terms of production because production is spatially organized on a regional level. This leaves consumption as the only possibility, without, in fact, providing any arguments in its support. The problem is that the points Castells uses to dismiss other possibilities can also be directed towards the conception of the city as a consumption unit. Just as in production, the city is not a unified and bounded segment of consumption space. To delimit the urban space of Coventry as a production unit would make little sense given the relationship of production in Coventry with production in other spatial areas. By the same token, to delimit Coventry's urban space as a consumption unit involves the same problems: Coventry's public transport is part of the West Midlands transport executive, its leisure facilities extend through the Cotswolds to Blackpool and the Costa del Sol, and its adult education services are linked to the University of Birmingham Adult Education Department. Just as one cannot specify a social structural element in terms of a spatial unit, so one cannot delimit a spatial unit in terms of one social structural element. Castells's two objectives do not neatly fit together to produce a mutually satisfactory solution.

Why does Castells adopt this strategy, of delimiting a relevant spatial unit in terms of a single social structural element, in the first place? Essentially, it is because he seeks to explore the function of urban space in the working of capitalist society as a whole: 'The ensemble of the so-called urban practices connotes the articulation of the process (of the reproduction of labour power) with the social structure as a whole.'[34] However, we must ask what is entailed in the phrase 'the social structure as a whole'. I suggest that the injunction to place the city in the context of the wider social structure can have two very different meanings which, following Mandelbawn,[35] I will refer to as methodological collectivist and holistic. It can mean that the social relations and groups of a city, say its political parties, have to be systematically related to other groups, organizations, and institutions in the rest of the society. To analyse the workings of a local Labour Party, one might have to note its domination by a particular trade union whose delegates are mandated by the unions' national policy. Further, the party might be committed to a regional group of MPs or have historical connections with the Fabian Society. Here, the whole notion of *the* social structure is a complex one, constituted by a host of institutions and groupings in varied relationships. By implication, a central research question becomes, 'How do elements of social structure relate to each other?' Here a spatial dimension is crucially important. At what spatial level do social relationships form so that one can speak of a 'village' community, a 'town's' business elite, an 'urban' labour market, a 'regional' arts group or a 'national' planning policy? In particular, if the national level of spatial structuring is causally most significant, if, for example, capital investment is centralized in a metropolitan capital market, or if the education policies of the national government override the policies of the local education authorities, then these are the relevant empirical and historical facts.

Alternatively, the injunction to place the city in the context of the social structure can lead one to ask, 'What are the functions of the city for the characteristic features of the social structure *as a whole?*' This seems to be what Castells has in mind. Space is organized into urban units in order to fulfil the requirements for the reproduction of labour power, itself a requirement for the workings of the social structure. Here, the concept of *the* social structure proposed is a fairly simple one. Castells defines the characteristic features of the whole system in terms of three 'instances': the economic, which functions to produce material life and reproduce labour power; the political, which functions to regulate the whole system in conjunction with the repression/integration of subordinate classes; and, the ideological, which functions to symbolically legitimate the system.

The methodological collectivist concept of social structure claims that the *pattern of relationships* between individuals, groups and institutions is causally significant in explaining social affairs. The methodological holistic concept of social structure claims that the characteristic features of the *whole system* are equally significant in explaining social affairs. While I cannot go into the differences at any length, in this context, I suggest that the latter is inappropriate to the study of urbanization in that it fails to make problematic variations in social organization over space and reifies the societal level of the structuring of social institutions.

There are numerous references to historical specificity, particular conjunctions and specific variables in Castells's work. One only has to note his distinctions between urbanization in advanced capitalism, peripheral capitalism, and socialism, to recognize his awareness of differential urban development. However, Castells does not make the differential organization of institutions in space a problem which itself requires theoretical conceptualization and research. This would appear to be for one of two reasons: either such differentiation is no more than the specification of the features of the whole in a particular historical conjuncture, or it represents the combination of two or more wholes in a concrete situation. With reference to the first, when discussing the location of industry in Paris, Castells says, 'The logic of this distribution ... expresses the social structure of advanced capitalism, articulated with the conditions of historical development of French society.' [36] The question which arises here is: does one simply leave differentiation as a matter of historical uniqueness or make it a theoretical problem? On the whole, Castells adopts the first option. To subject the problem of urbanization to theoretical explanation, 'There is no other way than that of concrete research, drawing out the signification of each social situation, on the basis of its specificity.' [37] At another point, Castells claims that one cannot simply work on the principle that any general model will have specific manifestations: 'it is not at all a question of explaining the "present" by the "past", but of showing the organization of the different social structures that merge at the level of a concrete social reality.' [38] However, the problem remains. It is the merging of different wholes which accounts for historical specificity. In either case, then, Castells takes the features of the whole as given, reifying the attributes of the whole, rather than seeing social structure as a historical patterning of institutions at the societal level.

I briefly summarize my remarks on the deficiencies of Castells. First, in conceptualizing what is problematic about urbanization, Castells leads us to the question of the social organization of the built environment, rather than of the organization of social institutions in space. Second, his theoretical scheme for explaining urbanization depends on the notion that a particular level of spatial organization, the city, is a manifestation of the social structural element of consumption. This is inadequate as there is no neat correspondence between a spatial segment and a social structural practice. At base, Castells operates with a conception of social structure which is ill-adapted to the differential organization of institutions in space because the societal level of such organization is taken as given.

III

I turn next to Mellor's recent book. [39] The book is rather puzzling to read in that her aims remain somewhat ambiguous. Is it a review of urban problems in Britain and the response of sociologists to these? Is it a critique of the classic theories of urbanization? Is it a proposal for a different theoretical approach to the urban? One can find elements of each. Part I reviews traditional areas of urban sociological concern: the regional city, the inner-city problem, housing, and planning; Part II represents an exegesis and critical evaluation of the German and Chicago theories of urbanization; and the Introduction and Chapter 1 argue for the employment of Frank's theory of underdevelopment to address urban and regional questions within advanced capitalist societies.

These various components do not hang together well, and Mellor is frankly disarming on this lack of coherence. For example, she writes,

'The theories of urbanization reviewed in the second part are in a sense an appendix.'[40] Of her review of urban problems she writes, 'A programme for the development of either urbanization or urban sociology in Britain cannot be derived from this survey of experience over the last century',[41] seeming to admit that her theoretical framework has not acted to inform her discussion of problems nor to form a basis for future work. After arguing for Frank's theory and attempting to employ it to comprehend British urbanization, she retracts by saying that 'The model of metropolitan dominance is too simplistic'[42] and cannot be employed to analyse the historical material.

Mellor's aims, then, are rather unclear, but the reasons for her equivocation are brought to light in the Preface. Her underlying interest is in the variation and differentiation of urban experience. This interest is frustrated by urban sociology. 'How could this diversity be aggregated in national statistics, or the localism of experience be denied in the rubric of "society"?'[43] Further, urban sociology in its various forms diverts the student from the experience of variation:[44]

> So, perhaps paradoxically, an interest in local differences, quirks and oddities, which set one place off from another, took one into the discussion of the 'universals' of urbanization, inner city blight and peripheral expansion, for instance, and the policies of government in oversight of property investment.

I take it that Mellor's interest is in variation, and not so much in 'quirks and oddities', but the differentiation of social experience across space motivated her development of a theory of urbanization. For this reason, we shall be concerned with this theory and not with her other discussion of urban phenomena and theoretical responses to the problems of urbanization. At the same time, the retraction of the theory, alluded to above, suggests that the theory has its acknowledged weaknesses. We will be concerned to isolate some of these weaknesses, but in a positive spirit, as it seems that they can be repaired and a modified framework developed to conceptualize just what is sociologically of interest in 'urbanization'.

Mellor's theoretical framework can be summarized fairly succinctly. The starting-point is the differentiation of communities:[45]

> Local communities are to be studied as definite articulations of the social structure, contexts specific in their life chances, their class system, their forms of political association, and their cultures.

This local variation is, however, not to be understood in terms of the *internal* character of villages, towns or cities, 'but always in terms of their relational situation in a "field" or matrix of other settlements'. [46] Each place 'has stood in a specific relation to "society" throughout its life cycle', and 'It is these relations of urban community to nation and world society that have been left unexplored and yet it is these that must underpin any more localized sociology.' [47]

To forge this link between the local and the societal, Mellor turns to Frank's theory of metropolitan dominance. This was, of course, originally developed to analyse the relationship *between* national economies and states, but Mellor, amongst others, employs it to examine the uneven distribution of resources *within* a national economy and polity such as Britain. The major claim, substantiated suggestively in her review of British urbanization, is that there is a basic trend in capitalist development towards the concentration of capital control in metropolitan centres. The increasing centralization of control of capital resources has spatial consequences in the distinction between metropolis, where the control of capital is located, and province. The dominance of capital is paralleled by the dominance of metropolis and the dependence of the province. But the principle can be extended further, not just between metropolitan and provincial regions within the national society, but also within the region as between *its* metropolitan centre and dependent satellites. So we have: [48]

> a polarization which is replicated down the chain of expropriation, world, national, provincial, local—at each level, there is a community which replicates the contradictions of capitalism. The global relations of imperialism are recreated with increasing intimacy as beads of a chain from world metropolis to remote hamlet.

It is at this point that the first weakness in Mellor's approach becomes apparent. Where are the boundaries between metropolis and province to be drawn? Within her own discussion of regional underdevelopment, Mellor is ambiguous as to whether London, south-eastern England, or the south-east and the Midlands constitute the metropolis. At one point she observes that a 'major cleavage' in British society is that between the provinces and the metropolitan south-east. However, a few pages later the dividing line is drawn differently: [49]

> There are in Britain, as in other developed societies, marked regional distinctions. One in particular is conspicuous, that between the stagnant economies of the provinces—Scotland,

Wales, South West and Northern England—and the prosperity of the Midlands and South East.

This is not a simple problem of whether or not to include the Midlands in the metropolis. For the dominance-dependence model is extendable within regions, within cities, and within local areas. This point is well made by Hechter. [50] Hechter also uses Frank's theory to analyse the relation between spatial areas in Britain but he draws the boundaries completely differently. For him, the metropolis is England, as a whole, with the Celtic lands as the dependent satellites. Perhaps this is what Mellor means in her retraction of the theory by observing that the theory's claims 'are so general that they can neither be corroborated nor denied.' [51] The drawing of boundaries seems an arbitrary business.

There is, however, a second and more basic problem, not to do with where the boundary between metropolis and province lies but with what sort of entities they are. In what terms are metropolis and province defined? We find three different possibilities in Mellor. First, metropolis and province designate *communities* where 'some communities are wholly dependent, others exercise dominance while themselves dominated.' [52] And she claims that we ought to analyse society 'in terms of metropolitan dominance and provincial dependency in which pre-existing variations deriving from the relational position of one community *vis-à-vis* the others are continually being reactivated.' [53] Second, metropolis and province can be identified in *spatial* terms. Speaking of the English Civil War, Mellor writes: [54]

> There was then evident a major antagonism, which was not that between classes, nor between town and country, but between the remote provinces and those regions subordinate to the major urban centre.

Similarly, in claiming that 'It is not hard to make a preliminary identification of the metropolitan centres of the developed world', [55] Mellor lists a number of indices of a spatial area: high rates of economic growth, labour shortages, immigration, housing shortages, etc. Third, metropolis and province are conceptualized as distinct *social groups* with their respective cultures. [56]

> The debate between 'dependency' and 'interdependency' needs to be discussed with reference to the extent of penetration of the local and regional cultures of Britain by the culture of the dominant bourgeoisies of the national metropole.

Mellor herself seems to recognize this variety of definition. [57]

> Urbanization can be considered either as the transformation of
> places as their status in the matrix of communities is altered, or,
> alternatively, as the incorporation of groups in society into the way
> of life of the controlling metropolis, and their acquiescence in the
> hegemony of those interests dominant in the metropolitan centre.

Clearly the three types of definition are not synonymous. To
conceptualize metropolis as community or spatial area implies that the
entity as a whole dominates the provincial community or province,
while a class definition would suggest the internal division of the
metropolis and possibly imply integration along class lines cutting
across the metropolitan-provincial distinction, the solidarity of metropolitan and provincial capital. Further, each definition, in itself, is
inadequate. If the class definition is taken, then the spatial dimension,
the whole notion of metropolitan dominance, becomes of minor
importance. Metropolis becomes merely the physical locale of a ruling
class. Mellor herself comments on the inadequacy of the community
definition. [58] To treat metropolis and province as communities which
dominate others and are dominated by others, plays down to excess
their internal differences and crosscutting solidarities. Mellor also
seems well aware of the weakness of a spatial definition. 'There may
be a distinction between *rural* province and dominant *metropolis* but it
is one that derives from the economic and political connections
between the two, rather than their ecological characteristic.' [59]

This last comment is important as it gets to the heart of the matter.
The difference between metropolis and province is to be understood
in terms of the economic and political, and, I would add, other
connections between the two; in other words, in terms of the way
institutions are organized. Dominance and dependence are functions
of institutional structures; for example, the control of capital supply
and investment by financial groups and enterprises whose spheres of
operations are national and international, the focus of political
organization on the administrative system of the nation-state, and the
centralization of media and cultural organizations, again on the
national level.

Are these institutions *metropolitan?* Is the dominance-dependence
relationship to be understood in terms of the dominance of provincial
institutions by the institutions of the metropolis? Surely not, for what
is significant about the institutional structures mentioned is not that
they are located in London but that they operate at the level of the
national society. For example, movements in the national economy

led to the differential experience of depression and suburban boom in
the 1930s. [60] Political decisions which impinge upon a particular
provincial area, such as the running down of deep-sea fishing, or the
refusal to implement import controls on textile goods, might be taken
in London but are taken in the interests of the nation and not in the
interests of London. Local radio's attempts to promote local popular
music are frustrated not by the dominance of London taste but by the
dominance of the national broadcasting system. What we have, then,
is the dominance of local institutions by nationally organized
institutions. This is not synonymous with metropolitan dominance.
For example, secondary education is to some degree dominated by the
entry requirements of British universities, which are nationally
organized but do not centre on the metropolis. Despite Colonial 'B',
no one would want to argue that Cheltenham is a metropolitan centre!

Mellor would, I think, agree that it is the national and the local
which is at issue. She says in her Preface, for example, that the book
was written in Hull but [61]

It is now a matter of personal regret that I did not attempt to map
out some dimensions of its class relations, economy and culture, to
tread through the interrelationships between national and local in
this one town. It is information and analysis of this kind that we
lack.

However, it is an error to make the national and local equivalent to the
metropolitan and the provincial, as when Mellor writes of 'the shifting
relationship between peripheral community and metropolitan
centre—between localism, or provincialism, and (national) hegemony'. [62]

IV

Three criticisms have been made of Mellor's work: the boundaries of
metropolis and province are arbitrarily drawn, the terms in which they
are defined are ambiguous and each one is individually inadequate,
and the concepts of metropolitan and provincial are not equivalent to
those of national and local. More positively, two suggestions are
implied by the above discussion. First, the units of analysis should be
institutions: the patterned ways in which relationships are routinely
organized by systems of norms and the distribution of the bases of
power. [63] Second, institutions can be analysed in terms of factors
which operate at various 'vertical' levels of spatial organization, from
the local to the international. A labour market in a particular town

might, for example, be effected by local redundancies, by its situation in a development area, by national trade union agreements, and by international sources of labour. This is one aspect of the spatial organization of social institutions. But this is just to look at one institution, yet a labour market is embedded in a matrix of other institutions; as well as there being 'vertical' links at different spatial levels there are 'horizontal' links with other institutions. The working of the labour market may well be affected by neighbouring political institutions, there may be a patronage system of allocating council jobs, the local housing system may, or may not, give advantage to long residence, and education system may, or may not, facilitate the geographical and/or social mobility of the young. Just as what happens at the local level is affected by influences from higher levels, so the impact of state policies, economic movements and other national and international phenomena is filtered through the local interconnections of institutions.

Margaret Stacey has attempted to develop this idea. [64] Stacey attempts to justify locality studies in the face of warranted criticisms of studies based on definitions of community given in terms of geographical areas or vague notions of solidarity feelings. Her initial point is that the sociological study of locality is concerned with the interrelations of institutions in a locality. Her main theme is that a local social system may exist which can be analytically isolated as a causal factor which, alongside others, materially affects the working of society. The key here is Stacey's definition of a 'local social system': [65]

> A *local social system* occurs when ... a set of inter-relations [between institutions] exists in a geographically defined locality. If there are *no* connections between the major social institutions in the locality, *that is connections which are specific to that locality*, there is *no* local social system. The set of inter-relations which compose the social system may be more or less complete.

To re-emphasize the crucial point: it is the specific mix of institutions within a spatial area which makes the difference and which justifies the locality study.

The main problem with the notion of local social system is one which has recurred throughout this discussion. Where does one draw the boundaries of local social systems? Most of the empirical material, to which Stacey alludes, is concerned with studies of fairly small-scale geographical areas, such as villages, country towns, or neighbour-hoods of cities. However, in principle, the idea of the interrelation of institutions in a given spatial area can be applied to whole cities, regions, or nations.

Mellor's work is important because she directly addresses the question of local variation. However, her attempt to employ Frank's theory of metropolis and province is inadequate. In its place, I suggest a focus on the social organization of institutions in space along two dimensions. Figuratively, I have called these the 'vertical' and the 'horizontal'. The 'vertical' refers to the spatial range of the factors which influence the working of a given institution, from the local to the international. The 'horizontal' refers to the interconnections between the various institutions at a given level. [66]

Further, it is this 'horizontal' aspect that is the particular domain of the 'urban' sociologist, though in no sense at the expense of the 'vertical'. There are, of course, spatial variations in the character and working of particular institutions (e.g. the labour process, political organization, health care, or education). However, these are the concern of specialists in institutional areas. In explaining the spatial variation of a given institution some causal factors lie within the nature of the institution itself; for example, the incidence of paternalist industrial capitalism. In a recent paper, Norris has identified the structural conditions for the occurrence of this particular manifestation of the labour process. [67] Some of these conditions are to do with the labour process itself, dependence of workers on an isolated labour market, the controlling influence of a local bourgeoisie, etc., but other relevant conditions take one out of the economic area *per se*. Hence, Norris argues that a further condition of paternalism is that the bourgeoisie have 'historical and contemporary links with the area', [68] manifested, for instance, in a family structure which maintains involvement and control in a firm over several generations. This is clearly a case of the horizontal connections between institutions. Yet Norris says very little about the nature of these 'historical and contemporary links', and says nothing about how this family structure is maintained. This is not a point of criticism, rather it is only to be expected, given Norris's focus on a single institution. However, it does illustrate the need to focus on the problem of the interconnections between the whole round of institutions. The effect of the mix of institutions in a given spatial context is then the concern of the sociologist of the spatial organization of social institutions.

The recurring question is, 'Which spatial context?' At what level of spatial organization is it empirically important to examine the mix of institutions—neighbourhood, village, town, city, region, state, or system of states? The major trap is reification, of taking some self-evident boundary (geographical, political, or cultural) as indicative of the existence of a real local social system. In many community studies the properties of the local area have been reified, while in other kinds of studies the state becomes a monolithic entity whose dictates have a uniform effect. The key point, which we continuously need to remember, is that any actual spatial ordering of social institutions is a historical phenomenon, which has developed and is developing. Then the main question, from the point of view of urbanization, is to what extent, in the development of nineteenth- and twentieth-century British capitalism, has the city been a significant local social system? To what degree has the interconnection of institutions at the level of the city, as a spatial unit, been a significant empirical phenomenon? In this sense, urbanization is not simply a demographic process, nor is it the growth of specifically 'urban' institutions in the Wirthian sense of an urban way of life, or in Castells's sense of the city as a mechanism of collective consumption. The study of urbanization involves, rather, the study of the empirical significance and effects of the connections and relationships between the various institutions at the level of the city.

So far, some simple theoretical ideas have been developed to focus attention on the spatial organization of social institutions. However, to leave matters at this point would be inadequate on two counts. First, it is deficient in suggesting 'institutional pluralism', that all institutions are of equal weight. Second, it is open to the charge of 'spatial particularism', that is, an emphasis on the unique institutional matrix of a given spatial context. To avoid these deficiencies, it is necessary to attempt to specify *which* institutions and what *range of variation* in their relationship are empirically important. Here, I want to return to Marxist political economy, not in the shape of abstract urban theories such as that of Castells, but in urban history.

We have some excellent examples of the interconnectedness of institutions in the towns and cities of Britain in the nineteenth century. Three studies deserve special attention here. The first is John Foster's exploration of the relationships between economic structure, class consciousness, and political organization in three English towns, bringing in kinship, residential community, religion and education. [69] The second is Gareth Stedman Jones's detailed analysis of the connection between the peculiarity of London's economy and its perennial housing problems. [70] Third, a recent study by Bryan Roberts compares the relation of economy, particularly the degree of labour mobility and the scale of enterprises, and the levels and form of state provision in the process of industrialization in Manchester, Barcelona, and Sao Paulo. [71]

These studies are exemplary in that they examine institutional interconnections in space, both 'horizontally', in the given spatial context, and 'vertically', in their sensitivity to wider spatial contexts. Further, they bring out the variability of 'urbanization' while avoiding the weaknesses of 'institutional pluralism' and 'spatial particularism' by the centrality granted to economic institutions. However, here we should be careful. Making economic structure central can be interpreted in two senses. First, a strong sense, in which centrality means determinancy, where variability in the interrelation of institutions is a result of changes in economic structure alone. Second, a weak sense, in which economic institutions are central in providing a reference point to which other institutions are related. Then variability can arise from the economy or from other institutional areas, but the organization of the labour process acts as a hub around which 'super-structural' institutions are organized.

It is in the second sense that I would advocate the centrality of economic institutions. The labour process as a reference point gives more theoretical direction without an overambitious theoretical closure. It specifies the institutional connections to look for and suggests empirical hypotheses to explore in research without preempting them. In this paper, I can hardly give a full justification for my preference for the weaker, rather than the stronger, sense of economic centrality. However, perhaps, I can provide some support by asking some questions of John Foster's study, which advocates the strong thesis but which seems unconvincing at some crucial points on this very issue.

Let me say at the outset that the following takes the form of a number of queries, rather than criticisms, as I simply do not have the empirical material on nineteenth-century Oldham to substantiate criticism. Foster traces changes in the political organization and consciousness of the Oldham working class, primarily in the second quarter of the nineteenth century. During this time there was a marked shift from a class-conscious, radical labour community, which employed illegal organizational techniques to control the various branches of local government, to a patriotic political consciousness, displaying deference to the bourgeoisie's control over politics and the wider cultural community. In explaining both the causes of labour militancy and power (as compared to their absence in South Shields and Northampton) and the causes of their demise, Foster draws upon economic conditions. In contrast to his other two towns, Oldham in the 1830s and early 1840s was characterized by large-scale factory production in which the consequences of competitive capitalism were self-evident to the working class in their experience of falling wages and unemployment. This was the essential basis on which Oldham's radicals built the labour community. But technical and economic changes, manipulated by the bourgeoisie, undermined this community. Employer promotion of a labour aristocracy in industry altered not only the authority structure of industry (the authority of labour leaders switching from discipline against employers to discipline on their behalf), but also the structure of the wider community. Labour solidarity was replaced by the differentiation in the labour force into 'rough' and 'respectable', leadership of labour organizations passed from class conscious radicals to the labour aristocracy, and labour's hold over local political institutions collapsed.

It is Foster's explicitly economic explanation which prompts my queries. In two instances there seem to be gaps and inconsistencies in Foster's analysis, which might suggest other institutional factors at work. Both relate to the reassertion of employer control. In the first place, Foster tells us very little about the ways in which employers regained control of the machinery of local government and the politics of that process. [72] He simply presents this as a more or less self-conscious use of state power by the bourgeoisie to displace labour from control of local government: [73]

> If the authorities eventually won, it was because Oldham was only a smallish town in a country which remained throughout under bourgeois control. The government was able to alter the rules of the game as it went along.

Two such changes of the rules involved the switching of control of the police from parish vestries to magistrates and then to the lord lieutenant of the county, and the incorporation of Oldham as a municipality. On the latter, Foster comments: 'In the twilight years of the late 1840s there was a half-hearted attempt at resistance [by the labour movement] when the employers decided to incorporate and get rid of the still potentially dangerous commission and vestry.' [74] Incorporation was simply a manoeuvre, which allowed the employers to continue their attack on the working class.

A study by Derek Fraser prompts me to express some doubts here. [75] A leading theme in this study is that the shift in levels of political organization, especially from the parochial to the municipal, involved a political struggle between factions of the bourgeoisie, factions which stood to gain in terms of economic rewards, patronage and status, as to whether local government was organized on parochial or municipal lines. Foster analyses the internal structure of the Oldham bourgeoisie but says nothing about its *internal* politics, other than noting 'the covert and sometimes open attacks which the Manchester group made on the county [group]', [76] a conflict which Foster stresses must not be overstated. Yet in the light of Fraser's evidence some attention should be given to bourgeois politics. The possibility remains that shifts in local government organization, which had the *consequences* of restricting labour's access to political control, were *caused*, in part at least, by the internal jockeying for power within the bourgeoisie as well as by a concerted bourgeois attempt to subvert the working class.

My second query relates to the break-up of the integrated labour community by the rise of a labour aristocracy. Foster argues that employer-promoted changes in industrial authority caused the splitting of the working class into two cultural groupings: the mass culture centred on the public house and the minority culture of 'self-educators' generating and controlling temperance, Sunday schools, and adult education. To sustain this argument Foster needs, firstly, to establish that the supervisory group in work consisted of the same people who controlled the self-education institutions of the wider community, and second, to establish the causal connection between work and extra-work situations. I do not think that either of these conditions are met. Foster establishes only that in both work and non-work a differentiation and status-ranking of the working class took place. No doubt changes in the authority structure of work did play a part here, but one or two points in Foster's evidence raise the possibility that there was not a neat correspondence between the supervisory workers and the self-educators, and that changes within the extra-work institutions of the community contributed to the differentiation of the working class.

Foster notes the expansion of Methodism and its occupational composition, i.e. the absence of 'big employers' and the presence of large numbers of tradesmen, clerks and supervisory workers. [77] The argument here is that Methodism was one of the institutions differentiating the *supervisory* workers from the *supervised*. Yet Foster's data cast some doubt on this. He uses information on marriages to support his claim that Methodism was the religion of supervisory workers. [78] While it is true that, as compared to all marriages (of which 10 per cent were between the children of supervisory workers), 30 per cent of Methodist marriages were between children of supervisory workers, it is also the case that 41 per cent of Methodist marriages were between the children of semi-skilled workers. [79] Using these data alone then, [80] a substantial proportion of Methodists were *not* supervisory workers. Methodism was not the preserve of supervisory workers 'surrounded by a cocoon of formal institutions', [81] to insulate them from those whom they supervised at work.

The second piece of questionable evidence comes from Foster's discussion of the incorporation of Oldham's coal miners into bourgeois society. [82] Here the checkweighman system developed, but Foster admits that this was hardly a labour aristocracy of supervisory workers. Yet he goes on to argue that 'in time there does seem to have developed a *cultural* receptiveness to employer attitudes among certain sections of the labour force [not necessarily just the check-weighmen], most typically expressed in the development of Wesleyan Methodism.' [83] The possibility is open, then, that developments within extra-work institutions (for example, Methodist chapels) contributed to the differentiation of the working class.

Let me repeat that the purpose of these remarks is to question the strong interpretation of the centrality of the labour process, but not to displace that process as the focus for the examination of the interconnections of institutions in space. It seems that within Foster's study there are gaps and inconsistencies which allow the possibility that developments within political and self-education institutions may themselves have contributed to the decline of the labour community. But the message from studies such as those of Foster, Stedman Jones, Roberts, and Fraser, is that the historical evidence points to the utility of the labour process as a reference point for research, for exploring the functional interconnections between political structures and the economy, on the one hand, and the links between cultural institutions and the labour process on the other.

I will now conclude by acknowledging my debts and briefly summarizing what I have tried to establish. I have proceeded by criticizing others, but I am essentially indebted to some of those whom I have criticized, for the ideas expressed in this discussion: to Briggs for the theme of differentiation, to Castells for making the notion of 'urban' problematic, to Mellor for the local-national dimension, to Stacey for the concept of local social systems, and to Marxist historians for the centrality of the labour process. The discussion has sought to weld these ideas together so as to sketch a framework for the study of urbanization in Britain.

For sociologists, urbanization cannot be conceptualized solely in terms of demographic movements, nor as some notion of an urban way of life. Rather, urbanization is one facet of the overall spatial organization of social institutions. In general this has two aspects: the 'vertical' incidence of factors from the purely local to the international level, and the 'horizontal' interconnection of institutions within a given spatial area. Within the sociology of spatial organization, the 'horizontal' is primary, but constant reference is required to the influence of factors located at different levels to any given context. The 'urban' is one such context, but it is empirically problematic whether a city is a significant local social system, e.g. a causally effective relationship between institutions. To further focus research, I suggest taking the labour process as the point of reference for institutional relationships. However, the task of research is not to engage in spatial particularism, but to isolate, through comparative analysis, which institutions, at a given level, are empirically important.

This discussion has been concerned to develop a framework of concepts with which to address the study of British urbanization. It might be used to conduct research on two important empirical topics. The first refers to the degree to which the city or town is a significant spatial unit for the working of social institutions in any given historical period. Does the city or town represent a 'sphere of operation' for the firm (raising of capital, supply of labour, organiza- tion of production, marketing, etc.), or the trade union movement (trade councils, shop steward groups, etc.)? In what sense is the city or town a political, educational, or religious unit? Of course, this is not a uniform or static picture. We know that the organization of social institutions in space has been varied, and that this is part of the wider processes of change. Yet, how these processes interrelate with spatial organization, and with the parameters of the interrelation of institu- tions in space, is obscure. Second, if at historical moments the city or the town is a unit of spatial organization for one or more institutions, what are the effects of this? I suspect that spatial variation in the interrelations of institutions might throw light on class formation, class consciousness, and class conflict, and their variations over time. If this is so, then, following through the suggestions outlined here might prove productive both for the question of class and politics at the societal level and for comparison between particular towns.

Notes

1 I would like to extend my thanks to Valdo Pons and Ray Francis for encouraging me to write this paper, and to Margaret Stacey, Margaret

Archer, and the late Philip Abrams for their helpful comments.

2 An exception is J. R. Mellor, *Urban Sociology in an Urbanized Society*, Routledge & Kegan Paul, London, 1977. A discussion of this work follows later in this paper.

3 B. J. L. Berry, *The Human Consequences of Urbanization: Divergent Paths in the Urban Experience in the Twentieth Century*, Macmillan, London, 1973.

4 A. F. Weber, *The Growth of Cities in the Nineteenth Century*, Reprints in Urban Studies, Cornell University, 1963. First published in 1899.

5 See, especially, G. Sjoberg, 'Theory and research in urban sociology', in P. M. Hauser and L. Schnore (eds), *The Study of Urbanization*, Wiley and Sons, London, 1965, pp. 157-89; R. E. Pahl, *Whose City?*, Penguin, Harmondsworth, 1975, pp. 115-22; M. Castells, 'Is there an urban sociology?' and 'Theory and ideology in urban sociology', in C. G. Pickvance (ed.), *Urban Sociology: Critical Essays*, Tavistock, London, 1976, pp. 33-59 and pp. 60-84. It should be noted that these criticisms stem from different standpoints.

6 See, for example, G. Stedman Jones, *Outcast London: A Study in the Relationship Between Classes in Victorian Society*, Oxford University Press, Oxford, 1976, for an excellent account of the peculiarities of the London housing market. The contrast in patterns of estate management in London and Sheffield can be found in D. J. Olsen, 'House upon house: Estate development in London and Sheffield', in H. S. Dyos and M. Wolff (eds), *The Victorian City*, vol. 1, Routledge & Kegan Paul, London, 1973, pp. 333-57. On the variety of working-class housing provision, see S. D. Chapman (ed.), *The History of Working Class Housing*, David & Charles, Newton Abbott, 1971.

7 J. Foster, *Class Struggle and the Industrial Revolution: Early Industrial Capitalism in Three English Towns*, Methuen, London, 1974.

8 D. Fraser, *Urban Politics in Victorian England: The Structure of Politics in Victorian Cities*, Leicester University Press, Leicester, 1976.

9 See the closing chapter of A. Briggs, *Victorian Cities*, Penguin, Harmondsworth, 1968.

10 Briggs, op. cit., 1968.

11 Ibid., p. 33. Briggs's claim is supported by J. Patten (1978), *English Towns 1500-1700*, Dawson and Sons, Folkstone. Patten's research focuses on pre-industrial towns where the emphasis is on the *lack* of differentiation but with the gradual development of a capitalist economy and the emergence of specialization.

12 Briggs, op. cit., 1968, p. 116.

13 Ibid., p. 34.

14 Ibid., p. 43.

15 H. S. Dyos and M. Wolff (eds), *The Victorian City*, vol. 1, Routledge & Kegan Paul, London, 1973.

16 E. E. Lampard, 'The urbanizing world', in Dyos and Wolff, op. cit., 1973, pp. 3-57.

17 For example, Berry, op. cit., 1973, B. London and W. G. Flanagan, 'Comparative urban ecology: A summary of the field', in J. Walton and L. H. Massotti (eds), *The City in Comparative Perspective*, Wiley and Sons, London, 1976, pp. 41-66; D. Slater, 'Towards a political economy

of urbanization in peripheral societies: Problems of theory and method with illustrations from Latin America', *International Journal of Urban and Regional Research*, vol. 2, no. 1, pp. 26-52.

18 H. S. Dyos and J. Wolff, 'Epilogue: The way we live now', in *The Victorian City*, vol. 2, Routledge & Kegan Paul, London, 1973, p. 907.

19 Ibid., p. 894.

20 Ibid., p. 904.

21 M. Castells, *The Urban Question: A Marxist Approach*, Edward Arnold, London, 1977, p. 17.

22 Ibid., p. 126.

23 Ibid., p. 64.

24 Ibid., chapter 9.

25 Ibid., pp. 237-42.

26 Ibid., p. 234.

27 Ibid., p. 234.

28 Ibid., p. 235.

29 Ibid., p. 236.

30 Ibid., p. 235.

31 Ibid., p. 237.

32 Ibid., p. 236.

33 Ibid., pp. 234-6.

34 Ibid., p. 237.

35 M. Mandelbawn, 'Societal Laws', in J. O'Neill (ed.), *Modes of Individualism and Collectivism*, Heinemann, London, 1973.

36 Castells, op. cit., 1977, p. 34. See also pp. 50, 65, 158, 176, 183 and 192.

37 Ibid., pp. 71-2.

38 Ibid., p. 58.

39 Mellor, op. cit., 1977.

40 Ibid., p. xiv.

41 Ibid., p. 18.

42 Ibid., p. 47.

43 Ibid., p. vii.

44 Ibid., p. xv.

45 Ibid., p. 13.

46 Ibid., p. 13.

47 Ibid., p. 9.

48 Ibid., p. 10.

49 Ibid., p. 19.

50 M. Hechter, *International Colonialism: The Celtic Fringe in British National Development 1536-1966*, Routledge & Kegan Paul, London, 1975.

51 Mellor, op. cit., 1977, p. 47.

52 Ibid., p. 13.

53 Ibid., p. 10.

54 Ibid., p. 26.

55 Ibid., p. 14.

56 Ibid., p. 15.

57 Ibid., p. 16.

58 Ibid., p. 8. Here Mellor quotes Halsey that 'There is no city which is

either autonomous or internally homogeneous. It cannot be the analytical unit for all life chances.'

59 Ibid., p. 16.
60 Ibid., pp. 36-45.
61 Ibid., p. xvi.
62 Ibid., p. 10.
63 My concept of institution is derived from Giddens's discussion of power and normative order. See A. Giddens, *New Rules of Sociological Method: A Positive Critique of Interpretive Sociologies*, Hutchinson, London, 1976, Chapter 3.
64 M. Stacey, 1974, 'The myth of community studies', in C. Bell and H. Newby (eds), *The Sociology of Community*, Frank Cass, London, 1974.
65 Ibid., p. 19. My emphasis.
66 After completing this paper, my attention was drawn to Roland Warren's *The Community in America*, Rand McNally, Chicago, 1963. Warren certainly shares my concern with the interrelations of social institutions in space and he uses the same terminology as I do in conceptualizing the interrelation of institutions within a given area ('horizontal') and the different spatial levels of analysis ('vertical'). He adopts a functionalist framework in order to develop his ideas. Whilst this allows for a considerably more developed scheme than that given here, it seems basically flawed in its principle of treating any social unit, whether the local community or the national society, as a social *system* and in analysing groups, institutions, and processes in terms of their functions for such a system.
67 G. M. Norris, 'Industrial paternalist capitalism and local labour markets', *Sociology*, vol. 12, no. 3, 1978, pp. 469-89.
68 Ibid., p. 479.
69 J. Foster, *Class Struggle and the Industrial Revolution: Early Industrial Capitalism in Three English Towns*, Methuen, London, 1974.
70 G. S. Jones, *Outcast London: A Study in the Relationship between Classes in Victorian Society*, Oxford University Press, Oxford, 1971.
71 B. Roberts, 'Mobility of labour, the industrial economy and state provision', paper presented at the Centre for Environmental Studies Conference on 'Urban Change and Conflict', Nottingham University, 1979.
72 Foster, op. cit., 1974, p. 65. Here Foster notes 'the reassertion of state power' as a phase in the class struggle, but devotes only one paragraph to it.
73 Ibid., p. 69.
74 Ibid., p. 61.
75 D. Fraser, *Urban Politics in Victorian England: The Structure of Politics in Victorian Cities*, Leicester University Press, Leicester, 1976.
76 Foster, op. cit., 1974, p. 184.
77 Ibid., p. 215.
78 Ibid., p. 215.
79 Ibid., p. 215. See Table 17.
80 In itself this is not a very satisfactory indicator, but then this is what Foster uses.

Ian Proctor

81 Foster, op. cit., 1974, p. 237.
82 Ibid., pp. 234-7.
83 Ibid., pp. 236-7.

114

Symbols, images and social organization in urban sociology [1]

Ray Francis

This paper seeks to restate the case for developing the study of the ways in which urban residents interpret, represent, and use their environments. My general concern is in keeping with the view expressed by Pons [2] that a better understanding of urban symbolism and imagery is essential for the development of our sociological understanding of cities within contemporary capitalist societies. In my view, however, this calls for a review and discussion of problems inherent in the study of the social and cultural organization of city life in general. I am therefore led to examine issues in contemporary sociology which go far beyond the analysis of urban symbolism and imagery as such.

To avoid the risk of misunderstanding, I would enter two categorical disclaimers at the outset. The first is that I am not driven by any concern to develop a more 'humanistic' perspective to somehow complement existing 'objectivist' perspectives on urban life. The second is that I am not pleading for, or seeking to promote, 'microscopic' studies for their own sake or for the purpose of somehow redressing any imbalance there may be between 'micro' and 'macro' approaches to urban society. To allow either of these views to harbour in the mind of the reader would be misleading. On the other hand, I would stress that a view implicit in this paper is that we do need to redress another imbalance, namely that between studies which focus mainly on the economic and political aspects of urban life and those which dwell on social and cultural aspects.

The fact that neighbourhoods, towns and cities are commonly imputed with meanings by their inhabitants was frequently alluded to in the urban and community studies of the 1950s and 1960s, and the general question of 'urban imagery' was the subject of an important position developed, at about the same time, by Strauss. [3] Since then, there has been a veritable surge of interest in 'environmental

115

perception' in the apparent belief that an understanding of how residents and commuters respond to their urban environments is important for policy-making and planning.[4]

The sociological relevance of 'environmental perception' is, however, far from clear, and some authors have expressed doubts over the ambiguous nature of the findings and interpretations of studies of individual perceptions.[5] This is not surprising, for it would be ludicrous to imagine that perceptions, symbols, and images of urban environments are invariably of fundamental significance. Yet there have been no systematic attempts to specify the ways and the situations in which representations of urban habitats enter into, and influence, patterns in social life. In short, there is a considerable gulf between the extensive body of literature built on psychological foundations and the largely undeveloped sociological position given thrust and form by Strauss.[6]

A central contention of this paper is that the two broad approaches in this field are too disparate to converge in any meaningful way until we have a more satisfactory context for studies of social and cultural organization in general. Unless such a context is developed, the current practice of viewing interpretations and representations of urban environments as 'mental maps', and the like, must be a barrier to any appreciation of the potential claimed for studies of symbolism and imagery in the understanding of urban-industrial life in capitalist society.

In order to elaborate these views, the rest of the paper takes the following form: Part I outlines the 'persistent malaise' long felt in British 'urban sociology'; Part II outlines the type of working conception of social and cultural organization which might be used; Part III highlights relevant directions in contemporary social theory and sociological analysis; Part IV evaluates the existing literature on perceptions, symbols and images; and Part V briefly summarizes the discussion and suggests lines for future research, following on the total stance of this paper.

I

Over the past twenty-five years, British 'urban sociology' has been the subject of a series of severe and wide-ranging criticisms. Few scholars regarding themselves as 'urban sociologists' have been happy with the state of their specialization.[7] Broadly, 'urban sociology' has been variously taken to task for focusing on a narrow, sterile, and fragmentary range of topics; for maintaining too great a distance from politics, policy-making and planning; for perpetuating its intellectual isolation from developments in other areas of the social sciences; and for being insufficiently concerned with the systematic development of its own theoretical foundations. Aspects of all these complaints were woven into a single trenchant passage of a critical essay by Ruth Glass in the mid-1950s. In her view, many urban studies of the period were of little significance for a variety of reasons and some of them made it unnecessarily difficult to see the wood for the trees. [8]

They tend to be devoid of general context and so microscopic that they get lost in the individuality of social phenomena: starting from a *tabula rasa*, sceptical of the objective validity of common social experience, the investigator, without knowing what to look for, can hardly see the social framework at all ... the institutions and relationships which are investigated—these are characteristically small-scale, mainly primary groups such as family, kinship, neighbourhood—may well have an urban background, but it is hardly visible. There is usually no theoretical background either: the striving for 'scientific' purity has so far led to plain piecemeal empiricism, barely disguised by some odd, *ad hoc* 'hypothesis'. The objects studied are so segmented that they can give no clue to social change, in terms of class and political alignments, for example. And they are observed in so intensive a fashion that the investigator himself needs to have no notion of social change, nor any commitments to value judgements and social theory: his families, for instance, are individuals, not representatives of social groups. As such, they are the most elusive of all objects of social study; as the research worker can never know enough about them, he cannot be expected to make generalizations.... Hence, though this approach to social research is apparently detached from politics and policy, it frequently serves as an apologia for the *status quo*, or results in nostalgia for an unhistoric past, despite the authors' insistence on the 'dynamics' of social roles and situations.

In a later passage from the same article, Glass adds an even more general indictment which suggests that our forebears sometimes served the cause of urban studies better than we do. [9]

The few, isolated attempts to view the urban social scene in wide perspective belong to the Edwardian and Victorian eras. Since the thirties, especially, there has been a total lack of comprehensive studies devoted to the characteristics of towns, to their historical diversity and changes. Neither their demographic and historical traits, nor their class relations, economy and culture have been systematically investigated; these aspects have not even been broadly mapped out.

Much has changed in British 'urban sociology' since the above passages were written. Yet, many of the criticisms remain relevant and the critiques of more recent years can be best understood if we read them partly as a continuation of, and partly as a response to, the assessment made by Glass. Dissatisfaction with ahistorical and piecemeal research, and with the general incoherence of intensive studies and of such frameworks of analysis as we have, continue to be expressed. This is so despite the substantial progress that has been made in developing interdisciplinary linkages and in placing urban studies within more general analyses of the component elements and structural properties of British capitalism. Perhaps the major achievement of recent years, largely emanating from the stimulus of Castells, [10] has been the firm location of urban studies in the context of debates on the nature of contemporary British capitalism, and especially of those which focus on the institutional structure and role of the state. [11] But, significant as these developments are, they have thus far provided little clear guidance on how to interpret intensive local studies of urban life, and the implications of the advances for the analysis of specifically social and cultural organization have not even been discussed. Indeed, the kind of assumptions, premises, and methods that prevail in contemporary British urban studies are so far removed from any implied in the analysis of social and cultural organization that it is difficult to see how the new literature can lead to an integrated analysis of social practices and social action.

The situation which confronts scholars wishing to develop analyses of social and cultural organization is fraught with difficulties. Community studies have fallen out of fashion since the 1950s and early 1960s, and they are unlikely to reappear in any more meaningful form unless their relevance to wider sociological debates can be demonstrated.

The crux of the problem seems to stem from the failure even to recognize that there is an imbalance between studies of the political economy of urbanization and studies of the social and cultural aspects of urban society. One consequence of this failure is that aspects of social and cultural organization are presented in a highly static and abstract manner. A diversity of assumptions and assertions is constantly made—implicitly or explicitly—regarding the nature of urban institutions and the significance of values, beliefs, motives, interests and purposes of urban dwellers. These assumptions and assertions are held to underlie social practices and to define social action in the urban setting. But they are scarcely subjected to investigation or analysis and they should not be accepted as valid bases for, or evidence in, theoretical arguments. They are, in effect, an *unexamined resource*, and our sensitivity to the problems entailed in using them would appear to be even lower today than at the time that Ruth Glass made her original strictures of the British urban literature.

In passing, we may note that it is not only 'urban' social and cultural organization which is in a state of relative neglect. National, regional, and local variations in social and cultural cleavages and alignments have also attracted little systematic attention in general. [12]

The more immediate 'reasons' for the current situation are not difficult to identify. Firstly, many contemporary urban sociologists still have a strong desire to distance themselves from the notion of urbanism handed down from the Chicago School and enshrined in Wirth's extremely influential, and oft-reprinted article, 'Urbanism as a Way of Life'. [13] It has often been demonstrated that Wirth's concept of urbanism and parallel notions such as the rural-urban continuum confuse the social and cultural aspects of liberal capitalism with the urban environment itself. [14] But rejections of the concepts involved have developed into a ritual, which is practised assiduously but is seldom accompanied by any constructive attempt to fill the vacuum left behind. The critics of the Wirthian position have thus far largely failed to come to grips with the nature and significance of personal, social and cultural organization in modern society.

Secondly, there has been a more recent, but equally pronounced desire to establish and perpetuate a sharp break with the methods used in local and 'community studies' of earlier generations. The arguments ranged against the 'community studies method' display many parallels with those advanced against urbanism. In Britain, these were powerfully supported, first by Dennis's attack on 'the popularity of the neighbourhood community idea' as ideologically conservative and sterile, [15] and then by sweeping condemnations of 'the community study as a method'. [16] This is not the place to argue for, or against, particular criticisms of 'community studies'. I simply want to stress that such studies yielded invaluable accounts of social and cultural organization and that, with their virtual disappearance, we no longer have any comparable sources of information for the present period. Yet many sociologists continue to use information drawn from past studies of this kind, while at the same time arguing, implicitly or explicitly, against the 'method' by which the data and their interpretation were established in the first place!

Thirdly, following the severe criticisms to which British 'urban sociology' in general, and local community studies in particular, have been subjected, there has developed a strong tendency to define urban studies as the political economy or urbanization, with an emphasis on the analysis of the state. [17]

The net effect of these developments has been a shift of focus from one set of wholly legitimate problems to another set of very different, but equally legitimate, problems, without any attempt to bridge the gap between them. The bulk of contemporary British 'urban sociology' takes the class structure as a constant factor, treats it in a largely unproblematic way, and then delegates the analysis of social and cultural organization to other sociological specializations, e.g. deviance, race relations, sex and gender, the mass media, and the like. In general, then, such changes as have taken place in the study of urban society have scarcely begun to resolve the unsatisfactory situation first brought to our attention by Ruth Glass in the 1950s.

It is one thing to argue that analyses of social and cultural organization in capitalist society take us 'beyond the urban', but it is quite another to argue that such analyses have no relevance for urban studies. Similarly, it is one thing to criticize the methodological inadequacies and shortcomings of 'community studies', but quite another to argue, or imply, that we can do without studies of this kind. They remain, in my view, the best means of grasping what Bell and Newby refer to as 'the very stuff of sociology, the social organization of human beings'. [18] If we argue, as many *in effect* do, that local and ethnographic-type studies have, by definition, no place in efforts to understand urban life, we are denying the importance of the relations between the localized processes of social and cultural organization and the supra-local processes of class formation, class conflict, and the activities of the state. Further, if we do not revive and develop the ethos and practice of 'community studies' and related forms of investigation, we will, by default, have to make do with crude reductionist analyses of social practices and social action.

We are already quite alarmingly dependent on community studies produced more than a decade ago for evidence on life-styles, life-cycles and class relations, patterns of family life, the significance of kinship and friendship networks, and the like. Moreover, we would appear to have a more systematic understanding of urban conditions and city life in the nineteenth century than we have of the present and the more recent past. This is due partly to the perceptive and detailed accounts provided by nineteenth-century observers, and partly to the fact that social and economic historians, [19] together with critics and evaluators of literary history, [20] have taken up issues central to the analysis of social and cultural organization more assiduously and systematically than contemporary 'urban sociologists'.

The major difficulty confronting those who would seek to orient contemporary sociological studies of urbanization is, however, not the absence of 'facts' or 'evidence'. A more serious obstacle is that we have not developed an adequate working conception of social and cultural organization itself. We clearly do need greater conceptual clarity and sophistication than was commonly displayed in the community and ethnographic studies of a decade or two ago. I therefore now turn to a brief discussion of the notion of social and cultural organization itself.

II

The search for a broad, all-inclusive, conceptual framework to guide and accommodate studies of urban social and cultural organization has had a chequered history. A major issue, commented upon by Glass and other critics, stems from the all too common division of labour between 'researchers' and 'theoreticians'. Field researchers have, on the whole, used conceptual schemes elaborated by others and they have done so in a selective and piecemeal manner. Limited aspects of Durkheimian, more specifically Wirthian, thought was widely used in the community studies of the 1950s, when there was a widespread concern with face-to-face relationships and with notions of neighbourhood spirit, social solidarity, and local community consciousness. [21] But these and similar studies did not lead to sustained attempts to establish new conceptual schemes. On the contrary, responses to them commonly took one of two forms. In the first form, there was strong criticism, even denunciation, of the core ideas, as in the critique launched by Dennis. [22] In the second form, the response undertook a review of possibly relevant theories and concepts, noting their utility and limitations but doing little more, as in the comprehensive review of British community studies produced by Frankenberg. [23] Interesting and insightful as these responses were, they were largely elaborated as criticism or as review and illustration without moving over to positively constructive innovation.

By and large, the same seems to have been true in other countries. Thus the limitations of Durkheimian ideas and of the Wirthian schema have long been recognized in the United States. [24] On the whole, intensive ethnographic-type urban studies gave rise to few new alternative conceptualizations of the processes of social and cultural change.

We are therefore left to consider more general formulations of social and cultural organization to be found in the broader spectrum of sociological and anthropological writings. For the purposes of a brief discussion, it is helpful to draw a contrast between two fairly clear-cut views. The first may be identified by referring to the names of Radcliffe-Brown and Merton, the second by reference to the work of Raymond Firth. [25] For Radcliffe-Brown and Merton, the phrase 'social and cultural organization' identified an analytic construct which encompassed whole societies. As such, it assumed the status of a theoretical object in its own right, imbued with heavy overtones of adaptation, integration, and continuity. In a very general manner, this conception of social and cultural organization is akin to that which suffuses Wirth's schema, and all its variants.

In Firth's work, however, the phrase 'social and cultural organization' does not assume the form of an analytic construct or theoretical object. It is, rather, a heuristic device which directs attention to 'the working arrangements of society': to the *processes* through which the normative and instrumental aspects of social relationships and social actions are ordered and re-ordered. On the one hand, these processes refer to the interests, experience, goals and activities of people engaged in everyday life. On the other, they refer to associational forms and groupings, to events and happenings, and to the constraints bearing on all social action through the operation of social, economic, political and cultural structures. In this perspective, 'organization' does not constitute a 'thing'. It is not a structure possessing certain functions or characteristics, nor is it a set of social actors possessing distinctive and static attributes. Rather, it refers to the bases of differentiation around which social relationships are structured—bases such as age, sex, race, occupation, residence, etc.—*and* to the constitution of action and practice in, and through, such fundamental processes as communication, co-operation and conflict, apposition and opposition.

As Portes [26] clearly sees, such a view of social and cultural organization questions the grounds for over-reliance on 'structuralist' or 'normative' views of social life. It directly challenges the validity of any position which takes 'structures' and/or 'norms' as the primary objects for analysis. Just as this view *questions* mechanistic, simplistic and reductionist conceptualizations, it *supports* and *advances* others. In particular, it promotes the view that members of society 'see' and 'use' existing social, economic, political, and cultural structures and institutions as *conditions* for action, but not as *imperatives* in, nor as determinants of, these.

Such a view of social and cultural organization has, in effect, been used more than it has been systematically elaborated. [27] It is a conception which lurks beneath a number of important urban studies. [28] As Silverman [29] points out, however, its value has long been more clearly admitted in the analysis of key problems in the study of bureaucracies or 'formal organizations'. In other fields of sociological enquiry, it has only been discussed explicitly from time to time. One good example is Boissevain's study of 'politics' in terms of small-scale, personalized networks and social relationships. As he himself puts it: [30]

> The subject-matter is familiar: the network of friends, relatives and
> work-mates; the visiting, bargaining, gossiping and manoeuvring
> that goes on between them ... the steps an ambitious man takes to
> build up his fund of credit among useful relations; and the
> operation of neighbourhood and workplace cliques and factions.
> These are the processes and situations with which we are all
> involved and they are the basic stuff of social life.

Concern in studies inspired by this conception is not so much with 'formal', persistent, even eternal relationships, as with those that are more 'informal', changing, and ephemeral, and which emerge as people 'do their thing', play their parts, negotiate their roles, choose their companions and friends, or make their enemies. The approach has much in common with the processes analysed in Elizabeth Bott's classic study, [31] in which the nature of the social networks of husband and wife are explained in relation to the developmental cycle of the family, and to geographic mobility and social class. (It is interesting to note, in passing, that many subsequent urban studies have made reference to this work, though usually without any sustained attempt to develop the width of its applicability.)

The importance of Firth's general conception of social and cultural organization resides in the way attention is drawn through it to the inadequacies of analyses couched primarily in terms of 'social structures', and thus to the severe limitations of the mechanistic and static use of such concepts as 'ideology', 'culture', 'role' and 'norm'. In common with many of the views to be found in the symbolic interactionist literature it shifts the focus of attention from, for example, 'roles' to 'role-players' and, even more, to the 'making and taking of roles'. [32] But the importance of the conception does not attach simply to its value in analyses of social interaction, for it closely resembles Williams's view of 'culture' and the tasks of 'cultural analysis'.[33] It is a conception that requires that we think with greater precision and thoroughness about the use of wider general concepts, such as 'social formation' and 'social practice', and indeed, about 'society' and 'culture' themselves. At the risk of stressing the obvious, it should be said that terms like 'society' and 'culture' refer to a whole range of inclusive and exclusive structures and processes, and to a host of diverse organizational arrangements and sets of social relationships, which all too often escape scrutiny and analysis in urban studies. One salient injunction of Firth's position, which needs to be stressed, is that sets of structures, processes, arrangements, and relationships cannot simply be identified and laid side-by-side, as in a mosaic. We are not dealing with inert pieces. The metaphor of 'mosaic', which has so often been used in relation to urban, industrial, capitalist society, is very misleading. 'Kaleidoscope' would be a much more accurate and relevant metaphor, if one is needed.

It must, of course, be acknowledged and stressed that the Firthian conception of social and cultural organization is not without its problems. It plunges us into more than one marshland. Most notably, there are those which lie between analyses of economic and political factors and of social and cultural factors, and, between these respectively and those which focus on social interaction. We have no 'mega-theory' to deal adequately with the trenchant theoretical, methodological and empirical issues encountered in the marshlands. Any advocacy for using the approach outlined above must therefore rest on heuristic grounds. The approach holds the promise of complementing and extending our analyses of a variety of substantive themes, topics, and problems. And it has the advantage of being more open-ended and far less restrictive than its rival perspectives.

It scarcely needs to be emphasized that the approach discussed here should *not* exclude historical, political economy, class and institutional analyses. Any serious attempt to deal systematically with social and cultural processes demands that these be carefully placed within the context of our fast developing knowledge of contemporary British capitalist society. The important point to be made is that current debates on the interrelations between capitalism, class conflict and the state tend, in varying degrees, either to *imply* analyses of social and cultural phenomena which have not been undertaken or to *preclude* by definition any serious consideration of social and cultural organization.

III

While the analysis of urban social and cultural organization has stagnated over the past ten to fifteen years, other aspects of urban studies have undergone far-reaching changes in response to new directions in general social, economic, and political theory. The main thrusts have been towards (a) the rejection of 'functionalism' and 'economism', and (b) a concentration on the component elements, systematic arrangements and structural properties of capitalism. Despite major differences in the perspectives and definitions of leading writers, their collective impact has been to clear the way for significant debates on the 'relative autonomy' of social, economic and political structures in capitalist society. The central problems here relate to the degree of 'autonomy' of different structures and to the nature of their 'interdependence', with particular emphasis on the total institutional structure and role of the state. The scope of these developments, and their implications for urban studies, have been well and fully documented. [34]

Without for one moment denying either the relevance or the significance of these developments, it must be stressed that there have also been *other* theoretical debates and explorations which merit the close attention of 'urban sociologists', but which have so far been accorded little recognition. I have in mind arguments and debates which focus on the following areas: (a) the adequacy of current analyses of social class; (b) the relations between ideology, culture, and legitimation; and (c) the relationships between social structure and social action.

An adequate overview of the issues involved in, and arising from, the relevant arguments and debates would demand far more space than is available here and would take us far beyond the scope of this paper. But a brief discussion of each area will be attempted with the twin aims of showing how developments in contemporary social theory invite, indeed demand, a reconsideration of the nature and significance of social and cultural organization, and of substantiating my view that 'urban sociologists' need to be more involved in, and more flexible towards, general social theory if their studies are to achieve a proper place in the analysis of capitalist society.

(a) There is widespread concern among British social scientists over the kinds of social class analysis which have flowed from different versions of the 'relative autonomy' thesis, and particularly over the neo-functionalist tendency to regard social classes as monolithic structures. [35] In recent years a number of important

125

attempts have been made to reformulate social class analysis in more dynamic, processual and multi-dimensional terms. [36] The objections to the cruder conceptualizations of the early 1970s are all too familiar to those attempting to utilize them. Parkin neatly catches the mood in the following statement. [37]

> The most damaging weakness of any model of class that relegates social collectivities to the status of mere incumbents of positions, or embodiments of systemic forces, is that it cannot account properly for those complexities that arise when racial, religious, ethnic, and sexual divisions run at a tangent to formal class divisions.

It is generally recognized that there are always a diversity of bases upon which social relationships may be formed and groups mobilized. In any given context, the bases of relationships, associations, and mobilization depend on the interaction of the class structure with more particular and localized factors. As seen by Giddens, Scott, and Urry, [38] the more particular structures requiring our careful attention, arranged roughly in descending order of importance, are as follows:
1.   the spatial organization of labour and of residence, e.g. nations, regions, cities, towns, countryside and neighbourhoods;
2.   the sexual division of labour, e.g. the differential allocation of gender into spheres of production and reproduction, and the organization of sexual relations;
3.   the religious, ethnic, and racial allocation of subjects;
4.   the differentiation of subjects on the bases of trade union and professional associations, artistic and leisure organizations, political parties, media institutions, etc.;
5.   the generational allocation of subjects.

All these principles of 'structuration', [39] and not simply 'class' and 'economic differentiation', form the bases of social relationships and social and cultural organization in varying degrees. Indeed, 'class relations' can only be truly understood in terms of the effects of the differential significance of such principles. [40] As Parkin points out, there is much evidence of considerable inconsistency in the way inter-class and intra-class relations are addressed. [41]

> Inter-class relations are conceived of as inherently antagonistic, a condition only to be comprehended through the idiom of dichotomy and conflict. At the intra-class level, however, the emphasis upon competitive struggle gives way to a rather blander concern with the niceties of social differentiation. The subject of

investigation here becomes (among the working class) variations in life-style and social consciousness or (among the middle class) variations in the social composition and recruitment of elites. Sociological ingenuity is directed to mapping out the social contours of a territory in which a truce has been declared in the *omnium bellum contra omnes*. Social differentiation within a given class, moreover, is analysed by reference to conceptual categories that generally do not correspond to existentially based groups with the capacity for mobilization; even less could they be said to constitute social collectivities in mutual competition for scarce resources.

If we collapse the principles of differentiation that are basic to co-operation and conflict alike into one monolithic structure, the concept of social class loses its explanatory power and critical thrust. While this point may be generally recognized, or at least conceded in debate, there appears to be a widespread reluctance to embark on the systematic and detailed research which it undoubtedly calls for in the sphere of urban studies.

(b) Since the mid-1970s it has been increasingly recognized that many aspects of ideology, culture, and legitimation call for concentrated attention and exposition. Broadly, there are here two significant strands in the literature. The first, to which Habermas, Gouldner, and Bell [42] have made prominent contributions, is concerned to explore in a variety of ways the trajectory of ideological and cultural development in capitalist society. The general implication of such contributions is clear. The analysis of ideological and cultural issues has received far too little attention and could well constitute the primary task for sociological work in the 1980s.

The second strand of writing in this area of concern is more specific in that it expresses a marked dissatisfaction with the tendency of views associated with the 'relative autonomy' thesis to foreclose upon a whole set of issues and questions regarding the relationships between social practices, ideology, and culture. Thus, several recent publications have been led to query the theoretical relevance and methodological implications of the concept of a 'dominant ideology' and its use to account for the maintenance of prevailing social, economic, and political orders. [43]

(c) Despite the importance of the above issues, perhaps the most fundamental and provocative theoretical debates of recent years have been those focusing attention squarely on the exceedingly complex issues of the relationship between social structures and social action—upon what Dawe terms 'the problem of human agency'. [44]

These issues have constituted the core of the writings of Bernstein and Giddens. [45]

To avoid any misunderstanding, it is worth quoting Giddens's categorical denial that these issues can be defined in terms of the 'micro' and the 'macro' [46]

the problem of the relation between the constitution (or, as I shall often say, production and reproduction) of society by actors, and the constitution of those actors by the society of which they are members, has nothing to do with a differentiation between micro- and macro-sociology; it cuts across any such division.

The relevant theoretical questions here cannot be distinguished methodologically in terms of 'scale' or 'level of analysis'. As raised by Dawe, Bernstein and Giddens, to name but a few, the issues refer equally to all levels of analysis. The central problem is how to bring together in one conceptual framework (a) the interpretations of actors as active, skilful, self-reflective and practical agents, and (b) the interpretations of social, economic, political, and cultural structures (within which social actors are scarcely visible) as having a more or less deterministic influence over social action.

Argument and debate on all three of the above areas of social theory and sociological analysis are manifestly crucial for the development of sociology in general, no less than for urban studies. The work of Giddens, Bernstein and Dawe, taken in conjunction with that of Habermas, Gouldner, and Bell, would seem to argue for a deeper and more systematic, yet more flexible, focus on 'ideology', 'culture' and 'legitimation' in the constitution of social action. Furthermore, we are reminded by all the participants in these debates that the very terms used in sociological analysis call for far more critical evaluation than they have hitherto received.

The debates concur on two important points in particular. Firstly, it is incorrect to think that there is one kind of sociology—'interpretive sociology'—which is solely and primarily concerned with explaining the relationships between 'culture', 'meaning', 'social organization' and 'social action', while other kinds of sociology disregard these issues. We should, rather, recognize that different sociological approaches define and explain these phenomena in different ways, e.g. in terms of 'social function', or 'rationality', or 'consciousness', or 'cathexis', and so on. Secondly, the analysis of social action, in whatever terms, must recognize the conditional and fragile nature of the way social practices and social relationships are related to wider social, economic, political, and cultural structures. In short, people regard and use their social environments as *conditions*, rather than as *imperatives*, for action.

With regard to substantive issues, the contributions of many writers are now inviting us to bring into consideration a host of topics largely excluded from the urban studies undertaken up to and during the 1980s. Urry virtually provides an inventory of such topics when he writes of the essential features of capitalist society that demand more adequate attention: [47]

> the existence of a multiplicity of social classes; the variety of social groupings based on gender, generational, racial, residential and national differences; and the importance of 'private' social relations within the family and within voluntary associations of very many kinds.

In effect too, he argues for fresh systematic studies of such features by adding: [48]

> The social relations of 'civil society' are not to be equated with either the state ... or with the economy.... They are not to be equated because they involve different forms of constitutive relations.

It is clear that the kind of disquiet expressed by Parkin over mechanistic class analyses and the relative neglect of intra-class divisions and conflicts, or by Urry in the above comments, is also felt by 'urban sociologists'. For example, Pickvance has expressed concern over studies of 'urban social movements' which ignore the problematic relationship between 'social base' and 'social force'. [49] And writers like Mellor, Lebas, Lloyd, Saunders, Dunleavy, and Elliott, also explicitly reveal their awareness and concern of the issues involved for British researchers. [50] The same is true for writers on urbanization in the Third World. [51]

The above comments cover an exceedingly wide range of issues, but they must suffice for the purposes of this paper. My concern is to direct attention to the *kind* of theoretical, methodological, and empirical questions which immediately arise when analyses of urban and social cultural organization are proposed. The theoretical and conceptual views which underpinned the urban and community studies of the 1950s and 1960s have changed out of all recognition. This has important implications. Whereas information on age, sex, income, occupation, place of residence, etc., are usually viewed simply as 'attributes', to be analysed for classificatory and descriptive purposes, one of the central points arising from the discussion in this section is that such 'data' are *not* simply 'attributes'. They should be viewed as more than that, as the bases of social and cultural organization, and as the *resources* upon which communication, co-operation and conflict, apposition and opposition, exploitation and discrimination, are developed, maintained, and changed. A plea for a return to the study of social and cultural organization is, therefore, not a simple plea for more studies of the kind undertaken in the 1950s and 1960s. It is, rather, a plea for, firstly, a more complex and problematic view of the relationships between social structure, social organization, and urbanization, and secondly, for a return to locality and ethnographic studies conducted with sensitivity to the range of themes and issues which have emerged in the last decade.

Against the background of these views on the analysis of social and cultural organization, I now turn to a review of existing studies of the way urban environments are experienced, interpreted and represented.

IV

Any attempt to respond to the suggestion that a deeper understanding of urban society requires 'more and better attention ... to the ways in which urban residents interpret their environments'[52] naturally demands an appraisal of past and current work in this field. The task is complicated in two respects. Firstly, the study of 'perceptions', 'symbols', and 'images' in social life is part of a long, rich, complex, and varied heritage derived from philosophy, theology, music, painting, and history. Secondly, the contemporary social scientific literature on the effects of urban environments on social life itself covers a host of themes and issues.

Focusing attention specifically on 'urban' perceptions, symbols and images, the recent literature would appear to contain two relatively distinct strands; the *psychological*, which is concerned with subjective representations of a quasi-sensory yet non-perceptual character[53]; and the *literary*, which is concerned with the emotional content of particular words, phrases, passages, or even whole works.[54] While research in urban environments stems from both the psychological and the literary perspectives, most individual studies have laid emphasis on one or the other. By and large, geographers, psychologists and planners have focused on the psychological aspects, stressing the connection between 'perceptions' and 'images', while historians and sociologists have emphasized the literary-based conception, stressing the connection between 'meanings' and 'images'. Each set of writings merits brief review.

Perceptions, images and 'mental maps'
Perception-based research on the effects of urban environments covers
a bewildering array of topics. This is apparent from even the most
casual reading of the literature which has burgeoned since the
innovative work of Lynch. [55] At base, linking the many diverse
studies of this area, there is a common concern with the perceptual-
cognitive devices (e.g., 'mental maps', 'spatial schemata', etc.) which
are taken to be the key organizing devices through which people
acquire, code, store, recall, and manipulate information about the
world in which they pursue their multifarious activities. In his
pioneering work, Lynch had sought to demonstrate that the 'memora-
bility' or 'imageability' of cities is largely determined by the physical
elements which comprise urban form and design. According to
Lynch, we negotiate the complex urban environment by perceiving
urban physical elements and by organizing these perceptions in terms
of 'edges', 'pathways', 'nodes', etc. This approach to the way urban
environments are perceived and used has been taken up and developed
by many researchers and writers, most notably Appleyard and Lee. [56]
Given the centrality accorded to the perception-design-use nexus, it is
not surprising that urban planners have found much to interest them
here. [57]

Broadly, this approach argues that there is a relationship between
the physical form or structure of urban environments and the
perceptual and cognitive processes of individuals. The 'images' that
are formed are the result of a two-way process between the observer
and the environment. The observer is held to select, organize, and
assign meaning to a limited number of environmental features which
are then further held to provide focal points and elements for the
construction of 'images', which in turn serve as the key orientation
points for further perceptions as individuals pursue their daily
activities.

Two additional notions are central to this kind of research. Firstly,
different arrangements of urban elements and form either facilitate or
inhibit the development of 'images' by individuals and, consequently,
also facilitate or inhibit behaviour patterns. Secondly, individuals are
more 'prone' or 'ready' to perceive those elements of urban environments which have a high probability of occurrence within their 'action
spaces'. Together these notions are used to analyse the processes
whereby environments are ordered in terms of hierarchies, boundaries, locations, and relationships between 'points'.

Finally, it is held that an individual's 'image' of any particular environment, and of the external world in general, develops with maturity and through progressive, perception-based, learning. Accordingly, there have been attempts to build a more systematic theoretical foundation on the basis of developmental psychology to account not only for a child's growing conceptualization of, and operations with, space, but also for the conceptualization of entire neighbourhoods, cities, and even nations.[58] At the same time, there has been a tendency to account for the variety of individual images uncovered through research by reference to such social factors as class, age, sex, occupation, and length of residence.[59]

Meanings, symbols and images

The study of the 'meanings' associated with localities, neighbourhoods, towns and cities, is less concerned with the relationship between urban form and cognitive processes and more with the way in which overlapping, and sometimes mutually exclusive, 'social worlds' may influence the process through which environments are both apprehended and presented. This view was pioneered in the United States by Strauss, and has been taken up most directly in Britain by Pons.[60] Similar, though less specific, views can be found in Briggs, Dyos and Wolff, Williams, and Relph.[61] The subject matter here often consists of the 'images' embedded in novels, diaries, official documents, songs, newspapers, textbooks, films, and the like.

Much of the work is concerned with the 'symbols' and 'images' used to identify and characterize whole cities in different historical contexts. The identities and characterizations are then examined for the quality of life they represent.[62] It is sometimes argued, though more often implied, that people make considerable methodological use of 'images' to reduce the complexity of their urban environments, thereby rendering them more orderly and meaningful. Hence, there is much interest in the use of metaphors, analogies, catch-phrases, clichés, stereotypes, and labels, which are used to classify, describe, and personify cities and parts of cities. Promotions by Chambers of Commerce, the persistence of local styles in architecture, and the construction and location of monuments may all play a part in the creation and maintenance of either generalized or particularized images. Similarly, the influence of local ceremonies and rituals, folklore and mass media may, individually or collectively, be influential.[63]

A basic theme in this type of literature is that in any city, or indeed in any differentiated population, we may expect to find a 'mosaic of social worlds', each of which has the potential to generate its own distinctive environmental imagery. In this respect, Strauss is following in the steps of the earlier well-known work of Firey, in arguing that in any urban environment different sets of people follow different 'orbits'. [64] Thus various sites and regions within cities acquire, or become invested with, distinctive symbolic associations and meanings. The public images, promoted and propagated in official, commercial, and academic circles, are in constant interplay with the idiosyncratic images which guide and escort individuals in all their activities in the city.

Echoes of the above themes, and of closely related issues, are encountered in a number of different kinds of sociological research. Perhaps their clearest manifestation is in the host of studies which focus on community and neighbourhood attachments and sentiments, local rituals and displays, social boundaries, and the like. [65] Similar themes reverberate through studies of 'community action', [66] and of the status-ascriptive dimensions of residential segregation. [67]

An evaluation

Collectively, this body of work has considerably expanded the traditional interest in environmental issues. It has clearly demonstrated that there is much to be gained from viewing the 'environment' in relation to the experiences, interests, and activities of individuals and groups. At base, linking all these approaches, is a view of the 'environment', not merely as the context within which social life takes place, but as itself an integral part of social life. 'Environment' becomes a fluid and relativistic notion, and our conceptions of it, our relations in and to it, are complex, multi-faceted and multi-layered affairs, and not to be understood in terms of a restricted causal chain or functional relationships linking particular stimuli or variables to particular responses. To paraphrase David Harvey, the question, 'What is the environment?', has been displaced by another, 'How is it that different human practices and life-styles make use of distinctive conceptualizations of their environments, and with what consequences?' [68] There are, however, a number of important criticisms to be made of the literature as it stands, particularly when we bear in mind the need to develop this kind of work in the future.

(a)   We are confronted with a diversity of quasi-theoretical notions (e.g. mental maps, spatial schemata, urban images, etc.), with little, if any, discussion of the severe theoretical and methodological difficulties inherent in them. Indeed, we are left in some doubt as to whether writers see their quasi-theoretical notions as constructions of the researcher or as models, maps, or images, held in the minds of

133

individuals, or both! There is, too, considerable blurring of different levels of analysis, and of the important distinction between 'perceptions' and 'meanings'.

(b) Both approaches describe and analyse perceptions and images largely divorced from the reality of social action and daily life. Both treat images as things in themselves, as relatively static products, located in the minds of individuals. They appear to assume that these images influence behaviour, and that they can be described and analysed *without* reference to particular contexts, interests and actions. Such a stance simply begs questions of validity and relevance—relevant to whom, for what, when, where, why, and with what consequences?

(c) The psychologically-based, perception-oriented approach dominates research in this field. Most of the work is overwhelmingly focused on design and incorporates a crude blend of behaviourism, gestaltism, and market research. Complex cognitive, communicative and social processes are reduced to simplistic and mechanistic terms, e.g. 'the man-environment relationship'. Ladd's plea for a more sophisticated concern with sociological factors, utilizing ethnographic studies, seems to have fallen on deaf ears. [69] The literary-based, meaning-oriented approach consists mainly of undeveloped programmatic statements. The framework employed resembles an assemblage of elements drawn at random from symbolic interactionism and content analysis. To date, this work has glossed over the social, economic, and political significance of 'urban images', largely because it has failed to establish the necessary links with the diversity of interests, relationships, and groupings found in capitalist society.

(d) Regardless of whether the descriptive, ascriptive, or prescriptive aspects of imagery are emphasized (and there seems precious little interest in exploring the relationships between these aspects), the representations are invariably viewed in 'pictorial' terms—as geographical, geometrical, or literary abstractions. The basic *communicative* significance of all representational devices is ignored. Now, this is not simply a methodological point. The anthropological literature, [70] not to mention the literature on 'deviance', [71] constantly makes the point that symbols and images cannot be reduced either to their 'essential meanings' or 'ideological functions'. Rather, they are characteristically partial, incomplete, and context-sensitive, such that attention must focus on the way they are derived, constructed, manipulated, modified, presented and disputed in communicative processes which are themselves embedded in social relationships. Further, there is no reason to assume that the symbols and images are either overtly 'pictorial' or overtly 'urban', in form, content or relevance. [72] They could just as relevantly be derivations from, or extensions of, representations constructed around linguistic forms related to class, age, sex, ethnicity, and the like, and for a diversity of purposes and audiences.

There are, however, a number of important contributions to this field which warrant special attention. Firstly, there is an emerging body of work which is concerned to explore the theoretical issues implicated in analyses of 'environmental issues' in the specific context of modern capitalist society. [73] Secondly, Pocock and Hudson have made a deliberate and highly relevant attempt to push the study of perceptions, symbols, and images into the sphere of urban planning and policy-formation. [74] Thirdly, Burgess's work can be taken as but one example of a much wider movement towards a broader approach to 'environmental perception', incorporating a wider social, economic, political, and historical framework, under the label 'sense of place'. [75] Fourthly, Pons has argued strongly for future analyses to focus on the social, economic, political and historical contexts within which image-makers, image-purveyors, image-users and image-breakers operate. [76]

In keeping with my own criticisms, and with the points made earlier in this paper, a particularly fruitful line of investigation would be to pursue the study of urban symbolism and imagery in localized studies of social and cultural organization. Attention here might focus on how symbols and images, developed and used by different individuals and groups in different contexts, have communicative significance, and are inevitably *partial entities*, whose existence and character depend on their relationship to *both* local and wider social, economic, political, and historical processes. The work of Suttles [77] is extremely suggestive in this regard. Among British studies, those by Boal and Damer are examples of research which give tantalizing glimpses of the potential insights to be gained from the position advocated here. [78]

V

A major weakness in contemporary British urban sociological work is the scant systematic attention paid to the nature and significance of social and cultural organization. This is most unsatisfactory, for aspects of social and cultural organization are traded upon as unexamined resources and writers are in consequence often led to crude, reductionist accounts of social practices and social action.

There is a widespread rejection of Wirth's notion of 'urbanism' but there is little evidence of any concerted effort to explore anew the parameters of the social and cultural aspects of urban, industrial, capitalist society. Indeed, there are good grounds for concluding that, despite the explicit rejection of 'urbanism', urban sociologists generally still accept that the social and cultural life of British urban dwellers can be adequately grasped using elements derived from the 'mass society' and 'social disorganization' theses which lie at the heart of Wirth's position.

A systematic focus on social and cultural organization is justified and required, partly because it is already implied in, and necessary for, existing work, and partly because it is difficult to see how urban sociologists can do without it if they are to come to grips with the general current of debate in social theory and sociological analysis. We urgently need to go beyond those elements of social and political theory which are relevant to the classic ecological analyses of urbanization. Current theoretical concern with the nature and significance of ideology and culture in capitalist society, with the inadequacies of social class analysis, and with the problematic relationship between social structure and social action would all direct our attention towards a far more complex view of the relations between social structure and spatial structure than is invoked by current urban research.

It is difficult to conceive of future progress in the study of, say, 'urban social movements', 'the labour process', 'local labour markets', and 'local political environments', [79] without the systematic analysis of issues stemming from and directly related to social and cultural organization. It would appear that this point is becoming more widely recognized. Thus, for example, in commenting on the 'curiously disembodied' character of much of the urban literature of the 1970s, Pahl has recently referred to what he considers to be 'the self-evident need' for social anthropological studies. [80] In a similar vein, Lebas comments on the serious absence of detailed historical, social, and political analyses of the forces which have structured urban places and the consciousness of their inhabitants. [81] If, and when, systematic studies of the social and cultural aspects of urban life are resumed, we may expect a rapid growth in the linkages between the work of urban sociologists and work in the fields of 'race', [82] 'deviance', [83] 'women', [84] and 'popular culture', [85] to name but a few.

There are clear methodological implications which flow from the theoretical and substantive issues discussed in this paper. It is surely time that a much more tolerant and sophisticated view be taken of ethnographic studies and community studies. The point is made very forcefully by Lloyd. [86]

> Despite the problems there is a clear need to get to theoretical grips with community studies particularly if we accept that the development of capitalism is typified by 'combined and uneven' development and that this has spatial manifestations, not only internationally but intra-nationally. In short we need to have a theory of consciousness that does not simply assume universality but takes some account of place.

A number of different writers have noted the importance of studies of 'urban' symbols and images for urban studies in general. [87] Ultimately, of course, the basic problem here is to locate a level of analysis which makes clear how the cognitive logic meshes with the communicative logic of social relationships, and how this logic meshes with the wider social, economic, and political structures. In the meantime, it is important to acknowledge that we cannot abandon interest in aspects of social and cultural organization. Otherwise we will have no way of identifying either the pertinent groupings to which symbols and images may be attributed, or the nature and relevant content of these. Formal abstractions or psychologistic generalizations will be equally suspect if we cannot locate them in, and demonstrate their efficacy in relation to, the sphere of social practices. How, and when, symbols and images enter into different areas of social life constitutes a key area for future research. McHugh's comment that people pay special attention to their 'environments' when their normal and orderly expectations regarding other aspects of their lives are disrupted or threatened would appear to be a particularly interesting theme to pursue. [88]

> Persons *assess* their environments in terms of relativity (typicality, likelihood, etc.), whereas they *assume* there will be certain emergent properties of the interaction (theme, fit, etc.).

Any renewed focus on social and cultural organization would undoubtedly have far-reaching implications for analyses of urban symbolism and imagery, which at present have no legitimate context to allow their contribution to urban studies to be realized. More specifically, I would like to suggest three broad areas within which future studies of symbolism and imagery could fruitfully be pursued.

(1) In the rapidly expanding sphere of 'urban' politics, policy-formation and planning, the work of Pocock and Hudson [89] appears to be particularly interesting and potentially important. Bell and Newby

have provided us with a most stimulating discussion, which raises again the hoary old issues of 'localism' and 'community', but in a new light.[90] There would appear to be a case for taking up the themes discussed by Bell and Newby, in relation to Long's classic notion of the local community as an 'ecology of games',[91] perhaps in conjunction with Pons's interest in image-makers, image-purveyors, and image-breakers. This could stimulate an interest in the mass media, an aspect of British society which has been largely ignored in urban studies.[92] It is important to remember that the kinds of urban symbols and images we are dealing with here resemble icons and rhetorical devices more than they do concepts, meanings, or 'definitions of the situation'.

(2) Whatever its shortcomings, there exists an extensive British literature on 'social images of class'.[93] This body of work has considerable substantive overlap with studies of 'urban imagery', and it displays considerably more theoretical and methodological awareness than can be found in either of the two approaches discussed in Part IV.[94] There are clearly good reasons and ample scope for the study of 'urban images' to be pursued in conjunction with studies of 'class images'. In particular, Davis's recent work,[95] and his point that 'images' are best viewed as 'projects for action', could well be coupled in future work with Lloyd's interest in the role of 'place' in the formation of class consciousness.[96]

(3) There is an extensive body of rather crude empirical research work on the persistence of strong sentiments and attachments to given localities, towns, etc. in British society.[97] These data have been coupled with similar work in the United States,[98] and have revitalized interest in the extent to which the persistence of local attachments may themselves be products of processes operating within mass, industrial, capitalist society. In short, these data query the notion that mass, industrial, capitalist society *necessarily* destroys more parochial social and communal forms. It is not necessary to see the two as antithetical, but rather as co-existing in a more complex structure of institutions and interests than that posited in unilinear models of social change and development. If these themes were systematically pursued, there would clearly be considerable scope for a wide range of important research. But if studies of 'urban imagery' were pursued in this context, it would be vitally important to maintain a relationship with the principles of 'structuration' (discussed in Part III) at local, regional, and national levels of analysis.

The concerns of this paper are substantive and eclectic, rather than theoretical or formal. This paper does not suggest that *all* urban sociologists should concentrate their attention on social and cultural organization, but simply that some of us can and should do so. Those who do so should not be dismissed out of hand for engaging in 'unfashionable' research. Whatever the precise future of urban perceptions, symbols, and images, it is almost certain to remain a minority activity within urban studies. Perceptions, symbols, and images may well serve to reduce the complexity of the 'worlds' we live in to a range of discrete and contrastingly defined units, which can then be used for a diversity of social, political, and ideological purposes. These units may well exaggerate the sharpness of boundaries, the uniqueness of resident populations, the 'identity' of neighbourhoods, and the like, but as representations they are an integral aspect of wider patterns of thought, knowledge, and organization, and I would argue that they are central to an understanding of city life. They enter into a host of every day situations in the forms of 'background assumptions' or 'rhetorical devices', both of which are fundamental aspects of social, economic, and political organization. It is important that we do not reify them, or trivialize them, but it is also crucially important that we should not ignore them. The task is to study them without removing them from the realm of action.

Notes

1 This paper would not have been written but for the support, advice, and stimulation of Professor Valdo Pons and my wife, Pat.

2 V. Pons, *Imagery and Symbolism in Urban Society*, University of Hull, 1975.

3 R. Wohl and A. L. Strauss, 'Symbolic representation and the urban milieu', *American Journal of Sociology*, vol. 63, pp. 523-58; A. L. Strauss, *Images of the American City*, Free Press, Glencoe, Ill., 1961; A. L. Strauss, 'Strategies for discovering urban theory', in L. Schnore (ed.), *Social Science and the City*, Praeger, New York, 1968; A. L. Strauss (ed.), *The American City: A Source Book of Urban Imagery*, Aldine, Chicago, 1968.

4 See, for example, B. Goodey, *Perception of the Environment*, Centre for Urban and Regional Studies Occasional Paper no. 17, University of Birmingham, 1973; R. Downs and D. Stea (eds), *Image and Environment*, Edward Arnold, London, 1973; D. T. Herbert and R. J. Johnston, 'Geography and the urban environment', in D. T. Herbert and R. J. Johnston (eds), *Geography and the Urban Environment*, vol. I, Wiley, London, 1978; D. Pocock and R. Hudson, *Images of the Urban Environment*, Macmillan, London, 1978; R. Sack, *Concepts of Space in Social Thought*, Macmillan, London.

5   C. Filkin and D. Weir, 'Locality', in E. Gittus (ed.), *Key Variables in Social Research Vol. I—Religion, Housing, Locality*, Heinemann, London, 1972; C. Bell and H. Newby, 'Community, communion, class and community action: The social sources of the new urban politics', in D. Herbert and R. Johnston (eds), *Social Areas in Cities Vol. II: Spatial Perspectives on Problems and Policies*, Wiley, Chichester, 1978.

6   This paper is primarily concerned with the literature which focuses specifically on 'urban environments'. I am well aware that there is a vast and rapidly expanding literature on general spatial and environmental orientations in psychology, geography, architecture, anthropology and sociology. I hope to explore the work neglected in this paper in a later essay.

7   Prominent among the critics have been R. Glass, 'Urban Sociology in Great Britain', *Current Sociology*, vol. IV, no. 4, 1955, reprinted in R. E. Pahl (ed.), *Readings in Urban Sociology*, Pergamon, Oxford, 1968; R. Glass, 'Urban Sociology', in A. Welford, M. Argyle, D. V. Glass and J. Morris (eds), *Society: Problems and Methods of Study*, Routledge & Kegan Paul, London, 1967; N. Dennis, 'The Popularity of the Neighbourhood Community Idea', *Sociological Review*, vol. 2, reprinted in Pahl (ed.), op. cit., 1968; J. Rex, 'The Sociology of a Zone of Transition', in Pahl (ed.), op. cit., 1968; R. E. Pahl, *Whose City?*, 2nd edn, Penguin, Harmondsworth, 1975; and C. G. Pickvance (ed.), *Urban Sociology: Critical Essays*, Tavistock, London, 1976. The views of these writers may be taken to represent those of a much larger number.

8   R. Glass, 'Urban Sociology in Great Britain', in R. E. Pahl (ed.), *Readings in Urban Sociology*, Pergamon, Oxford, 1968, pp. 61-2.

9   Ibid., p. 73.

10 M. Castells, 'Y-a-t-il une sociologie urbaine?', *Sociologie du Travail*, vol. I, 1968, reprinted in C. G. Pickvance (ed.), op. cit., 1976; M. Castells, *The Urban Question: A Marxist Approach*, Edward Arnold, London, 1977; M. Castells, *City, Class and Power*, Macmillan, London, 1978.

11 See, for example, M. Harloe (ed.), *Captive Cities*, Wiley and Sons, Chichester, 1977; J. R. Mellor, *Urban Sociology in an Urbanized Society*, Routledge & Kegan Paul, London, 1977; P. Saunders, *Urban Politics: A Sociological Interpretation*, Hutchinson, London, 1979; P. Dunleavy, *Urban Political Analysis*, Macmillan, London, 1980; B. Elliott, 'Manuel Castells and the new urban sociology', *British Journal of Sociology*, vol. XXXI, no. 1, 1980, pp. 151-8; and P. Saunders, *Social Theory and the Urban Question*, Hutchinson, London, 1981.

12 See the comments made by Mellor, op. cit., 1977, and J. Eldridge, *Recent British Sociology*, Macmillan, London, 1980.

13 L. Wirth, 'Urbanism as a way of life', *American Journal of Sociology*, vol. 44, 1938, pp. 1-24. Reprinted in P. K. Hatt and A. J. Reiss (eds), *Cities in Society*, Free Press, Glencoe, Ill., 1957.

14 See, for example, H. J. Gans, 'Urbanism and Suburbanism as Ways of Life', in Pahl (ed.), op. cit., 1968; R. E. Pahl 'The Rural-Urban Continuum', in Pahl (ed.), op. cit., 1968; and C. G. Pickvance, 'Introduction: Historical Materialist Approaches to Urban Sociology', in Pickvance (ed.), op. cit.

15 N. Dennis, op. cit., 1958.

16 Especially by M. Stacey, 'The Myth of Community Studies', *British Journal of Sociology*, vol. 20, 1969, pp. 134-45.
17 See, for example, Dunleavy, op. cit., 1980, and Saunders, op. cit., 1981.
18 C. Bell and H. Newby, *Community Studies*, Allen & Unwin, London, 1971, p. 250; C. Bell and H. Newby (eds), *The Sociology of Community*, Frank Cass, London, 1974.
19 M. Anderson, *Family Structure in Nineteenth Century Lancashire*, Cambridge University Press, Cambridge, 1971; H. J. Dyos, 'Agenda for Urban Historians', in H. J. Dyos (ed.), *The Study of Urban History*, Edward Arnold, London, 1968; H. J. Dyos and M. Wolff (eds), *The Victorian City: Images and Realities*, vol. I, Routledge & Kegan Paul, London, 1973; and J. Foster, *Class Struggle in the Industrial Revolution*, Weidenfeld & Nicolson, London, 1974.
20 R. Williams, *The Country and the City*, Chatto & Windus, London, 1973; M. Vicinus, 'Literary voices of an industrial town, Manchester 1810-1870', in H. J. Dyos and M. Wolff (eds), *The Victorian City*, vol. 2, Routledge & Kegan Paul, London, 1973.
21 See, for example, L. Kuper, *Living in Towns*, Cresset Press, London, 1953; C. D. Mitchell, T. Lupton, M. W. Hodges and C. S. Smith, *Neighbourhood and Community*, Oxford University Press, Oxford, 1964; J. M. Mogey, *Family and Neighbourhood*, Oxford University Press, Oxford, 1956; M. Young and P. Willmott, *Family and Kinship in East London*, Routledge & Kegan Paul, London, 1957; R. Frankenberg, *Village on the Border*, Cohen & West, London, 1957.
22 Dennis, op. cit., 1958.
23 R. Frankenberg, *Communities in Britain*, Penguin, Harmondsworth, 1966.
24 See, for example, M. Stein, *The Eclipse of Community*, Princeton University Press, Princeton, 1960; and H. J. Gans, op. cit., 1968.
25 R. Firth, *Elements of Social Organization*, Watts, London, 1956; R. Firth, *Essays on Social Organization and Values*, University of London Press, London, 1964; R. Firth, J. Hubert and A. Forge, *Families and Their Relationships*, Routledge & Kegan Paul, London, 1969.
26 A. Portes, 'Rationality in the slum: An essay on interpretive sociology', *Comparative Studies in Society and History*, vol. 14, 1972, pp. 268-86.
27 M. E. Olsen, *The Process of Social Organization*, Holt, Rinehart & Winston, New York, 1968.
28 See, for example, J. Rex and R. Moore, *Race, Community and Conflict*, Oxford University Press, Oxford, 1967; P. Willis, *Learning to Labour*, Saxon House, London, 1977; J. Rex and S. Tomlinson, *Colonial Immigrants in a British City*, Routledge & Kegan Paul, London, 1979; and K. Pryce, *Endless Pressure*, Penguin, Harmondsworth, 1979.
29 D. Silverman, *The Theory of Organizations*, Heinemann, London, 1970.
30 J. Boissevain, *Friends of Friends*, Blackwell, Oxford, 1974, p. 4. Also relevant here are, J. Boissevain, 'The place of non-groups in the social sciences', *Man*, vol. 3, 1968, pp. 542-56; and J. Boissevain and J. C. Mitchell (eds), *Network Analysis*, 2nd edn, Tavistock, London, 1973.
31 E. Bott, *Family and Social Network*, 2nd edn, Tavistock, London, 1971, (first published in 1957). Also see U. Hannerz, *Exploring the City*, Columbia University Press, New York, 1980.

32 See R. H. Turner, 'Role-taking: Process Versus Conformity', in A. M. Rose (ed.), *Human Behaviour and Social Processes*, Routledge & Kegan Paul, London, 1962.

33 R. Williams, *The Long Revolution*, Penguin, Harmondsworth, 1965; and R. Williams, *Culture and Society 1780-1950*, Penguin, Harmondsworth, 1968.

34 See, for example, Pahl, op. cit., 1975; Harloe, op. cit., 1977; Mellor, op. cit., 1977; Saunders, op. cit., 1979; and Dunleavy, op. cit., 1980.

35 E. P. Thompson, *The Poverty of Theory*, Merlin, London, 1978; F. Parkin, *Marxism and Class Theory*, Tavistock, London, 1979; J. Urry, *The Anatomy of Capitalist Societies*, Macmillan, London, 1981.

36 See, for example, F. Parkin, 'Strategies of Social Closure in Class Formation', in F. Parkin (ed.), *The Social Analysis of Class Structure*, Tavistock, London, 1974; K. Roberts, F. Cook, S. Clark and E. Semeonoff, *The Fragmentary Class Structure*, Heinemann, London, 1977; S. Giner and M. S. Archer (eds), *Contemporary Europe: Social Structures and Cultural Patterns*, Routledge & Kegan Paul, London, 1978; R. King and N. Nugent (eds), *Respectable Rebels*, Hodder & Stoughton, London, 1979; J. Scott, *Corporations, Classes and Capitalism*, Hutchinson, London, 1979; T. Bottomore, 'Structure and History', in P. M. Blau (ed.), *Approaches to the Study of Social Structure*, Open Books, London, 1975.

37 Parkin, op. cit., 1979, p. 4.

38 A. Giddens, *The Class Structure of Advanced Societies*, Hutchinson, London, 1973; Scott, op. cit., 1979; Urry, op. cit., 1981.

39 A. Giddens, *Studies in Social and Political Theory*, Hutchinson, London, 1977.

40 Urry, op. cit., 1981.

41 Parkin, op. cit., 1974, pp. 1-2.

42 J. Habermas, *Legitimation Crisis*, Heinemann, London, 1976; A. W. Gouldner, *The Dialectic of Ideology and Technology*, Macmillan, London, 1976; D. Bell, *The Cultural Contradictions of Capitalism*, Heinemann, London, 1976.

43 N. Abercrombie, *Class, Structure and Knowledge*, Frank Cass, London, 1980; N. Abercrombie, S. Hill and B. S. Turner, *The Dominant Ideology Thesis*, Allen & Unwin, London, 1980; Urry, op. cit., 1981.

44 A. Dawe, 'Theories of Social Action', in T. Bottomore and R. Nisbet (eds), *A History of Sociological Analysis*, Heinemann, London, 1978.

45 F. J. Bernstein, *The Restructuring of Social and Political Theory*, Blackwell, Oxford, 1976; A. Giddens, *New Rules of Sociological Method*, Hutchinson, London, 1976; A. Giddens, op. cit., 1977; A. Giddens, *Central Problems in Social Theory*, Hutchinson, London, 1979.

46 Giddens, op. cit., 1976, p. 22.

47 Urry, op. cit., 1981, p. 4.

48 Ibid., p. 4.

49 C. G. Pickvance, 'On the Study of Urban Social Movements', in Pickvance (ed.), op. cit., 1976; C. G. Pickvance, 'From Social Base to Social Force', in M. Harloe (ed.), *Captive Cities*, Wiley, London, 1977.

50 J. R. Mellor, op. cit., 1977; E. Lebas, 'Regional Policy Research: Some Theoretical and Methodological Problems', in M. Harloe (ed.), op. cit.,

1977; J. Lloyd, 'Neighbourhood, community and class: The role of place in the formation of class consciousness', *Papers in Urban and Regional Studies*, no. 3, Centre for Urban and Regional Studies, Birmingham, 1979, pp. 63-76; Saunders, op. cit., 1979; Dunleavy, op. cit., 1980; and Elliott, op. cit., 1980.

51 See for example, T. McGee, *The Urbanization Process in the Third World*, Bell & Sons, London, 1971; R. E. Pahl, 'Instrumentality and community in the process of urbanization', *Sociological Inquiry*, vol. 43, nos 3/4, 1973, pp. 241-60; B. Roberts, *Cities of Peasants*, Edward Arnold, London, 1978; R. G. Oliven, 'Culture rules OK: Class and culture in Brazilian cities', *International Journal of Urban and Regional Research*, vol. 3, no. 1, 1979, pp. 29-48; D. Butterworth and J. Chance, *Latin American Urbanization*, Cambridge University Press, Cambridge, 1981.

52 Pons, op. cit., 1975, p. 3.

53 D. Stokols (ed.), *Perspectives on Environment and Behaviour*, Plenum, New York, 1977.

54 T. Ziolkowski, *Disenchanted Images*, Princeton University Press, Princeton, 1977.

55 K. Lynch, *The Image of the City*, MIT Press, Cambridge, Mass., 1960. For a more detailed outline of the main developments, see, Goodey, op. cit., 1973; Downs and Stea, op. cit., 1973; Pocock and Hudson, op. cit., 1979.

56 D. Appleyard 'Notes on Urban Perception and Knowledge', in Downs and Stea (eds), op. cit., 1973, pp. 109-14; T. Lee, 'Cities in the Mind', in D. T. Herbert and R. J. Johnston (eds), *Social Areas in Cities, Vol. II: Spatial Perspectives on Problems and Policies*, Wiley, London, 1976.

57 See, for example, M. Stewart (ed.), *The City: Problems of Planning*, Penguin, Harmondsworth, 1972; P. F. Smith, *The Syntax of Cities*, Hutchinson, London, 1977; and D. Soen (ed.), *New Trends in Urban Planning*, Pergamon, Oxford, 1979.

58 See, for example, D. Stea and J. M. Blaut, 'Notes Toward a Developmental Theory of Spatial Learning', in Downs and Stea (eds), op. cit., 1973, pp. 51-62.

59 D. Prokop, 'Image and Functions of the City', in *Urban Core and Inner City*, Proceedings of International Study Week held at the University of Amsterdam, Brill, Leiden, 1967; Appleyard, op. cit., 1973.

60 Strauss, op. cit., 1961; Strauss, 'Strategies for discovering urban theory', op. cit., 1968; Strauss, *The American City*, op. cit., 1968; and Pons, op. cit., 1975.

61 A. Briggs, 'Urban perspectives: A review article', *Urban Studies*, vol. IV, 1967, pp. 165-9; H. J. Dyos and M. Wolff (eds), op. cit., 1973; Williams, op. cit., 1973; and E. Relph, *Place and Placelessness*, Pion, London, 1976.

62 Strauss, op. cit., 1961, p. 5.

63 Pons, op. cit., 1975.

64 W. Firey, 'Sentiment and Symbolism as Ecological Variables', *American Sociological Review*, vol. 10, 1945, pp. 140-8.

65 For overview, see Filkin and Weir, op. cit., 1972. For example, see Frankenberg, *op. cit.*, 1957.

66 See, for example, P. Leonard (ed.), *The Sociology of Community Action*, Sociology Review Monograph no. 21, University of Keele, 1975.

67 See, for example, B. Robson, *Urban Analysis*, Cambridge University Press, Cambridge, 1969; D. Timms, *The Urban Mosaic*, Cambridge University Press, Cambridge, 1971.

68 D. Harvey, *Social Justice and the City*, Edward Arnold, London, 1973, pp. 13-14.

69 F. C. Ladd, 'Black youths view their environment: Neighbourhood maps', *Environment and Behaviour*, vol. 2, 1970, pp. 64-79.

70 R. Firth, *Symbols: Public and Private*, Cornell University Press, Ithaca, 1973; J. Dolgin, D. Kemnitzer and D. Scheinder, 'As people express their lives, so they are ...' in J. Dolgin, D. Kemnitzer and D. Scheinder (eds), *Symbolic Anthropology*, Columbia University Press, New York, 1977; and L. Holy and M. Stuchlik, 'The Structure of Folk Models', in L. Holy and M. Stuchlik (eds), *The Structure of Folk Models*, Academic Press, London, 1981.

71 H. S. Becker, *The Other Side: Perspectives on Deviance*, Free Press, New York, 1964; K. Plummer, 'Misunderstanding Labelling Perspectives', in D. Downes and P. Rock (eds), *Deviant Interpretations*, Robertson, Oxford, 1979.

72 This point is made most forcibly by R. Glass, 'Urban Images', in G. A. Harrison and J. B. Gibson (eds), *Man in Urban Environments*, Oxford University Press, Oxford, 1976.

73 See, for examples of a rapidly expanding literature, D. Gregory, *Ideology, Science and Human Geography*, Hutchinson, London, 1978; J. Anderson, 'Geography, political economy and the state', *Antipode*, vol. 10, no. 2, 1978, pp. 87-9.

74 Pocock and Hudson, op. cit., 1978.

75 J. Burgess, *Image and Identity*, Occasional Papers in Geography, no. 23, University of Hull, 1978.

76 Pons, op. cit., 1975.

77 G. D. Suttles, *The Social Order of the Slum*, University of Chicago Press, Chicago, 1968; G. D. Suttles, *The Social Construction of Communities*, University of Chicago Press, Chicago, 1972.

78 F. W. Boal, 'Territoriality on the Shankill-Falls Divide, Belfast', *Irish Geography*, vol. VI, no. 1, 1969, pp. 30-50; F. W. Boal, 'Territoriality and Class: A study of two residential areas in Belfast', *Irish Geography*, vol. VI, no. 3, 1971, pp. 229-48; S. Damer, 'Wine Alley: The sociology of a dreadful enclosure', *Sociological Review*, vol. 22, no. 2, 1974, pp. 221-48.

79 On 'urban social movements', see Pickvance (1976), op. cit., 1976; on 'the local labour process', see Roberts op. cit., 1978; on 'local labour markets', see R. Kreckel, 'Unequal Opportunity Structure and Labour Market Segmentation', *Sociology*, vol. 14, no. 4, 1980; on 'local political environments', see Dunleavy, op.. cit., 1980.

80 R. E. Pahl, 'Employment, work and the domestic division of labour', *International Journal of Urban and Regional Research*, vol. 4, no. 1, 1980, p. 8.

81 E. Lebas, 'Introduction—The new school of urban and regional research: Into the second decade', in M. Harloe and E. Lebas (eds), *City,*

Class and Capital, Edward Arnold, London, 1981, p. xxxix.

82 See, for example, Rex and Tomlinson, op. cit., 1979; Pryce, op. cit., 1979.

83 See, for example, S. Henry, *The Hidden Economy*, Martin Robertson, Oxford, 1978.

84 See, for example, M. Evans and D. Morgan, *Work on Women*, Tavistock, London, 1979; and Lebas, op. cit., 1981.

85 See, for example, Willis, op. cit., 1977; T. Bennett, G. Martin, C. Mercer and J. Woollacott (eds), *Culture, Ideology and Social Processes: A Reader*, Batsford Academic and Educational Ltd., London, 1981.

86 Lloyd, op. cit., 1979, p. 64.

87 The list includes Glass, op. cit., 1955; R. E. Pahl, *Patterns of Urban Life*, Longman, London, 1970; W. Michelson, *Man and His Urban Environment*, Addison-Wesley, Reading, Mass., 1970; L. S. Bourne (ed.), *Internal Structure of the City*, Oxford University Press, Oxford, 1971; Stewart, op. cit., 1972; and Pons, op. cit., 1975; K. Young 'Urban Politics: An Overview', in K. Young (ed.), *Essays on Urban Politics*, Macmillan, London, 1975.

88 P. McHugh, *Defining the Situation*, Bobbs-Merril, Indianapolis, 1968, p. 107.

89 Pocock and Hudson, op. cit., 1978.

90 Bell and Newby, op. cit., 1978.

91 N. Long, 'The local community as an ecology of games', *American Journal of Sociology*, vol. 64, 1958, pp. 251-61.

92 D. Murphy, *The Silent Watchdog*, Constable, London, 1976.

93 See J. Goldthorpe, D. Lockwood, F. Bechhofer and J. Platt, *The Affluent Worker in the Class Structure*, Cambridge University Press, Cambridge, 1971.

94 See the discussion in M. Bulmer (ed.), *Working-Class Images of Society*, Routledge & Kegan Paul, London, 1975.

95 H. Davis, *Beyond Class Images*, Croom Helm, London, 1979.

96 Lloyd, op. cit., 1979.

97 See, for example, Royal Commission on Local Government in England, 'Community Attitudes Survey', *The Redcliffe Maud Report*, Research Studies 9, HMSO, London, 1969; A. R. Townsend and C. C. Taylor, 'Regional Culture and Identity in Industrialized Societies: The case of North-East England', *Regional Studies*, vol. 9, 1975, pp. 379-93.

98 H. Kasarda and J. Janowitz, 'Community attachment in mass society', *American Sociological Review*, vol. 39, 1974, pp. 328-39; A. Hunter, 'Persistence of Local Sentiments in Mass Society', in D. Street and Associates (eds), *Handbook of Contemporary Urban Life*, Jossey-Bass, London, 1978; M. Janowitz and D. Street, 'Changing Social Order of the Metropolitan Area', in Street, op. cit., 1978.

Town planning and sociology

E. J. Reade

I

The main outlines of the relationship between these two fields seems fairly clear, and fairly generally accepted; sociology and town planning have common intellectual origins, but in their subsequent development have become separated, and to such an extent that discourse between members of the two fields has become all but impossible. What remains is to document this separation a little more fully, to explain it, and to suggest how it might be overcome.

The shared origins lie in nineteenth-century social philosophical reactions to industrialization, and centre on distaste for large industrial cities, and a desire to recapture lost community. [1] To these, Mellor would add shared distaste for excessive individualism, and reassertion of tradition. [2] Sociology in Britain, at least until the First World War, and arguably until well after the Second, consisted largely of social philosophical criticism of social conditions, backed up by a very policy-oriented tradition of social survey. From the onset of agricultural depression in the 1870s, there developed in Britain a very strong social and political movement for land reform, taxation of 'betterment' and even land nationalization. In the 1906 Parliament, for example, 130 MPs were supporters of the Land Nationalization Society, committed to abolition of all private property in land. [3] Ten out of the fifteen demands of the 'Radical programme' of 1885 had been concerned with land. [4] Politically, strong efforts were made to portray rural regeneration as inseparable from solutions of the social problems of the big cities, often by dispersal of their populations to new settlements, and the writings of town planners such as Howard and Geddes are probably best seen in relation to this wider social and political interest in the land question. Given these two things, the policy-orientated nature of the sociology of the period, and the prevailing political interest in the social consequences of land tenure and population distribution, it is not surprising that a number of the early advocates of town planning were among the founders of the Sociological Society.[5]

The separation of sociology and town planning seems to date from about the time of the First World War. Thus it cannot be entirely explained in terms of 'academic' desire on the part of the sociologists to free their sociological work from overt social and political commitment, for in British sociology, this came rather later. Two factors which do seem to have played a part are first, that political interest in the land question itself diminished, after 1918, and second, that some of the leading personalities in the planning movement lost their influential positions in the Sociological Society, after the war.[6] Those who founded the Town Planning Institute, in 1914, were drawn mainly from the professions of architecture, engineering and surveying, and once this domination of the design and land use professions had been established, it no doubt exercised a cumulative effect, causing those with primary social and political concerns to withdraw even further. Whatever the reasons the thesis of separation between the two fields seems valid. It is clear that by the time that social and political conditions once more led sociologists to interest themselves in town planning, around the end of the Second World War, they found many of its social and political assumptions questionable. Ruth Glass, for example, though co-operating with town planners in the early years after the Second World War, ultimately became fairly critical of their implicit or unconscious social assumptions.[7]

In the inter-war period, town planning as an activity of government had been of only marginal significance. The very few sociologists there were at this time may well have felt that other aspects of public policy were of greater interest and importance. With the Second World War and its immediate aftermath, however, a new problem of explanation arises. For there now developed a high level of public interest and political debate on post-war reconstruction and planning, in which it was widely assumed that physical and social reconstruction were inseparable. Though not among planners themselves,[8] political and social objectives undoubtedly played a large part in the thought of those who created the post-war system of town and country planning.[9] In view of this, the relatively small involvement of sociologists in planning in this period is rather puzzling.

Quite possibly, the explanation lies in a continuation and reinforcement of the factors already mentioned. Sociologists were still

147

extremely few. The domination of town planning by the design and land use professions had no doubt been even further consolidated. Since town planners were now seen by politicians and by the public as among the main creators of a new and better Britain, the more eminent among them increasingly yielded to the temptation to pronounce on the social purposes of their plans. Given the characteristic sociological naivety and social utopianism of such pronouncements, it would not be surprising if this had the effect of alienating even further those sociologists who might otherwise have become involved.

From 1951 onwards, of course, planning itself went out of favour, both as an approach to policy in any sphere, and even as a word. [10] But with the rather surprising conversion of the Conservative government, around 1962, to indicative planning in the economic sphere, and to a revival of the long dormant New Towns programme, we entered a new period, which has persisted until the present day. Throughout this period, 'planning' has been widely accepted as necessary, and normal, and has even, at least in certain quarters, been from time to time quite fashionable. Throughout this period, too, an increasing tendency to question the actions and decisions of planners has not led, in general, to a rejection of planning itself. Rather, the feeling has been that the process of planning should be improved. Often, the argument has been that the way to do this lies primarily in giving ordinary people a greater say in it.

Like the mid-1940s, therefore, the period from the early 1960s to the present day presents us with a problem of explanation. For the 'gulf' in mental orientations, between planners and sociologists, still persists. The relationship between the two fields remains largely one of mutual incomprehension. Planners and sociologists seem to inhabit different worlds of discourse with mutually incompatible intellectual assumptions. And all this despite a high level of concern, among planners, politicians, and the public, for the social implications of town planning. It also exists, despite one very important change in the situation; since the 1960s, the number of sociologists in Britain is no longer insignificant.

Since the 1960s there have of course been developments in sociology, and especially, perhaps in 'urban sociology', which some writers see as leading to a better understanding of town planning, and thus, to better planning practice. [11] The work of Rex and Moore, for example, certainly brought 'urban sociology' into a better relationship with certain central concepts in sociology, and especially those of *class* and *power*. [12] Others see the emergence of the new 'Marxist urban sociology' as having had a similarly beneficial effect, first on sociological understanding, and second on policy. [13] The present writer doubts this, broadly sharing Ruth Glass's evaluation of this body of work. [14]

McDougall and her colleagues suggest that a number of developments in public policy have brought sociology and town planning closer. These include such things as the Community Development Projects, the wider 'Urban Programme', the 'Inner Cities' initiatives, the emergence of 'community planning', 'social planning', 'corporate planning' approaches in local government, and so on. Sociologists have also been increasingly employed in town planning departments of local authorities, and in planning schools, of course. [15] This kind of an analysis seems to mistake rhetoric for reality. A number of the developments mentioned seem best understood as political stratagems, designed to absorb youthful energy and social concern, to no effect. Others of them seem best understood as ideologies promoting various professional imperialisms. As for employment of sociologists, local planning authorities and planning schools could hardly afford to be seen *not* to employ them, given the prevailing public rhetoric. It does not follow, however, that their potential contribution is wanted, or even understood. From the point of view of those who are influential in town planning, the object is to *portray* practice as resting on sociological understanding and advice, while simultaneously *preventing* this sociological understanding from exerting significant influence on practice. For, as in most fields, sociological criticism of practice creates doubts among practitioners.

The acid test of the thesis advanced by McDougall lies in practice, and what seems usually to happen in reality is that concern for the social consequences of town planning is strongly discouraged. Wherever socially concerned planners attempt to write social considerations into structure plans, for example, they generally get 'written out' again, or at least, translated into language so bland as to have no real meaning. And central government itself, whenever it fears that social concern among planners could become an embarrassment, does not hesitate to issue directives reminding local authorities that planning is limited to the physical and the spatial.

There is, however, one factor in the period since the early 1960s, not mentioned by McDougall *et al.*, but which could create increased understanding of the relationship between sociology and town planning, and thus, some greater social awareness in town planning practice. This is the part played by the mass media, and especially television. Awareness of all those things which McDougall and her colleagues mention, all put together, is probably limited to relatively tiny coteries. The questioning of planning by the media, by contrast, has created some awareness throughout society generally. Even among planners themselves, and even academic planners, more pause for thought seems to be occasioned by television programmes than by arguments put forward, for example, in CDP reports. Thus, discussion of planning in the media, if it increases, could eventually lead to a situation such as existed in the mid-1950s, of a high level of public and political interest in town planning, but with the difference that this time, public attitudes towards planning would probably be more critical.

For present purposes, it is assumed that the thesis of an intellectual 'gulf' between sociology and planning is not disproved. The next section, therefore, seeks to identify the causes of this gulf.

II

Two broad areas within sociology are relevant to town planning. The first is those specialisms within sociology which explore spatial and locational behaviour, and the social creation and social meaning of physical environment. The second is the sociology of politics, public administration and 'decision-making'. The importance of the second broad sociological specialism, relative to the first, has increased over time, due to three trends in planning thought, and, to a lesser extent, planning practice. Firstly, even *within* town planning, the main emphasis of thought has shifted considerably out of the 'substantive' and into the 'procedural' sphere; planners have increasingly avoided saying that any particular environmental outcomes are more desirable than others and instead have increasingly portrayed their expertise as lying in possession of a *technical procedure* for deciding what environmental outcomes should be sought. Secondly, town planners (now, significantly, preferring to be known simply as 'planners'), have publicly urged that knowledge of this planning method, as possessed by themselves, is knowledge which can be applied in *any* sphere of public policy, and not only to those governmental policies which shape our physical surroundings. Thirdly, they have urged not only that all aspects of physical, economic and social policy be planned, but that they be planned jointly (i.e. 'co-ordinated'). [16]

It is not possible here to explore in detail the reasons for this profound shift of emphasis from the substantive to the procedural. Broadly, one might hypothesize, it results from a *valid* appreciation that to urge any particular type of physical environment, as the early proponents of town planning did, is to align oneself with particular political interests, together with an *invalid* belief that to urge planning in the abstract does not have this effect, and is therefore safer. Due to the prevalence of unconscious technocratic assumptions in the socialization of town planners, the profession tends to see the adoption of this abstract planning method as merely the most rational and efficient way of approaching any public question, and therefore as purely technical, and politically neutral. It is not, of course. In reality, it is a political philosophy, in that it constitutes a prescription, or at least a partial prescription, for government and administration. [17] We could ask many questions about it, but perhaps for the present purposes the most important question is whether this planning method is empirically possible, whether applied to the creation of physical environment, to government generally, or to the co-ordination of governmental policies in the physical, economic, and social spheres. The assumption of this paper is that in broad terms, the answer must be that it is not. The question cannot be argued here, but it is suggested that the first reason for the existence of the 'gulf' between sociology and town planning can be stated as follows:

(1) *Town planners tend to a political philosophy which sociologists see as unrealistic.* It may be added that this approach to questions of politics and government, which can be broadly characterized as technocratic, is known to be more common among those in the physical sciences, engineering, technology, and design professions, than among those whose education has been in literature, history, or the social sciences. It is difficult, of course, to divorce the question of whether this 'planning' is empirically possible from the question of its appeal. To the present writer, it appears frightening. [18]

One might be less frightened were such social technology urged as an unavoidable means of achieving some actual state of affairs, which the writer clearly desired. It is the *contentlessness* of such writing which is its most chilling feature. This reminds us, however, that it is its empirical validity and not its subjective appeal which should be our test; for it is this contentlessness which would seem to render such work sociologically unsound.

Next it is necessary to turn to the 'substantive' area of town planning. Town planners do after all continue to concern themselves with physical outcomes. Increasingly, however, they do this in a way which differs radically from that in which the founders of their profession did so. The latter had the boldness to advocate specific spatial patterns and environmental forms, usually on the grounds that these would yield specific cultural, economic or social benefits. Present-day planners, by contrast, tend to the entirely opposite

151

method, of first ensuring legitimation for 'planning' itself. Only secondly, it seems, do they raise the question of what particular physical outcomes should be sought. The answer to this last question is often seen as being provided by the planning *method*: 'planning as a method' will tell you what to put in your 'plan as a physical design'. Here the two meanings of 'planning', both equally important to town planners, are brought together. To some extent, this changed order of procedure may be attributed to the influence of sociologists, who have doubted whether the physical forms advocated by the earlier proponents of town planning do in fact have the effects claimed for them. But in addition to believing that planning as a method will tell them what to put in their plans, present-day town planners also exhibit a more general tendency to see the purposes or objectives of their plans as being supplied by others, rather than by themselves. They variously assume the determination of these objectives to be the responsibility of elected representatives, or of the 'planned' themselves, bypassing these representatives ('participation'), or as being derived from direct investigation of 'needs' or 'preferences'. It is the third of these assumptions, that the content of the plan can be derived from study of 'needs' or 'preferences', which is of most direct concern to us here, for it is generally linked with the further assumption that it is the sociologist's job to discover these needs and preferences.

Thus, quite simply, the planners' belief is that the sociologist can show them what they ought to put in their plans. The word 'ought' here, is chosen advisedly. Whether it implies a categorical or a conditional imperative is left unclear, for the planning literature and planners themselves leave it unclear. But the strength with which town planners cling to this belief is in no way impaired by the lack of clarity in their explanation of it. To explain contemporary town planners' tendency to believe that social science can tell them what objectives to pursue, it seems useful to look at an example of urban development in a period when social science did not exist. Summerson [19] documents the way in which residential development was carried out in eighteenth-century London, largely by speculative builders, and generally without architects. The models which these builders followed lay in the houses of the aristocracy and upper-middle class. Often, they used actual 'copy books'. At each social level, domestic buildings tended to be a simplified and scaled-down version of the houses inhabited by those at a slightly higher level in the social hierarchy. Thus, there was to a great extent a single set of values, in society, as to what constituted a desirable home; from the aristocracy right down to the level of the artisan, architectural styles were broadly similar. It is of interest, though it is not crucial to the present argument, that the residential quarters thus created are today highly regarded by architects and town planners, and often by other people too. The social assumptions implicit in the above manner of proceeding would seem to be as follows:

Firstly, that at any given social level, particular types or styles of house will be seen as desirable, and desired, not because they reflect some values, attitudes, preferences or needs supposedly inherent in the life-style of those at that social level, but because they are valued by, and have hitherto been the prerogative of, a higher class.

Secondly, that perception as to what is desirable will tend continually to percolate downwards, through the social structure, and at any level, a common source of happiness or contentment will lie in obtaining those things which were previously the prerogative of one's betters.

These implicit social assumptions seem sound. Indeed, they are sociologically sounder than those apparently held by present-day town planners. Human beings obtain satisfaction from getting what *seems* desirable, not from getting what *is* desirable, for to the question of what is desirable there can be no answer.

As a second illustration, we can take the major British exception to the rule of planning in the twentieth century, the Inter-War speculative builders' suburbs. These too produced an environment which is apparently highly prized by many, but which, unlike Georgian development, is only now beginning to be admired by architects and planners. These areas too were largely constructed without architects, and certainly without sociologists, unless it be argued that speculative builders, estate developers and house agents tend to have a good sociological understanding of their own business. This last may well be true, however, for it is clear that the social assumptions implicit in their mode of operation are precisely the same as those underlying residential development in eighteenth-century London. There is the same understanding that what gives satisfaction will be socially determined by emulation, and fashion. There is the same understanding that this being so, aspirations will be constantly both changing in content and moving from one part of society to another. Inter-War suburbs, like areas of eighteenth-century lower-middle-class and artisan's housing, consist of houses which are scaled-down versions of the homes of the aristocracy and gentry.

Next, it is necessary to look at the totally contrasting present-day assumptions concerning these same questions, prevalent especially among town planners and architects. Firstly, it tends to be assumed that needs and preferences are objective facts, which can be ascertained, rather than subjective perceptions, which are inevitably susceptible to modification in the light of new experience or new knowledge. This is ironic, for new knowledge is a much more common factor than it was in the eighteenth century. Secondly, it tends to be assumed that differering needs and preferences are characteristic of particular social groups, classes or subcultures, and are sufficiently stable within any such stratum to justify their being reflected in rather permanent building forms. This too is ironic, for society is if anything somewhat more, rather than less, fluid today than it was in the eighteenth century. Thirdly, of course, and following on from the above two assumptions, it tends therefore to be supposed in some vague way that social science can show architects and planners what to put in their plans. The latter do not usually explain in any detail their reasons for making these assumptions, but in general, they seem to centre on the notions of 'need', and of 'wants', or 'preferences'. It is suggested that three factors can help to explain the emergence of these questionable assumptions. These will be labelled 'the rise of science' (to which can be related the concept of 'need'), 'the rise of democracy' (to which we can ascribe 'preferences') and the relative powerlessness of the planners themselves.

(a)   *The rise of science*   In a scientific age, neither politicians nor officials can afford to be seen to be basing plans on mere opinions. Thus, and often in something approaching desperation, they look to social research to demonstrate 'scientifically' that their proposals meet the carefully ascertained needs of those they will affect. But the inconvenient truth is that human beings have *no* needs. [20] Certainly, some things are necessary for life itself, but these are hardly at issue in the field of policy with which we are concerned. Beyond this, all one can say is that people need what they think they need, but that, even then, they can usually adapt fairly readily if they do not get it. For unlike animals, our possession of language and culture enables us to put meanings on artefacts and experiences. Thus, they do not affect us directly, but through these meanings. Sociology can discover a great deal about *why* we believe we need particular things, but it cannot show that we *do* need them, and even less, unfortunately, that we should have them. And since our perceptions of our needs are constantly changing, partly in response to what is available, it makes little sense to take them as 'given', and to legitimate further provision by reference to them. To do so may be politically expedient, but it is epistemologically and methodologically nonsensical. [21] Planners adopt this approach, nevertheless, because it enables them to evade responsibility for the objectives of their plans.

(b) *The rise of democracy*   In a democratic age, no politician or official can afford to be seen as ignoring the wants or preferences of the electorate. Again, the somewhat desperate hope is that plans can be legitimated by demonstrating that they reflect carefully observed preferences. But, as in the previous case, this assumption turns procedural logic on its head. It makes little sense to take preferences as given, without asking what causes them. [22] And once architects and planners do ask this, it is clear that their own actions may be among these causes, firstly because one of the main components in present preference is past experience and, secondly, because architects and planners take part in the public debate (for example in the mass media) as to what constitutes a desirable environment. As in the previous case, the explanation seems to lie in political expedience, and evasion of responsibility. Planners and architects seem unable to face up to the fact that they might actually help to *shape* preferences for particular kinds of physical milieu. Sociologically, it is difficult to see how they could avoid doing so. Sociologically too, it is clear that they are among the best fitted to do so. For if their training has any real content, it enables them to inform those without that training of the relative costs, benefits, and conseqences of the various locational and environmental choices available to them.

(c) *The relative powerless of planners themselves*   Not *all* public policy makers behave as described above. The Foreign Office does not invite us to share in formulating its China policy, though expertise in foreign policy making, unlike expertise in town planning, is not claimed to be the prerogative of a 'profession', nor to rest on a clearly defined field of validated knowledge. Nor does the local education department usually offer us any great say in deciding how our children are to be educated, despite educationists' ready acceptance that educational policy must rest on social values as much as on technical or scientific knowledge. But few arms of the state, at central or local level, are as weak as planning. 'Participation' is a desperate search for legitimation.

   The above discussion has identified three further causes of the 'gulf' between sociology and town planning.

   (2) *Planners tend to assume that sociologists can tell them what forms particular environments ought to take.* The three constraints discussed above tempt planners to give the impression that what

constitutes a good environment is a matter of fact, and not of opinion. Planners seem unaware of this, and actually to *believe* that social science can show what ought to be done. This alienates sociologists, for it makes their own position untenable.

The issue of 'environmental determinism', usually given prominence in published discussions of the causes of the 'gulf', [23] seems best regarded as a *part* of the wider problem. It does not seem very fruitful to ask whether the assumption of this determinism is or is not a fallacy. The truth would seem to be that physical milieu *can* affect perceptions and attitudes, and thus behaviour, but to varying degrees, depending on the strength of other factors in the situation (such as whether we *believe* it will do so, or wish it to do so). These other factors are mainly social, in some sense or other. The interplay between the effects of the physical milieu itself, the effects of the social meaning placed upon it, and the effects of other social factors in the situation, seems likely to be complex. All that it seems necessary to say here is that if a truly applied sociology actually existed in this area, then the sociologists concerned probably *could* find ways of using physical environment as a means of influencing perceptions, values, and attitudes, and thus behaviour. After all, physical environment is one of the most potent of all social symbols. After sex, and possibly dress, it is probably the main vehicle of advertising. It is one of the great themes of literature. And it has been used effectively in a number of societies to help shape political and social attitudes. [24] Even in societies where it is not thus used consciously by the state, characteristic landscapes and townscapes are commonly interpreted as symbolizing specific life-styles and values, and thus play a part in maintaining them. [25] Thus, one might identify a third source of the 'gulf'.

(3) *The issue of 'environmental determinism', due to the way in which it has been formulated, has tended to obscure more fundamental sources of intellectual misunderstanding between sociologists and planners.* To suggest, however, that there could exist an 'applied sociology' in this area—that is, that sociologists could assist planners in realizing their objectives—raises the question of what these objectives are. And from the above discussion, it seems that on this, one can hardly avoid pointing to the following, as a further cause of the 'gulf'.

(4) *Planners seem unwilling to state what patterns of behaviour or, more generally, what outcomes, they wish to produce* (except, of course, with the both odd and vague exception of 'community'). Indeed, such is the bland and vague nature of the language in which planners usually discuss the 'contribution of sociology' that the very notion

that the purpose of the Town and Country Planning Acts is 'behaviour modification' may seem slightly shocking. On the other hand, what is planning for? It is difficult to justify the existence of any governmental intervention which leaves the social structure, the pattern of relationships in society, and social behaviour, unchanged. If town planning seeks to promote certain spatial and physical patterns, presumably this is because these are believed to promote certain changes in the way people live. The question, 'What is planning for?', identifies the fifth and sixth sources of the 'gulf', ones which the present writer would agree with Faludi [26] are the major ones.

(5) and (6) *Town planning lacks any credible theory and any credible social philosophy.* To make the theoretical and socio-philosophical basis of governmental policies *publicly* explicit, of course, is likely to be impossible; ambiguity is a political necessity. But it is less excusable to be *privately* muddled. If we look at a field of public policy which has certain affinities with town planning, that of education, we see a very different situation. There, the existence of an intellectual tradition means that both the theory and the social philosophy of the activity are relatively well-developed, enabling individual teachers and educationists both to make sense of their own lives, and to engage on a basis of intellectual equality with those who carry out social research in their field. Few things are so destructive of successful practice as the false theories of those who deny having any.

It is suggested here that planners *overvalue* the sociologist's contribution, in supposing them to be able to show *what* should be aimed at, rather than how it might be achieved. Simultaneously, they *undervalue* the sociologist's contribution, by supposing that it is *facts* which demonstrate what policies ought to be adopted, and by assuming that sociology is the discovery of these facts (i.e. that it is 'social survey'). All three misunderstandings have political utility, for the planners themselves, for politicians, and for those who channel research funds. For they conceal values and interests. Thus, a fourth group, consisting of *some* sociologists, may fail to point out those misunderstandings, where research funds are available. [27] This seems to explain why the 'gulf' persists, despite the existence of a fairly well-developed 'urban research industry'. The latter addresses itself largely to 'problems' as defined by the planning system itself, and carefully avoids asking those questions elucidation of which would actually reveal the workings and consequences of planning. The last is left to independent researchers, [28] and by tacit agreement the 'Planning Establishment' dismisses their findings as irrelevant. [29]

157

(7) *There is a lack of independent sociological research into town planning of the type which would clarify issues and make the contribution of sociology clearer,* This is both a consequence of the 'gulf', and an important factor in its perpetuation.

(8) *The planning doctrine that social data is merely one, among many types of data, all of which the planners must evaluate, and to all of which they must give due weight.* Faludi sees this as a particular aspect of the 'generalist' orientation of planners, which helps to perpetuate the gulf between sociology and planners.[30] As Faludi writes, reporting the results of an empirical study of sociologists in planning, '... one respondent commented, for planners there are "physical needs" and "social needs", which must both be fulfilled.'[31] One could add that characteristically, planners recognize a whole range of categories of 'physical needs', but restrict 'social needs' to a single category. Summarizing his findings, Faludi observes:[32]

> ... to a large extent, the difficulties of collaboration result not so much from the attitudes and outlooks of the social scientists but rather from the 'generalists' role-concept which the planners hold for themselves.

Heraud,[33] accepting an argument put forward by Faludi,[34] suggests that the difficulties would be reduced if planning education moved, in Bernstein's terms from a 'collection code' to an 'integrated code'.[35] It is difficult to accept this line of argument. Planning education, like planning practice, is *already* based (in its rhetoric) on the 'integrated code'. The only freedom which exists for sociologists in planning schools to study planning, rather than to *advocate* it, results from the planners' failure to follow their own rhetoric in practice, so that some disciplinary independence still remains. As Musgrove comments, 'Only one man wins when you integrate subjects—the man at the top'.[36] Bernstein himself pointed out that the integrated approach is likely to require a 'high level of ideological consciousness' and that the adoption of the 'integrated code' is likely to lead to students' progress being evaluated not in terms of the intellectual understanding they have gained but in terms of the extent to which they have adopted the 'right attitudes'.[37] Finally, in his Postscript, Bernstein remarks that the integrated approach, 'would stand a better chance of successful institutionalization in societies where there were strong and effective constraints upon the development of a range of ideologies.'[38] The conclusions seem clear. A discipline such as sociology can only aid an activity such as town planning if the working relationship between the two is one of equality. The 'integrated code', since it subordinates sociology to planning, prevents any real sociological contribution. But further, as is clear from Bernstein's analysis, the 'integrated code' has inherently totalitarian implications. This is also made clear in Faludi's own advocacy of it.[39]

A further possible source of the 'gulf' between sociology and town planning which is often suggested[40] may be stated as follows: sociologists are trained to be sceptical, to reserve judgement, to seek explanations of *why* things are as they are, to be as 'neutral' or 'impartial' in their analyses as possible, and so on. Planners, by contrast, have to make decisions, often on insufficient evidence, and in general are concerned with action, rather than with understanding. As suggested by, for example, Faludi,[41] however, this argument seems rather to miss the point. The sociologist is not alienated by the planner's need to make a recommendation. Rather, he is alienated by the grounds upon which those recommendations are currently based.

(9) *The planner's denial that recommendations must reflect interests and values, and his assertion that they can be derived from rational analysis alone.* Sociologists do not differ from other human beings in being less ready to make value judgements or to recommend what ought to be done. Rather, they differ, at least from town planners, in being more aware as to *when*, and *to what extent* they are making these value judgements, or recommending actions which would promote interests. This source of misunderstanding is related to a wider phenomenon.

(10) *Planners tend to confuse fact and value, science and politics, analysis and interest-based recommendations.*

(11) *Planners overrate the capacity of the social sciences to predict future states of affairs.* There appears to be a quite specific misunderstanding among planners concerning the nature of sociology, and of the social sciences generally.[42] It is hardly surprising that the misunderstanding has created some resentment, on the part of those sociologists who have attempted to work with town planners.[43] In response to them, and in an attempt to summarize them in a phrase, Pahl has asked whether what is needed is 'sociology *for* planning', or 'sociology *of* planning'.[44] Other applied fields, of course, had already reached this point, one by one.[45] The argument was that though planners did not appreciate the fact, they would be aided more by 'pure' sociological research into planning practice, designed only to promote the sociologist's own understanding of society, than by sociological research designed to solve planning problems as these were perceived by planners.[46] The argument seems valid, but only if its validity is in fact understood and accepted by planners themselves

(see the discussion leading to point (7) above). And until this understanding is reached, there is the difficulty that analyses and findings which are resented are unlikely to be acted upon. In the meantime, we can identify a twelfth reason for the 'gulf'.

(12) *That discussion, by sociologists, of planning, and of research on planning, understandably creates resentment among planners.* There is a further point to note here. The choice posed, between a 'sociology *of* planning' and a mistaken 'applied sociology' based on false premises, may be misleading. There is a third alternative, and this is an 'applied sociology' based on *valid* premises. Exploration of this third possibility is the main concern of the next section of this paper.

III

We can identify a number of ways in which sociology could contribute to town planning practice. [47] Pahl has suggested a typology of the various roles which the sociologist in planning is characteristically *expected* to play. [48]

(i) *As a general liberal-educational or liberating influence.* The somewhat patronizing ring of this is hopefully excused by the fact that it is only suggested in relation to town planning *education.* [49]

(ii) *As a means of promoting among planners an awareness of the position of town planning in society.*

(iii) *As a means of increasing planners' understanding of what is and what is not politically feasible.* There seems little that the sociologist could tell most town planners here. But why, if planners do have this realistic understanding of these things, do planning reports, and the planning literature generally, purvey an unworldly technocratic rhetoric which denies this understanding?

(iv) *As a means of explaining the existence and content of planning rhetoric, and of planning ideology generally.* More especially, it would seem useful to raise the question as to whether the very high level of output of this 'stuff' is strictly necessary. Would town planners necessarily suffer, if they said at least some of the things a little more plainly? This 'making plain', of course, is another name for providing town planning with credible theory and credible social philosophy.

(v) *As a means of clarifying planning objectives, and putting them into 'operational' terms.* Because planners see themselves as reconciling competing demands, the task generally associated with politicians, they have found it necessary also to take over the language style of politicians. Thus, planning objectives as stated by planners are almost invariably bland and ambiguous, such that they are capable of meaning all things to all men, and so that virtually *any* actual decisions or designs can be said to be derived from them. [50] In this respect, the position is less difficult in socialist countries, for there it can be clearly stated that the object of environmental planning is to reduce environmental inequalities. In Western countries, by contrast, it is apparently often difficult to say anything more precise than that the object of planning is to produce good planning. 'In the interests of good planning', has actually been used, by local planning authorities, as a reason for refusing permission for development, and for imposing conditions on permissions granted. In taking over this language style, however, planners have accentuated it. It is still relatively easier to discuss the political implications of policy in the public political arena than in the rather closed bureaucratic-professional sphere. The social scientist would point out that objectives can only be achieved, and progress towards their achievement can only be measured, if these objectives are made explicit and operational. He thus finds himself urging that planning be 'politicized' to a far greater extent than it now is. Strictly, the sociologist can only urge particular objectives in his capacity as a citizen, and not as a sociologist. But there seems no reason why he should not operate in these two roles simultaneously. [51]

(vi)   *As an aid in achieving planning objectives.* Assistance in achieving objectives is presumably the justification for applying *any* social science to *any* area of public policy. But in the case of planning, it would seem that successful completion of tasks (ii) to (v) above is a *precondition* of the use of sociology in its 'primary' purpose (vi). In addition, it is also necessary that the planners have a good understanding of the nature of sociology itself, and of what it can and cannot do.

Assuming that these preconditions are not impossible of attainment, what can be said about the application of sociology to the achievement of planning objectives? One of the best discussions of what would be possible, and of the way in which it might be achieved, is provided by Jameson. [52] While Jameson's concerns focus on social research for architecture, his views seem equally valid in the case of town planning. Confusingly, Jameson terms the approach which he advocates 'instrumental social research', and the approach which he depreciates 'sociology'. The approach which he advocates seems better characterized as 'good sociology', and the approach which he depreciates as 'bad sociology'. These semantic problems will be dealt with by translating his terminology into that appropriate to this discussion.

The nub of Jameson's argument is that the planner must himself take responsibility for the objectives which he pursues. Secondly, the planner must accept that this choice of objective is a matter of moral or political commitment, and not a technical matter. For Jameson, 'The objective ... lies outside the realm of the research enquiry, and its morality or immorality is neither proved nor disproved by the research findings.' [53] Jameson suggests that the proper question to ask is not, 'What do people want?', but rather, 'How can people be made to want what we [the planners] have to offer?' This formulation has led to much criticism of Jameson's entire approach. However, it seems to be methodologically sounder than the way in which the problem is usually formulated in this field, as one of discovering the respondents' needs and preferences. [54] Jameson does seem to have exaggerated the position somewhat, suggesting that the planner is committed to *one* solution, or policy, which he insists on 'selling' to the consumer. It is clear from reading Jameson's article, that this was not his intention. All he is in fact suggesting is that the planner, together with his sociological researcher, must know the *range* of possibilities which are objectively available, and must, therefore, succeed in reconciling the consumer to *one or other* of them (or to some combination of them).

It seems reasonable to assume, following Jameson, that the planner, since he devotes his working life to the matter, will have knowledge which the consumer cannot have, on the question of what types of physical milieu it is possible to create, of their relative costs, of the various advantages and disadvantages which each is likely to offer, and of the implications of these various environmental choices generally. It is clear that Jameson sees the consumer as free to reject what is offered, or to partially reject it (i.e. to secure modification of it), but it is equally clear that the consumer *must* become informed as to what it is objectively possible to provide, and must settle for something within these bounds. The point would seem to be that if there is any technical content at all, in the body of expertise which planners claim to possess, then planners must know, better than those for whom they plan, the probable consequences of the various options.

Central to this approach is the concept of *dialogue* between planner and planned. The planner makes the various possibilities known to those he plans for, and the latter informs the planner of the importance which they attach to various features of the plan. Thus the planner in turn is able to concentrate on more detailed investigation of the precise cost at which specific desired or undesired features can be obtained or avoided. Because he questions the conventionally fashionable view that all that is needed is to discover people's 'wants' and 'preferences', Jameson was attacked as 'undemocratic'. For example, Young and Willmott, commented on his article in the following terms. [55]

> ... his kind of research is more concerned with manipulating the customer to make him want the architect's product than with trying to find out about people's own needs ... But really there is no substitute for respecting people's own experience and wishes. This means trying to find out ... what basic social needs have to be met, and even what people themselves think they might actually like.

This criticism seems misplaced. Firstly, it assumes that 'needs' and 'preferences' can be taken as given, without facing up to the probability that those who act as our expert advisers in any sphere of life must inevitably help to create our perceived needs and preferences in that sphere. Secondly, it ignores the fact that even to the extent that needs and preferences *can* be ascertained, there is no way of deriving policy from them. [56] Thirdly, it is mistaken in suggesting that Jameson's approach is manipulative. As Jameson himself makes clear, it is Young and Willmott's approach to policy-making which is manipulative, for in its assumption that policies can be derived from observed preferences, it conceals the role of values.

This is made clear by comparing Young and Willmott's study of Bethnal Green with Rosser and Harris's study of Swansea, also concerned with the impact of public policy on traditional community patterns. [57] Unlike Young and Willmott, Rosser and Harris make it very clear that *no* policies are necessarily implied by the research findings. Rather, the research findings show the probable consequences of choosing various policies; the choice between them can only be made in the light of values. Thus, policy can hasten, or retard, the rate at which traditional community patterns disappear and can hasten, or retard, the rate at which attitudes and patterns of behaviour spread from the middle class to the working class. Jameson takes the argument further, by suggesting that this choice should be arrived at through a process of dialogue between planners and planned, in which the main task of the planners is to ensure that the planned are made fully aware of the likely consequences of *all* possible choices.

It is unfortunate that the approach pursued in the Bethnal Green study has been so influential in architectural and town planning circles. Every student, for example, knows that we must not break up communities, and must not impose middle-class values on working-class areas. This unfortunate influence is itself a result of sociologists' criticisms of these professions. Such has been architects' and planners' consequent lack of morale, and such has been their consequent exaggerated and mistaken respect for what they see as a 'democratic' approach, that to suggest to them that they might claim to understand anything better than their clients do has been for many years to find oneself accused of 'elitism'. The same mistaken understanding of 'democracy' is found, for example, in the Educational Priority Area policy. To suppose that because people are found to have certain values, and certain patterns of behaviour, public policy should be used to reinforce and perpetuate these patterns seems profoundly mistaken.

IV

The preceding section sought to identify the epistemological and methodological preconditions for the successful use of sociology in town planning. But there are also institutional preconditions. This section proposes just *one* such institutional precondition. This is that town planning should cease to be seen as the concern of a planning 'profession'. The grounds on which this thesis hinges were touched upon in Section III, where the question of the clarification of planning objectives was discussed. It was suggested there that this clarification implies greater 'politicization' of town planning.

What this means, in effect, is that 'public participation' in town planning should be greatly enlarged in scope, its main emphasis shifting to quite another level. Rather than being seen as concerned with such things as whether a particular new road should or should not take a particular route, or development be encouraged in one place or another, it should be conceived as public debate about the purpose of town planning itself. This means asking precisely what outcomes can be achieved with planning, which cannot be achieved without it, and precisely why this is. It also implies debate about the desirability of these outcomes, and thus the desirability of planning itself. Such debate, clearly, must rest both on social scientific findings, and on clarification of socio-philosophical values. It is thus a debate which can only be carried on if contributions are forthcoming from many different disciplines, as well as from political philosophy. As to why such open debate implies the 'deprofessionalization of planning', there would seem to be two main reasons.

Firstly, the existence of a planning profession, which arrives at recommendations supposedly on the basis of 'technical' appraisal of expert evidence provided by all relevant disciplines, has the effect of taking *out* of the public political arena questions which should properly remain within it.

Secondly, there would seem to be attributes inherent in professionalism itself, both as ideology and as practice, which tend to discourage open questioning and open discussions of existing procedures. This seems true of professions generally. More crucially to this discussion, however, is that in the case of the planning profession, there are additional factors, greatly accentuating this general tendency. These hinge on the fact that town planning is not a profession in the traditional meaning of that word. [58] Rather, it is a field in which the institutional control of the occupation (as exercised by the professional body, the RTPI), and the governmental control of the activity (as exercised by central and local government) have become to a very large extent 'fused' into a single web of power and influence, with a single subculture. This represents a very 'closed' situation, in intellectual terms. Because those within this planning system have every reason to preserve or enlarge it, the system is unlikely to offer incentives to those who question its practices. To say 'question its practices' is, in effect, to say 'to seek to discover the extent to which planning rests on valid scientific theory and on coherent social philosophy'. Thus, town planning theory is undeveloped. Because it is undeveloped, planners feel vulnerable, and react badly to those who demonstrate this weakness, and almost as badly even to those who seek to strengthen it. In a characteristically circular process, the situation becomes constantly exacerbated. This vulnerability of town planners both to social scientific and to social philosophical criticism seems so great that at times their reaction takes the form of an almost overt anti-intellectualism. This consists, for example, of greatly exaggerating the demands made upon them to 'act decisively', to 'make crucial decisions on behalf of society as a whole, which cannot be delayed until all the evidence is available', and so on, and generally to assert the value of action and minimize the value of understanding.

The suggestion here is that this situation can be summarized as one in which planners are substituting power for knowledge. If *any* public policy is to be improved, society must offer incentives to those who question it. Town planning as at present institutionalized in British society, by contrast, offers incentives much more positively to those who *accept* its ideology and who *refrain* from making its theory and its philosophy a matter for debate. This constitutes a forced translation of such questions, by redefinition, out of the intellectual sphere, and into that of power relationships. On occasion, too, such questioners are asked whether they do not 'believe in' planning. This is odd, for the question of whether planning does or does not have the consequences claimed for it can hardly be a matter of belief. It is a matter of empirical research. Use of the word 'believe' suggests what a number of writers have noted, that 'planning' often becomes in effect a kind of secular religion. [59]

These points can be illustrated by reference to existing research. Knowledge which could inform town planning is not lacking. Rather, it is largely untapped. Yet at the same time, planners constantly call for more research. [60] Some explanation of this apparent paradox lies in the fact that planners only accept as 'relevant' research which is based on their own definition of the situation, and of the nature of the 'problems'. For example, at the moment funds are available for research into the problems of 'inner cities', but to many sociologists such a definition of the 'problems' seems itself ideological, and to reflect particular interests. It is suggested, following a strong tradition in sociological thought, [61] that to be of value to practice, research must be carried out by independent researchers, institutionally unconnected with the bureaucracies and policies which they study. Such independent research on British planning as has been produced, however, has been largely ignored by the planning profession. [62] To create a situation in which it would no longer be ignored, but instead harnessed to the improvement of practice, would necessitate taking planning out of the control of a professional body. Findings which question the official definition of the situation, which are unsought, unwanted and inconvenient to those in office, are likely only to be considered to the extent that planning problems become the subject of social scientific, socio-philosophical, and thus, political, controversy.

Notes

1 For sociology, see R. A. Nisbet, *The Sociological Tradition*, Heinemann, London, 1966. For town planning, see N. Dennis, 'The popularity of the neighbourhood community idea', *Sociological Review*, vol. 6, no. 2, 1959, pp. 191-206 (reprinted in R. E. Pahl (ed.), *Readings in Urban Sociology*, Pergamon, Oxford, 1968, pp. 74-92).
2 J. R. Mellor, *Urban Sociology in an Urbanized Society*, Routledge & Kegan Paul, London, 1977, p. 156.
3 H. V. Emy, *Liberals, Radicals and Social Politics, 1892-1914*, Cambridge University Press, Cambridge, 1973, p. 209; R. Douglas, 'God gave the land to the people', in A. Morris (ed.), *Edwardian Radicalism, 1900-1914*, Routledge & Kegan Paul, London, 1974, chapter 9.

4 D. A. Hamer (ed.), *The Radical Programme 1885*, Harvester Press, Brighton, 1971.

5 See L. Mumford, 'Patrick Geddes, Victor Branford, and applied sociology in England: The social survey, regionalism and urban planning', in H. E. Barnes (ed.), *An Introduction to the History of Sociology*, University of Chicago Press, Chicago, 1948; R. J. Halliday, 'The sociological movement, the Sociological Society and the genesis of academic sociology in Britain', *Sociological Review*, vol. 16, no. 3, 1968; W. Peterson, 'The ideological origins of Britain's New Towns', *Journal of the American Institute of Planners*, vol. 34, no. 3, 1968, pp. 160-70.

6 Mumford, op. cit., 1948.

7 R. Glass, *Middlesbrough: The Social Background of a Plan*, Routledge & Kegan Paul, London, 1948; R. Glass, 'Urban sociology in Britain: A trend report and current bibliography', *Current Sociology*, vol. IV, no. 4, 1955, pp. 5-19 (reprinted in Pahl, op. cit., 1968, pp. 47-73); R. Glass, 'The evaluation of planning: Some sociological considerations', *International Social Science Journal*, vol. 11, no. 3, 1959 (reprinted in A. Faludi, (ed.), *A Reader in Planning Theory*, Pergamon, Oxford, 1973).

8 M. Harrison, 'British town planning ideology and the welfare state', *Journal of Social Policy*, vol. 4, no. 3, 1975, pp. 259-74.

9 See J. Uthwatt, *Interim Report of the Committee on Compensation and Betterment*, Cmd. 6291, HMSO, London, 1941; J. Blackwell and C. Dickens, 'Town planning, mass loyalty and the restructuring of capital: The origins of the 1947 planning legislation revised', *Urban and Regional Studies Working Paper No. 11*, University of Sussex, 1979; G. Schuster, *Report of the Committee on Qualifications of Planners*, Cmd. 8059, HMSO, London, 1950; J. B. Cullingworth, *Reconstruction and Land Use Planning, 1939-1947*, HMSO, London, 1975; P. Healey and J. Underwood, *Professional Ideals and Planning Practice: A Report on Research into Planners' Ideas in Practice in London Borough Planning Departments*, Town Planning Department (mimeo), Oxford Polytechnic, Oxford, 1977; M. Hebbert, *The Evaluation of British Town and Country Planning*, unpublished PhD thesis, University of Reading, 1977.

10 J. Westergaard, 'Land use planning since 1951: The legislative and administrative framework in England and Wales', *Town Planning Review*, vol. 35, 1964, pp. 219-37, documents this in the case of town planning itself.

11 See G. McDougall, G. Foulsham and J. Porter, *Sociology in Planning: A Redefinition*, Occasional Paper no. 3, Sociology in Polytechnics Organization, 1977.

12 J. Rex and R. Moore, *Race, Community and Conflict*, Oxford University Press, Oxford, 1967.

13 McDougall *et al.*, op. cit., 1977.

14 R. Glass, Review of M. Castells, 'The Urban Question', 1977, M. Harloe (ed.), 'Captive Cities', 1977, *New Society*, 29 September 1977, pp. 667-9.

15 McDougall *et al.*, op. cit., 1977.

16 For an outstanding example of all these trends, see Royal Town Planning Institute, *Planning and the Future*, Report by a Working Party of the Royal Town Planning Institute, the Institution of Civil Engineers, and the Royal Institution of Chartered Surveyors, RTPI, London, 1976.

17 P. Healey and M. Hebbert, *Urban Governance: Some Critical Comments on the Royal Town Planning Institute Paper 'Planning and the Future',* Town Planning Department (mimeo), Oxford Polytechnic, Oxford, 1977.

18 To this writer it is 'frightening' as advocated, for example, in G. Chadwick, *A Systems View of Planning,* Pergamon, Oxford, 1971; A. Faludi, op. cit., 1973; J. Friend, J. Power, and C. Yewlett, *Public Planning,* Tavistock, London, 1974; W. Solesbury, *Policy in Urban Planning,* Pergamon, Oxford, 1974; Royal Town Planning Institute, op. cit., 1976; A. Faludi, 'Sociology in planning education', *Urban Studies,* vol. 13, 1976, pp. 121-32; for comments on Faludi's paper and a rejoinder see *Urban Studies,* vol. 14, 1977, pp. 215-24. Also of relevance here are E. J. Reade, 'Sociology in planning education', *Official Architecture and Planning,* October 1971, pp. 783-4; E. J. Reade, 'Education and Planners' Ideology: Cause for Alarm?', *Town and Country Planning,* November 1976, pp. 491-4; and, E. J. Reade, 'Research for environmental planning: Are we on the right lines?', *Planning,* December 1976, pp. 10-11.

19 J. Summerson, *Georgian London,* Penguin, Harmondsworth, 1962.

20 R. Plant, *Ideology and Community,* Routledge & Kegan Paul, London, 1974.

21 J. Platt, 'Survey data and social policy', *British Journal of Sociology,* vol. 23, no. 1, 1972, pp. 77-91. See also R. Gutman, 'The questions architects ask', *Transactions of the Bartlett Society,* vol. 4, 1966, pp. 49-82.

22 Platt, op. cit., 1972.

23 See, for example, Town Planning Institute, *Contributory Disciplines in Planning: Report of the Sociology Working Party,* Amos F. Convenor, unpublished internal paper, 1970, p. 3; M. Broady, *Sociology in the Education of Planners,* unpublished paper prepared for the Town Planning Institute Working Party on 'Sociology in Planning Education', 1968; M. Broady, *Planning for People: Essays on the Social Context of Planning,* National Council of Social Service, London, 1968; M. Broady, 'Sociology in the education of planners', *Salzburg Conference on Urban Planning and Development Bulletin,* no. 6, 1969, pp. 40-2, also published by Department of Town and Regional Planning, University of Sheffield; and B. Heraud, *Sociology in the Professions,* Open Books, London, 1979.

24 A. Speer, *Inside the Third Reich,* Weidenfeld & Nicolson, London, 1970.

25 R. Huntford, *The New Totalitarians,* Allen Lane, London, 1972.

26 A. Faludi, *Sociology in Planning Education,* Department of Town Planning Working Paper no. 4, Oxford Polytechnic, 1970, pp. 37-41; A. Faludi, 'The experience of sociologists in their collaboration with planners', Paper presented at conference on *Uses of Social Sciences in Urban Planning,* Planning and Transport Research and Computation Ltd., London, 1971, p. 7.

27 A. Buttimer, 'Sociology and planning', *Town Planning Review,* vol. 42, no. 2, 1971, pp. 145-80.

28 For examples, see N. Dennis, *People and Planning,* Faber, London, 1970; N. Dennis, *Public Participation and Planners' Blight,* Faber, London, 1972; and J. G. Davies, *The Evangelistic Bureaucrat: A Study of*

a Planning Exercise in Newcastle-upon-Tyne, Tavistock, London, 1972.

29 D. Eversley and M. Moody, *The Growth of Planning Research Since the Early 1960's*, Report to the SSRC Planning Committee, Social Science and Research Council, London, 1976.

30 Faludi, op. cit. 1971.

31 Faludi, op. cit., 1970.

32 Ibid., p. 5.

33 Heraud, op. cit., 1979, pp. 115-16.

34 Faludi, op. cit., 1976.

35 B. Bernstein, 'On the classification and framing of educational knowledge', in M. F. D. Young (ed.), *Knowledge and Control*, Collier-Macmillan, London, 1971.

36 F. Musgrove, 'Power and the integrated curriculum', *Journal of Curriculum Studies*, vol. 5, no. 1, 1973, p. 8.

37 Bernstein, op. cit., 1971, pp. 64-6.

38 Bernstein, op. cit., 1971.

39 A. Faludi, 'The knowledge code of planning education', *Newsletter of the Education for Planning Association*, vol. 4, no. 1, 1974, pp. 18-22; and A. Faludi, op. cit., 1976.

40 See Broady, op. cit., 1969; and Town Planning Institute, op. cit., 1970.

41 Faludi, op. cit., 1971, pp. 5-6.

42 On this point, see, for example, Town Planning Institute, op. cit., 1970, p. 2; R. E. Pahl, 'Playing the rationality game: The sociologist as a hired expert', in C. Bell and H. Newby (eds), *Doing Sociological Research*, Allen & Unwin, London, 1977, p. 131. For a thorough analysis, see J. H. Goldthorpe, 'The future of futurology', *European Journal of Sociology*, vol. 12, no. 2, 1971, pp. 63-88.

43 For a fuller statement of these see, Faludi, op. cit., 1971.

44 R. E. Pahl, *Social Research and Planning*, paper prepared for SSRC Seminar, 5 May 1971, and subsequent seminar at Department of Sociology and Social Administration, University of Durham. Published in *Forma* (Journal of the Association of Student Planners, Midlands and Wales Branch), vol. 1, no. 3, 1972, pp. 3-12.

45 P. Banks, *The Sociology of Education*, Batsford, London, 1968, pp. 7-9: Broady, op. cit., 1968, p. 101.

46 E. J. Reade, 'Some notes towards a sociology of planning', *Journal of the Town Planning Institute*, vol. 54, no. 5, 1968, pp. 214-18; Buttimer, op. cit., 1971, pp. 173-5; McDougall *et al.*, op. cit., 1977, p. 7.

47 See Town Planning Institute, op. cit., 1970, p. 4.

48 Pahl, op. cit., 1977, pp. 145-6.

49 Faludi, op. cit., 1970.

50 D. Foley, 'British town planning: One ideology or three?', *British Journal of Sociology*, vol. 11, no. 3, 1960, pp. 211-31, provides a well-known analysis.

51 A. B. Cherns (ed.), *Sociotechnics*, Mallaby, London, 1976, pp. 297-8; M. Albrow, 'The role of the sociologist as a professional: The case of planning', in P. Halmos (ed.), *The Sociology of Sociology*, Sociological Review Monograph no. 16, University of Keele, 1970; and A. W. Gouldner and S. M. Miller (eds), *Applied Sociology: Opportunities and Problems*, Free Press, New York, 1965.

52 C. Jameson, 'The human specification in architecture: A manifesto for a new research approach', *Architects' Journal*, vol. 46, 27 October 1971, pp. 919-41.
53 Jameson, op. cit., 1971, p. 928.
54 J. Platt, *Social Research in Bethnal Green: An Evaluation of the Work of the Institute of Community Studies*, Macmillan, London, 1971; J. Platt, op. cit., 1972; and J. Platt, *Realities of Social Research: An Empirical Study of British Sociologists*, Chatto & Windus, London, 1976.
55 M. Young and P. Willmott, 'We are misrepresented', *Architects' Journal*, vol. 46, no. 154, 1971, p. 1139. For other comments on Jameson, see *Architects' Journal*, vol. 46, no. 154, 1971, pp. 1139-42, pp. 1277-8, and pp. 1414-15; *Architects' Journal*, vol. 47, no. 155, 1972, pp. 239-43.
56 Platt, op. cit., 1972.
57 M. Young and P. Willmott, *Family and Kinship in East London*, Routledge & Kegan Paul, London, 1957; C. Rosser and C. Harris, *The Family and Social Change: A Study of Family and Kinship in a South Wales Town*, Routledge & Kegan Paul, London, 1965 (abridged each 1983).
58 P. Elliott, *Sociology of the Professions*, Macmillan, London, 1972; T. Johnson, *Professions and Power*, Macmillan, London, 1972; P. Halmos (ed.), *Professionalization and Social Change*, Sociological Review Monograph no. 20, University of Keele, 1973.
59 See J. M. Power 'Planning: magic and technique', in Institute for Operational Research, *Beyond Local Government Reform*, London, 1971; J. G. Davies, op. cit., 1972.
60 See D. Eversley and M. Moody, op. cit., 1976; D. Eversley, *The Planner in Society*, Faber, London, 1973; and R. E. Pahl, 'The urban research industry', *New Society*, 13 November 1969, pp. 783-4.
61 C. W. Mills, *The Sociological Imagination*, Penguin, Harmondsworth, 1960; W. W. Gouldner and S. M. Miller (eds), op. cit., 1965; I. Horowitz, 'Social science and public policy: Some implications of modern research', in I. Horowitz (ed.), *The Rise and Fall of Project Camelot*, MIT Press, Cambridge, Mass., 1967; M. Rein, *Social Science and Social Policy*, Penguin, Harmondsworth, 1976; and C. Bryant, *Sociology in Action: A Critique of Selected Conceptions of the Social Role of the Sociologist*, Allen & Unwin, London, 1976. For 'applied sociology', see P. Lazarsfeld, and J. Reitz, *Introduction to Applied Sociology*, Elsevier, New York, 1975; and, P. Lazarsfeld W. Sewell and H. Wilensky (eds), *Uses of Sociology*, Weidenfeld & Nicholson, London, 1967. Of more general relevance, see J. Bailey, *Social Theory for Planning*, Routledge & Kegan Paul, London, 1975; A. Cherns *et al.* (eds), *Social Sciences and Government: Policies and Problems*, Tavistock, London; 1972; M. Komarovsky (ed.), *Sociology and Public Policy: The Case of the Presidential Commissions*, Elsevier, New York, 1976; T. S. Simey, *Social Science and Social Purpose*, Constable, London, 1968; and J. Ziolkowski, 'Sociological implications of urban planning', in J. C. Fisher (ed.), *City Planning in Poland*, Cornell University Press, Ithaca, New York, 1966.
62 Dennis, op. cit., 1970 and 1972; and Davies, op. cit., 1972.

The spatial dimension:
geographers and urban studies [1]

David T. Herbert

After a long period of relatively slow and conservative evolution, urban geography has since the early 1960s experienced a number of paradigmatic shocks; which have both re-oriented its perspectives and left the sub-discipline with internal tensions which have yet to be resolved. One central feature of this period has been decreasing isolation of human geography at large within the social sciences; this trend has found both external and internal expressions. 'Externally', there is a much greater awareness in other social sciences, especially in economics, sociology, and political science, of a need at least to recognize and accommodate the roles of space in the comprehension of human behaviour. [2] 'Internally', there is an enlarged willingness to adopt derivative concepts and theories and, perhaps more significantly, to pay a much greater regard to the philosophies of the social sciences. The tensions arise from the speed with which new paradigms appear and the dominance which they threaten to assume. As the advance of quantitative methods and a much more scientific urban geography subsumed more traditional research activities and some of their established practitioners in the 1960s, so the radical critique of the 1970s is seen in a similar light. Reactions are inevitable and by no means particular to urban geography. [3]

There is one form of tension, however, which has particular meaning for urban geography; this concerns the 'adjectival' significance of urban. In more recent years, some social sciences, notably economics and sociology, have in their empirical work at least been of less interest to urban geographers. The retreat from 'place' and an unwillingness to view the city as a definable space with special characteristics removed much of the common ground. In sociology, this withdrawal was evidenced by the partial demise of social ecology, by the sterile outcome of the urban-rural differences debate and the gradual disappearance of urban sociology as a component of schemes

171

of study. Urban geographers have responded to this potential isolationism in several ways. They have increasingly turned to other subject areas as complementary derivative sources, notably to social psychology and other behavioural sciences, and to political economy, and more significantly have sought to develop a more broadly-based indigenous body of theory and methodology. Ironically, it is from these indigenous changes that the tension has primarily arisen. In the 1960s, as quantification and model-building became the vogue, the thrust was to analyse the geometry of space rather than the meaning of place and to seek explanations in spatial processes. Such a scheme, resting upon categories such as flows, networks and nodal regions, [4] could scarcely accommodate an 'urban' geography *per se*. In the 1970s, the radical critique, founded in Marxism and finding expression as radical geography, [5] has launched a more general frontal attack upon the use of space as a central focus of analysis. In this perspective, spatial outcomes, urban or otherwise, are mere manifestations of the encompassing political economy which should be the prime reference for all studies. Political economy, it is argued, includes human beings in their relationships with the real material world and this analytical framework therefore involves a spatial dimension; the objection is to the extraction of 'space' and the tendency to regard it as an independent social force.

That none of these sources of tension have had any major effect to date on the 'identity' of urban geography as a sub-discipline is a product of many factors. Principal amongst these is a continued belief in the qualities of place as an assemblage of the realities of urban life. The city is a reality as an entity both within society and within the experiences of its occupants; special features emerge from the synthesis of societal characteristics within a limited territory; there are problems *of* as well as *in* the city. [6]

If the conclusion to the last paragraph implies a continuing conservatism within urban geography, it is neither intended nor accurate. There have been many major changes and re-orientations since the early 1960s, the full outcomes of which have yet to be realized. In the discussion which follows, the aim will be to identify the more traditional bases upon which urban geography developed, to analyse the major changes which have been experienced within the last two decades, and to define the framework within which urban geographers now work. From this may be judged the roles, both independent and integrated, of a spatial dimension to urban studies.

Traditional paradigms and contemporary change

The three distinguishing hallmarks of human geography may be summarized as the study of man-nature relationships, of distributions and interactions in space, and of the meanings of place. Although the ways in which these have been studied and the weight given to them individually has varied considerably over time, they remain core features which can be traced to a number of paradigms which have formed the discipline. Exploration, environmentalism and regionalism—each developing during the nineteenth century [7]—are the most venerable of these paradigms. The exploration ethic is sustained in institutions like the Royal Geographical Society but the charting of new lands is now less significant than more mundane tasks of collecting and systematizing new forms of geographic data from sources as wide-ranging as census returns and satellite imagery. Environmentalism retains a stronger conceptual hold as the source of the man-nature relationship and finds continuity in urban studies in studies of ecological association and of behaviour in man-made environments. The key roles of regionalism have been maintained in geography as a teaching discipline and through its translation into regionalization at a variety of scales.

The traditional paradigms retain their validity but during the 1960s the pace of methodological change quickened considerably and nowhere has the impact of this change been felt more immediately than in urban geography. Within this 'contemporary' period [8] one major new paradigm has become established and other significant trends, which may yet acquire that status, have appeared. Chorley and Haggett [9] presented the case for a spatial analysis paradigm with their advocacy of more numerical and model-based studies: 'In general we feel that geometrical analysis offers a logical, consistent and geographically more relevant alternative to the "element orientated" approach with its inevitable tendency to subdivide geography and force it outwards towards the relevant external systematic disciplines.' The statement is interesting both in terms of its push towards the methodology of positivist science and in its aversion towards fusion with other disciplines.

As a paradigm, with an associated set of methodologies and techniques, spatial analysis has recently dominated contemporary geography, generating a voluminous research literature. There is clear evidence in the 1970s however that this dominance is disappearing and that other methodological and philosophical positions are becoming increasingly available and attractive. The trends which are producing these alternatives within geography are not unique and are diffusing from the wider framework of the social sciences with much shorter time-lags than have typified earlier events. An interest in 'subjectivism' entered geography in a fragmented way and there are contrasted perspectives to be disentangled. Behaviourism *per se*, which did influence some studies, has strong links with the biological sciences and experimental psychology and belongs to the tradition of positive science. The more significant 'behavioural murmurings', [10] however, were much influenced by Simon [11] and his concepts of bounded rationality and of satisficer as opposed to economic man. It is this latter trend, finding expression as studies of decision-making, perception and spatial cognition, which has found more collective identity as 'humanistic' geography with increasing reference to the philosophy of phenomenology and its derivatives, a branch which attaches particular significance to the meaning of place.

Another trend which is commonly, though perhaps not accurately, [12] held to have begun at the Association of American Geographers conference in 1971 is that towards relevance. Again, from being an initially diffuse reaction against the abstractions of spatial analysis, this trend has crystallized into a critique, which encompasses both a structuralist and essentially Marxist approach [13] and a more welfare-orientated interest in territorial justice. [14] Under this broad umbrella of relevance, the traditional concept of applied geography has taken new and often sharply divergent forms.

In summary, therefore, the three traditional paradigms continue to influence urban geography but since the early 1960s a quickening pace of change has enabled the establishment of one new paradigm and the emergence of two new influential perspectives. The ways in which these innovations have entered the mainstream of research and practice in human geography will now be examined.

Human geography remained in a relatively 'cocooned' position long after significant events began to change the character and status of the social sciences. Economics, for example, had passed through the Keynesian revolution and obtained both public (political) and scientific recognition for its role in ameliorating the ills of the 1920s and 1930s. Psychologists had been deeply involved in the war effort as studies by Stouffer [15] and others indicate and they, together with associates in sociology, had begun to launch large programmes of survey research into human behaviour. [16] All of this work had the following characteristics:

(a) It was nomothetic rather than idiographic, focusing on

general trends and patterns and interpreting specifics within a theoretical matrix rather than stressing the unique and the exceptional.

(b)   It used numerical methods to analyze its data and so was 'scientifically' respectable.

(c)   It apparently had predictive power and so could be used—at least in an evaluative and forecasting role—in the development of public policy.

Two statements can be made about the conditions under which these characteristics became translated into geography as spatial analysis. Firstly, many of the ideas were derived from other disciplines and reflected the general impact of normative scientific approaches on the social sciences. Secondly, although one can find examples of generalizations in human geography from much earlier periods, [17] the discipline in practice was centrally concerned with exceptionalism and stood in sharp contrast, for example, with the search for general laws in several branches of physical geography. During the early 1960s, the isolated examples of spatial models [18] assumed greater significance in the general drift towards a nomethetic discipline, in which the search for laws and models was a central concern. Associated with this shift was a much greater emphasis on quantitative analysis and statistics, an emphasis which both added a degree of difficulty to the new paradigm and better equipped geographers to develop the new methodology.

During the 1960s, the methodology of these investigations was both extended and made more precise. The aim was to be more scientific and to provide quantifiable theories and laws; the language of advanced models became more symbolic and mathematics rather than the now accepted statistics was advocated as the *desideratum*. [19] Doubts about this trend developed as many quantitative analyses remained descriptive and added neither new insights into urban problems nor, with any consistency, proved to have usable practical outcomes. Optimizing solutions tended to serve the needs of the suppliers rather than the consumers of goods and services. Besides these doubts originating 'internally' to the discipline and the social sciences, there were also the pressing imperatives of historical events in the 1960s and the increasing impossibility of remaining apart from contemporary urban crises.

Spatial analysis, developing with an emphasis on the geometry of space and locational analysis as part of a more general move towards a positive science [20] had produced theories based on mechanistic assumptions of human decision-making. These involved the concept of economic man, a perfectly rational being who based decisions on perfect knowledge and in a locational context became 'spatial man', [21] whose choice of location was based on a minimization of movement costs. Later there were models adapted from Parsonian functionalism which accepted a view of society as composed of individuals allocated to particular places within the economic and social order from which, by dint of personal effort, they might escape to a higher level. The members of these various groups then compete for territory, with the resulting spatial order representing a consensus acceptance of a certain pattern. These derivative sources and the ways in which they were translated into geographical models and theories ensured an essentially positivist and functionalist suite of postures. As quantification itself and the question of scientific bases for the discipline were the natural handmaidens of these philosophies, urban geography by the 1960s had assumed a stereotyped and rather abstracted character. During the 1970s, the influence of spatial analysis, although still significant, has declined. The changed nature of its role will be considered but first some of the key reactions to the paradigm need to be identified.

'Subjectivism' has a long heritage in the literature of human geography but retains the quality of being most easily identifiable as a critique rather than as a precise methodology with a cohesive structure. Increasing interest in phenomenology, idealism and related schools of thought suggest that a philosophical underpinning to provide cohesion may be forthcoming, but the perspective can presently be most clearly seen as a reaction against the mechanistic, aggregative, and 'dehumanizing' characteristics of spatial analysis. [22] Earlier reactions in the 1960s were reflected in Kirk's [23] identification of a behavioural environment, in Lowenthal's [24] advocacy of a humanistic concern for landscape, and in Wolpert's [25] interpretation of the decision-making process in migration. As the spatial analysts aimed to characterize geography as a geometry of space, subjectivists sought to re-assert the role of human values in the way in which space is regarded and to study the meanings which underlie a sense of place—man was to become more than a 'pale, entrepreneurial figure'. [26]

By the early 1970s, both the quantitative-theoretical and the subjective-humanistic approaches were being questioned on new grounds. This development, which has been variously termed a shift towards 'structuralism', 'radicalism', and 'political economy', [27] had strong methodological roots in the social sciences; its entry into human geography, however, was initiated at a more pragmatic level

with civil rights and anti-Vietnam movements in the United States
in the later 1960s. There were several fronts to this radical critique in geography.[28] One reaction was against the assumption of a
society in which there was 'fair' competition between buyers and
sellers; another sought to establish an understanding that an economy
based upon 'accumulation for its own sake' would be crisis-ridden;
whilst a third focused upon the contradiction of participatory
democracy through electoral procedures in the political sphere and its
absence in the workplace—the production sphere. Established science
had mistakenly claimed an objective, value-free, politically neutral
role and in so doing was working to serve the existing social system
and enable its survival. A second criticism concerned the assumption
of consensus arrangement among social groups. From a radical
viewpoint, capitalist society comprises socio-economic groups among
which the real processes are conflict and dissensus rather than merely
competition and consensus.[29] Geographical patterns could, it was
argued, only be interpreted through this conflict among unequal
groups in terms of their control of resources. A third criticism
suggested that spatial analysis had only a limited descriptive role and
could predict only in a mechanical way within the prescriptions of
existing orders.[30] Finally, subjective approaches were dismissed as
reductionism and a return to the idiographic and exceptional stances
which had proved so inhibiting in the past. The mainsprings of this
critique are undoubtedly derived from Marxism but many geographers are prepared to accept the validity of many of the points of
criticism without embracing the overall philosophy upon which it is
founded.

Contemporary urban geography

Against the backcloth of changing methodological bases in the social
sciences and their repercussions, urban geography in the 1960s and
1970s became the main platform for innovation and redirection within
human geography. The first shift, from an emphasis upon urban
morphology with its focus on physical form and land-use in a
historical and topographic setting to one on the economic and
functional bases of urban places was gradual. It drew upon earlier
work of land-economists and early location theorists such as Christaller but had a strong bias towards problems of classification and
regionalization. At the inter-urban scale, a growing literature centred
on the economic functions of cities and several classifications were
proposed; a strong focus on marketing and retail studies picked up the

threads of early work [31] aimed at identifying hierarchies of central places and delineating market areas and formed the bases of a strong suite of studies on systems of cities. [32] At an intra-urban scale, the general issue of land values, rents and land-use attracted attention whilst the analyses of central business districts (and commercial structures) stimulated a great deal of empirical urban study. These topics retained research attention but were eclipsed in overall significance by a rapidly growing interest in the social aspects of urban life. This interest grew from a dissatisfaction with the limited perspectives of traditional urban geography and its failure to recognize and study the social dynamics of urban life. A social geography of the city had advantages of being able to refer to a whole suite of models, concepts, and empirical work which had been developed outside the discipline. Whereas much of the early theory of social ecology had already been labelled as redundant, its obvious spatial qualities and empirical generalizations had enormous appeal to urban geographers and the early seminal paper by Harris and Ullman [33] provided a key link.

For some years this new work on the social geography of the city centred on the traditional objectives of classifying and defining residential sub-areas and the rapid development of the spatial analysis methodology provided numerous techniques which could be used to this end. Residential differentiation studies moved through analyses of natural areas and diagnostic variables, to social area analysis and factorial ecology [34] in a considerable and still growing literature. In a less prominent but still significant related research field, the 'dissimilarist' techniques were used to identify levels of spatial segregation, especially of ethnic minorities. [35] Over a period of some fifteen years from the mid-1950s, the balance and content of research and teaching in urban geography changed considerably. Whereas interest in more traditional themes such as urban morphology declined [36] there was a remarkable overall increase in research output centred on economic functions and social qualities of urban places. [37] This upsurge was closely related to the rise of the spatial analysis paradigm and mirrored its impact.

By the latter part of the 1960s, urban geographers had passed through their 'revolution'. The trail-blazers were now the established figures in the discipline and for new graduate researchers the form which urban geography had assumed represented the conventional truth. The period of stock-taking which began can again only be understood against the background of changing perspectives, new 'paradigmatic shocks' within the social sciences at large and major events in the real world. From both the behavioural and the radical/ relevance perspectives, dissatisfaction with the type of positivist science which urban geography had become grew. A nearly positive reaction emerged from the awareness that although, for example, multivariate analyses were slowly improving an understanding of residential patterns and probabilistic models were allowing some predictive power, these were retaining a focus on patterns and had limited perspectives. Concern with process as opposed to pattern had always been evident in geographical studies; themes of movement and change had received consistent attention. But process *per se* became a much more central focus for concern as behavioural concepts became absorbed into research practice. [38] The impact of the relevance/radical perspective, arising out of the urban crises of the late 1960s when the problems of cities found expression in dramatic and often violent ways, reinforced this dissatisfaction with pattern studies. Urban geographers quickly became aware of the limited practical value of their detailed quantitative researchers into urban structures. Factorial ecologies of Detroit or Belfast could justifiably stand as academically sound and statistically rigorous pieces of work but they seemed to bear little relationship to the urban realities of burning fires and exploding bombs. Urban geography began to diversify and the many threads can be summarized into three main categories, as shown in the diagram.

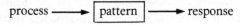

process ⟶ pattern ⟶ response

Pattern studies

Study of patterns represents a continuation and development of a traditional concern in urban geography, sustained by the legitimate argument that pattern identification is a basic starting-point for geographical research. Issues, questions and problems may be revealed by patterns; clustering, dispersal and the infinite variety of intermediate forms which patterns may take help identify research questions. Pattern identification remains an important stage in geographical study and has been considerably strengthened by technical procedures developed within the spatial analysis paradigm. The social area studies which dominated many analyses during the 1960s have continued to develop with more advanced forms of factor analysis and an interest in other techniques such as multi-dimensional scaling. By the early 1970s the numerous replications of 'factorial ecologies' in North America had consistently identified economic, family, and ethnic status as bases of residential separation and had also allowed accompanying spatial generalizations of sectors, zones and 'districts'. Similar results were obtained in several European studies though migrant status often emerged as a surrogate for ethnicity and the generality of results was affected by the extent to which there was public sector intervention in the housing market. Both the more general changes in foci of interest and the feeling that continuing replications of factorial ecology were producing diminishing returns led to a move away from studies of residential differentiation in the 1970s. The significant work which is ongoing is either concerned with applying established analytical procedures to understudied parts of the world, notably to Third World and to Socialist societies, or else is involved in the resolution of methodological issues such as the invariance of factorial solutions and with the development of improved or different forms of analysis.[39] Some preliminary generalizations upon the bases of residential separation in both Third World and Socialist cities are already possible but more empirical work is needed in these contexts; elsewhere social area studies will be used as stages in more widely based research strategies rather than as end results in their own right. Pattern identification studies of this kind can also be used in association with diffusion and probabilistic forecasting procedures in order to obtain useful though necessarily limited models of change over time.

A significant development in pattern studies is associated with a response to the call to relevance. Interest in territorial social indications has to be set against a more broadly-based movement within the social sciences[40] to obtain better social data for research purposes. Territorial social indicators are defined as 'quantitative measures of the incidence of given types of social problems in each of a number of spatial subdivisions'[41] and although geographers have become heavily involved in more general conceptual issues,[42] their basic roles have comprised the improvement of spatial statistics and their analysis. For the pattern identification procedures, the methodology of residential differentiation was available and although multivariate analyses have generally been used, there is some feeling that simpler statistical procedures more adequately linked to social theories are preferable. The priority should be one of asking better questions rather than one of seeking confirmations of established knowledge by using increasingly unwieldy analytical procedures. For the second task of relating quality of life to other measures of the urban environment, spatial analysis has formed the basis of study. Within the constraints of available data and aggregate analyses, correlational exercises have allowed some better understanding if not explanation of social problems. Territorial social indicators have key roles in identifying and portraying the varying quality of urban life,[43] and have been extensively used in the formulation of area policies.[44] Allied to the more general forms of territorial social indicator research have been analyses of more specific problems such as mental illness[45] and crime[46] which incorporate a pattern identification component.

Process studies
The initial resurgence of research interest in processes had close links with behaviourism. In its more straightforward form, this involved a stronger reference to the decision-making processes which underlay spatial patterns, a push towards individual rather than aggregate scale data, and the direct transference of concepts, such as place utility, stressors, stimuli, and awareness space from the behavioural sciences. At the intra-urban scale, the analysis of residential mobility provided a focal point. At least for North American and British cities, residential differentiation studies had laid down the detailed mosaic of residential areas and had provided some spatial generalizations. The task now was to understand how the patterns emerged and to recognize that aggregate patterns were in fact summations of a myriad of individuals' decisions on where to live. An early empirical study by Rossi[47] proved highly influential and a range of studies analysed processes in particular cities whilst others[48] placed the analysis of urban residential processes in the conceptual context of behaviourism.[49] Whereas these process studies related to residential patterns, similar studies examined the locational decision-making of firms and businesses and investigated consumer behaviour in a market/retail trade context. A basic deficiency with much of the earlier empirical work, and indeed of the conceptual models upon which it was based, was the emphasis on choice and the relative disregard for constraint. More recent work has corrected this imbalance and has been strongly influenced by the concept of 'housing classes' as initially introduced by Rex and Moore.[50] The transition from a view of process as a choice mechanism to one involving constraint, conflict and competition for resources[51] has merged this research area into the more general field affected by new perspectives of the radical relevance critique.

Response studies
Studies falling into the 'response' categories had innovative qualities but were in some ways linked to established modes of analysis. Response studies can be defined as those which use patterns as bases of

much more detailed investigations. These may be concerned with the characteristics of pattern itself, with detailed studies of selected areas, or with analyses of interactions over time and space. There are many antecedents of such studies. The concept of community, for example, has a long lineage in the literature of both social geography and urban ecology; social area analysts have frequently used classifications of areas as sampling frameworks. [52] The general re-emphasis of the subjective meanings of place have added new dimensions. As in Firey's [53] essay on sentiment and symbolism in Boston, and Emrys Jones's persistent emphasis on the social values with which space is imbued, [54] so Buttimer's [55] characterization of the 'anchoring points' in urban space which are stamped by human intention, value and memory, reinforces the need to comprehend the subjective qualities of the urban life-world. In similar vein, Ley and Cybriwsky [56] have demonstrated new ways of revealing the social dynamic in urban areas. From Boulding's [57] work on the image, allied research on mental maps, spatial images, and cognitive mapping has developed. [58]

The use of territorial social indicators in pattern identification has focused attention both on urban problems in general and in the identification of problem areas in particular. [59] Here again there are strong strands of development which can be traced to the type of social ecology initially studied in Chicago in the 1920s and 1930s. Epidemiological studies of ill health and mental illness can be classified in this way as can analyses of the spatial ecology of urban social problems such as crime and delinquency. Basic features of such studies continue to be the identification of the spatial patterning of incidence rates of such phenomena within urban areas, attempts to generalize upon these spatial patterns, and statistical analyses of the associations of the 'problem variable' with other measures of the social environment at an aggregate scale. Beyond these basic stages of analysis there has been a development of attempts to study varying forms of behaviour within identified 'problem areas' in greater detail. A good deal of interest has been revealed in the characterization of the 'subjective' as opposed to the 'objective' environment and examination of its role as a reference point for behaviour. Several studies have proposed the existence of a 'neighbourhood effect' which has some role in modifying attitudinal and behavioural characteristics at the local 'interface' of urban life. [60] Such studies acknowledge the overall significance of societal structure and an individual's position within society but have found some confirmation of the hypothesis that the local environment may add its own distorting effect on social behaviour.

An important development in this response mode is related to wider conceptual developments and increased awareness of the conflict and dissensus dimension to social relationships. Many conflicts may occur over externalities or 'goods' which households consume but do not produce themselves. Positive externalities are benefits produced by the actions of others—nearby residents or owners of adjacent properties —an example would be the re-zoning of a piece of land which causes neighbouring properties to appreciate in value. Negative externalities are the opposite; costs or disadvantages induced by the actions of others, such as pollution from a nearby factory. Residential location is therefore competition for externalities in which the better-off, most able to exercise choice have considerable advantages. In Tiebout's [61] analysis, people buy entitlement to public services through their choice of district of residence. Once individuals are located, their place of residence identifies them with a group which is given coherence by a common need to preserve or attract positive externalities and to repel negative ones. For many public utilities, such as schools, the conflict may be over spatial externality fields such as catchment areas, and decisions on the location of public services are therefore critical. As those with most power and influence are likely to prevail in conflict situations, best neighbourhoods may be enhanced. As negative externalities tend to be overproduced and positive underproduced, [62] externality effects may detract from overall social welfare.

In the context of response studies, and especially with reference to behaviour, a more persistent attempt has developed in the 1970s to specify the time dimension to spatial activities. [63] Pred [64] distinguishes between the 'life-path', with its spatial and temporal attributes, at the macro-level, and the daily interactions or path convergences in time and space; Tranter and Parkes [65] have attempted to apply the concept of an environmental image that is both spatial and temporal, a 'time-place'. This perspective is producing both some valuable insights and also some rather less useful 'truisms' and new jargonese; its potential has yet to be fully tested.

Urban geography's focus on problems in 'response' studies led to the intention to contribute to policy. Work on territorial social indicators, for example, had contributed to the development of area policies at both national and local level and a range of positive discrimination measures on area bases. [66] Most urban geographers would argue that area policies are valuable if not sufficient ways of tackling problems in the city. The more broadly-based notion of territorial or spatial justice [67] has been developed in more explicitly spatial terms from early work such as that by Davies [68] on personal

David T. Herbert

social services. Territorial justice may be said to exist where the distribution of key urban facilities—schools, hospitals—is such that it matches the distribution of need; it is essentially therefore a welfare concept as normal competition—as suggested in the discussion on externalities—will produce an imbalanced distribution in which the disadvantaged are the least well served. Measurement of need and provision is one element of this group of studies; nomination of more satisfactory facility locations is another. [69]

A new framework for urban geographical study

With these studies of the later 1960s and 1970s, summarized into the categories of pattern, process and response, the work of the urban geographer has diversified considerably. There is a greater diversity of patterns studied and a vastly improved 'technology' to enable this analysis, there is a strong focus on processes of many kinds and scales, and response studies are adding new dimensions and advancing the applied tradition. The focus of all these studies, however, remained the local interface or the urban environment *per se*. As the radical critique developed during the 1970s, its most valuable contribution has been its questioning of the primacy of this focus. Although urban geographers have always tried to place their research efforts in a broader context, preferably one which allows comparisons, the need to give the 'antecedents' of pattern, process and response as spatial outcomes greater primacy in research attention was gradually accepted. New levels of analysis had to be identified as context for continuing work at the local scale.

These levels can be summarized as shown in the diagram.

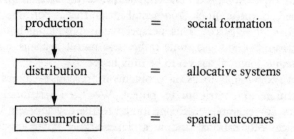

Under this scheme, the large majority of studies so far described under the headings of pattern, process and response can be located within the consumption level. It is no part of this argument that such studies are redundant. If, as will be shown, the research emphasis is

184

shifting to other 'levels', it is to redress a balance rather than to discard or replace. Analyses at production and distribution levels can contribute significantly to the understanding of those forces which underpin urban environment and to which, ultimately, key features of pattern, process and response can be retraced.

We will briefly define our terms. Research at the *production* level incorporates those studies concerned with 'institutions' at the macro-scale within society which give that society its particular form and character at a given point in time. The concept of social formation [70] as a historically determinate, 'real' society composed of economic, political and ideological levels finding expression as a complex whole most adequately expresses the scale of this level of analysis. By *distribution* level research is meant the study of allocative systems, with their roles in relationship with the means of production, and with the agencies—managers or gatekeepers—which filter policies and resources down to the *consumption* level. At this last level of *consumption* the scale is the urban environment, the local interface between societal forces and their spatial outcomes. Research trends at the two 'new' levels, production and distribution, will now be discussed.

Production level analyses
At the production level of analysis, it is possible to identify at least two broad categories of research. One group, centrally concerned with issues of methodology and philosophy, contains some diversity of stances, but is dominated by those with a central allegiance to Marxism—the 'radical geographers'. [71] For this methodological group at large, the issues, although material and real world, are not specifically spatial; indeed a unifying feature is the reaction against the 'fetishism' of space. Radical geographers and others in this 'group' argue, for example, that space should be seen in its limited context rather than given primacy; that disciplinary boundaries are an irrelevance within the goal of a unified social science which seeks to answer central questions on the nature of society; and that urban geography has failed to provide itself with either a sound integrating theory or to generate good theories. The terms of reference of the neoclassical economic model on which much of spatial analysis is predicted, for example, are 'hopelessly inadequate and misleading'. [72] In response to these deficiencies, the historical materialism of Marx has attraction through its ability to provide an overall theory of society and its development. It is the strength of the theoretical framework which has academic appeal and although other theories

may be recognized, they are either dismissed or counted as insignificant variants which can be encompassed within the general framework of historical materialism. Pragmatically, Marxism offers the basis for a severe critique of the capitalist system which dominates the Western world; a system which through its processes of production and reproduction is the basic cause of 'problems' which may eventually manifest themselves in urban environments: 'capitalist society must of necessity create a physical landscape ... in its own image, broadly appropriate to the purposes of production and reproduction', [73] and 'the choice of urban "solutions" is sharply circumscribed by the structural imperatives of the capitalist mode of production.' [74] If the inequalities in the urban environment are the product of the system, so their solution must involve change of the system. Marxists would discount ameliorating and welfare solutions as long-term strategies; 'urban life must become increasingly mediated by the state, and hence, directly politicized', eventually leading to a 'socialist political praxis'. [75] For many other geographers, however, the welfare state contains acceptable solutions.

Whereas ideological positions divide this group, the critique of spatial analysis and of positivist social science masquerading as objective knowledge provides common ground. Typical reactions are against the use of data, which are neither neutral nor absolute facts, in unexamined and atheoretical ways. [76] Aspects of this question have been well discussed in sociological literature. [77]

There are more explicitly empirical studies at the production level and these can be taken to comprise the second group. Two initial qualifications are needed. Firstly, the practitioners are diverse and largely autonomous and do not constitute a 'group' in the stricter sense of the term; secondly, most empirical work tends to 'straddle' production and distribution levels rather than remain exclusive to either one. Harvey's essay on Baltimore housing provides a Marxist interpretation which is couched in the context of federal policies and financial infra-structures. 'At the national level, then, policies appear to have been designed to maintain an existing structure of society intact in its basic configurations, while facilitating economic growth and capital accumulation, eliminating cyclical influence and defusing discontent'. [78] Walker's analysis of American suburbanization sees its origin in the early nineteenth century when 'the capitalist development process began to force rapid urbanization, new patterns of production, and new divisions of social life.' [79]

Not all recent work on macro-structures has begun from an established ideological position. Multinational corporations, or major economic institutions functioning in differing social formations, have received scrutiny.[80] In Western societies, multinational corporations are viewed as agents of capitalism with very large effects; investment strategies, for example, which determine the expansion or contraction of firms, have considerable local effects. Interestingly, as geographers move toward studies of the internal structures of large corporations in order to understand local outcomes, so organization theory is increasingly acknowledging the role of environmental uncertainty and the influence of local factors on firms. Other published work on the macro-economic structure has involved analysis of the effect of structural change—for example, through mergers—on the behaviour of individual firms.[81] Macro-political structure provides another study context and here an issue is the extent to which the state acts to sustain the social formation; Harvey[82] argues that the US federal housing subsidies serve the interests of capitalism.

Much of the empirical work at the production level remains exploratory and is hampered by the absence of good data. More generally the radical/relevance critique has served a valuable purpose both in stimulating recognition of the need for such research and in raising awareness of the necessity of studying in depth the philosophies of the social sciences. For empirical work at this level, qualitative rather than quantitative data are likely to provide the clearest insights into the nature of the social formation; conceptually, Marxism provides the most persuasive philosophy but for many its critique is more acceptable than its ideological premises.

Distribution level analyses

At the analytical level of distribution, work by geographers has related both to a conceptual assessment of the managerialist thesis and an empirical examination of the ways in which allocative systems actually work. During the early 1970s a flurry of empirical studies of managerialism in the housing market were initiated but tended to become subsumed by the more attractive theoretical contexts which Marxism provided. In the latter part of the 1970s a renewed interest, now more founded on social theories—particularly Weber's concept of ideal types—has found new empirical applications.[83] Early work by Pahl[84] and Rex and Moore,[85] although since revealed as possessing conceptual frailty, has been influential. For geographers, the distribution level with its proximity to traditional research at the local interface has obvious appeal. The housing manager deciding where to locate problem families and the building society manager deciding where not to allocate mortgages provide some immediate antecedents to spatial outcomes.

Most geographical studies recognize the realities of the allocative system and the mediators who run it. For the Marxists, the system works in the interest of capital. Roweis and Scott [86] identify a 'class monopoly' arising from the alliance of finance capital and real estate interest in the Canadian housing market. This monopoly works through red-lining, mortgage-fixing and the rest to manipulate the housing market. Harvey [87] casts the outcomes in the Baltimore housing market in the context of macro-structures but also recognizes 'taps and regulators' in the allocative system.

The issue of how the allocative system works is important but more critical for the managerial thesis is the question of how much discretion the managers or gatekeepers retain. Problems associated with the concept of managerialism [88] are well-known but many geographers regard the issue as worthy of more research. As Pahl suggests, 'specific agents ultimately control and allocate resources. States may attempt to centralize in the interests of equality or efficiency but discretion must remain at all levels.' [89] Whereas decision-makers have to be viewed in structural contexts, influenced by the policies of the institutions they serve, a refusal to treat them as puppets seems closer to the realities of urban life. Managerialism provides a useful way of penetrating the complex of relationships that structure urban areas at the points of contact between consumers and the allocators of scarce resources; it may help to expose both the allocative processes and the bases upon which they rest.

Conclusions

After a long period of slow change and a typical conservatism, urban geography has diversified considerably since the early 1960s. Each major new perspective has involved a critique but has also offered positive qualities which the sub-discipline has so far proved able to accommodate without disintegrating; Herbert and Johnston [90] suggested a branching model as the appropriate description for the framework which has evolved. Spatial analysis added a methodological rigour and scientific practice; radical geography has successfully argued the case for starting analysis from the organization of society rather than from the spatial expressions of inequality. Subjectivism with its affirmation of the significance of place has, in many ways, longer roots in geography and is allied to the arguments that an 'urban' analysis should be retained. In a phase of apparently competing paradigms, the need is for some bases for conciliations and positions which are sufficiently flexible for alternative perspectives to be accommodated within an overall framework.

In these respects the situation in urban geography offers striking parallels with that evidenced both in terms of general methodological issues in contemporary sociology, as in Eisenstadt and Curelaru's call for 'openings', [91] and also in the more specific applications of sociological perspectives to special fields such as criminology. [92] This points to a series of convergences in the social sciences at a methodological level as the various disciplines find themselves faced with the same issues and influenced by the same underlying philosophies. A further feature which may exist at the present time is that the time lags which often typified earlier innovations are less evident.

Geographers working with quantitative procedures in the spatial analysis paradigm have found little to interest them in recent sociology and it has been economics with its strong statistical basis which has offered the most valuable models and techniques. As a more general interest in the political economy approach develops, the potential for interchange again seems strongest in some forms of economic analysis allied with the political sciences. In this and other areas however the attractions of sociological perspectives to geographers are likely to remain strong. More generally there is persistent evidence that sociologists, geographers and others are playing significant roles in the identification, clarification, and development of the pervasive methodological and philosophical issues which face the social sciences. Whereas the writings of Castells [93] and others have general importance, those of geographers have added their own weight and dimension to the larger questions of urban analysis. [94] On more specific issues, geographers and sociologists have some ground to make up following the divergences in research practice which have been more typical of the last decade. The community studies theme which was a significant point of conflux has continued to interest geographers though sociologists have shown less interest in notions of 'community', at least as a territorial concept. Recent research by geographers into the subjective meanings of place may have something to offer in furtherance of this debate. It is from those sociologists who have continued to acknowledge the roles of place and space and who work at the interface between sociological and geographical concerns that geographers continue to derive positive advantage and look for a sustained exchange of ideas. Studies concerned with the emergence of 'problem areas' within cities and the associated roles of labelling theory; [95] studies of conflict theory and alternative views of classes in the context of the housing market; [96] and more direct attempts to incorporate spatial qualities into analyses of social space [97] are all examples of recent work by sociologists in this mode. In several study areas there is already clear evidence of the mutual advantage to be obtained by geographers and sociologists working on similar problems in different but related ways. Studies of ethnic minorities in Britain provide good evidence of such interaction of ideas and methodologies. [98]

The geographer's contribution to urban studies will continue to be distinguished by the attention which it focuses on the spatial dimension—on place, space and man/environment interaction. Most geographers would admit however that spatial processes in themselves are rarely explanatory processes; it is necessary to probe deeply into social, political, and economic forces at a variety of levels of analysis. This may take us some way towards a unified social science but will more likely see students of the city retain their disciplinary labels and identity whilst working in increasingly overlapping orbits to their mutual benefit and, hopefully, to those of the phenomena they seek to analyse.

Notes

1 I would like to acknowledge the extremely helpful comments offered by Jim Bohland, Carolyn Hock, and Chris Smith, all of the Department of Geography at the University of Oklahoma, on an earlier version of this article.

2 O. P. Williams, *Metropolitan Political Analysis, A Social Access Approach*, Free Press, New York, 1971; R. E. Pahl, *Whose City?*, Penguin, Harmondsworth, 1975.

3 S. N. Eisenstadt and M. Curelaru, *The Form of Sociology, Paradigms and Crises*, John Wiley, London, 1976.

4 P. Haggett, *Locational Analysis and Human Geography*, Edward Arnold, London, 1965.

5 R. Peet, 'The development of radical geography in the United States', *Progress in Human Geography* 1, 1977, pp. 64-87.

6 D. T. Herbert and R. J. Johnston (eds), *Social Areas in Cities*, John Wiley, London, 1978.

7 D. T. Herbert and R. J. Johnston (eds), *Geography and the Urban Environment*, vol. 1, John Wiley, London, 1978.

8 P. E. James, *All Possible Worlds: A History of Geographical Ideas*, The Odyssey Press, New York, 1972.

9 R. J. Chorley and P. Haggett, *Models in Geography*, Methuen, London, 1967, p. 34. See also P. Haggett, 'The spatial economy', *American*

Behavioural Scientist, 22, 1978, pp. 151-67, for a modified view.

10 D. T. Herbert and R. J. Johnston, *Geography and the Urban Environment*, op. cit., 1978.

11 H. Simon, *Models of Man: Social and Rational*, Stanford University Press, Stanford, California, 1957.

12 D. R. Stoddart, 'Kropotkin, Reclus, and "relevant" geography', *Area*, 7, 1975, pp. 188-90.

13 D. Harvey, *Social Justice and the City*, Edward Arnold, London, 1973.

14 D. M. Smith, *Human Geography: A Welfare Approach*, Edward Arnold, London, 1977.

15 S. A. Stouffer *et al.*, *Measurement and Prediction, Studies in Social Psychology in World War 2*, Princeton University Press, Princeton, New Jersey, 1950.

16 P. F. Lazarsfeld, B. Berelson and H. Gaudet, *The People's Choice*, Columbia University Press, New York, 1944.

17 P. E. James, op. cit., 1972.

18 W. Christaller, *Central Places in Southern Germany*, Fischer, Jena, 1933; and A. Lösch, *Economics of Location*, Yale University Press, New Haven, 1954.

19 A. G. Wilson, 'Theoretical Geography: Some Speculations', *Transactions, Institute of British Geographers*, 57, 1972, pp. 31-44.

20 D. Harvey, *Explanation in Geography*, Edward Arnold, London, 1972.

21 J. D. Nystuen, *Identification of Some Fundamental Spatial Concepts*, Papers of Michigan Academy of Science, 57, 1963, pp. 401-22.

22 D. Gregory, *Ideology, Science and Human Geography*, Hutchinson, London, 1978.

23 W. A. Kirk, 'Problems of geography', *Geography*, 48, 1963, pp. 257-71.

24 D. Lowenthal, 'Geography, experience and imagination: towards a geographical epistemology', *Annals,* Association of American Geographers, 51, 1961, pp. 244-60.

25 J. Wolpert, 'Behavioural aspects of the decision to migrate', *Papers Regional Science Association*, 15, 1965, pp. 159-69.

26 D. Ley, 'Social geography and the "taken-for-granted" world', *Transactions, Institute of British Geographers*, new series 2, 1977, pp. 498-512.

27 B. T. Robson, 'Houses and People in the City: Editorial Introduction', *Transactions, Institute of British Geographers*, new series, vol. 1, no. 1, 1976, p. 1.

28 R. Peet, op. cit., 1977.

29 R. R. Cox, *Conflict, Power and Politics in the City*, McGraw Hill, New York, 1973.

30 R. A. Sayer, 'A Critique of Urban Modelling', *Progress in Planning*, 6, 1976, Pergamon, Oxford.

31 R. E. Dickinson, 'The distribution and functions of the smaller urban settlements of East Anglia', *Geography*, 7, 1932, pp. 19-31.

32 L. S. Bourne and J. W. Simmons (eds), *Systems of Cities: Readings on Structure, Growth and Policy*, Oxford University Press, New York, 1978.

33 C. D. Harris and E. L. Ullman, 'The nature of cities', *Annals*, American Academy of Political and Social Sciences, 242, 1945, pp. 7-17.

34 D. T. Herbert, *Urban Geography: A Social Perspective*, David & Charles, Newton Abbot, 1972.

David T. Herbert

35 G. C. K. Peach (ed.), *Urban Social Segregation*, Longman, Harlow, 1976.
36 J. E. Vance, *This Scene of Man: The Role and Structure of the City in the Geography of Western Civilization*, Harper & Row, New York, 1977.
37 J. E. Vance, 'Geography and the study of cities', *American Behavioural Scientist*, 22, 1978, pp. 131-49, offers some estimates of this growth.
38 D. T. Herbert and R. J. Johnston, *Geography and the Urban Environment*, op. cit., 1978.
39 D. T. Herbert and S. de Silva, 'Social dimensions of a non-western city: a factorial ecology of Colombo', *Cambria*, 1, 1974, p. 139-58; G. Weclawowicz, 'The structure of socio-economic space in Warsaw, 1931 and 1970: a study in factorial ecology', in F.E.I. Hamilton and R. French (eds), *The Socialist City*, John Wiley, London, 1979, pp. 387-423; W. K. D. Davies, 'Alternative factorial solutions and urban social structure: a data analytical exploration of Calgary in 1971', *Canadian Geographer*, 22, 1978, pp. 273-97; R. J. Johnston, 'On the characterisation of urban social areas', *Tijdschrift voor Economische en Sociale Geografie*, 70, 1979, pp. 232-8.
40 R. Bauer (ed.) *Social Indicators*, MIT Press, Cambridge, Mass., 1966.
41 D. G. Pringle, 'The social indicators approach to the study of urban social problems', unpublished paper, St Patrick's College, Maynooth, Eire, 1979.
42 P. L. Knox, *Social Well-being: A Spatial Perspective*, Oxford University Press, London, 1975.
43 F. W. Boal, P. Doherty and D. G. Pringle, *Social Problems in the Belfast Urban Area: An Exploratory Study*, Queen Mary College, Occasional Papers in Geography 12, London, 1978.
44 J. Eyles, 'Area-based policies for the inner city: context, problems and prospects', in D. T. Herbert and D. M. Smith (eds), *Social Problems and the City*, Oxford University Press, London, 1979, pp. 225-43.
45 J. A. Giggs, 'The distribution of schizophrenics in Nottingham', *Transactions, Institute of British Geographers*, 59, 1973, pp. 55-76.
46 D. T. Herbert, 'The study of delinquency areas: a social geographical approach', *Transactions, Institute of British Geographers*, new series 1, 1976, pp. 472-92.
47 P. A. Rossi, *Why Families Move*, Free Press, Glencoe, Illinois, 1955.
48 D. T. Herbert, 'Residential mobility and preference: a study of Swansea', *Institute of British Geographers*, Special Publication no. 5, 1973, pp. 103-21.
49 L. A. Brown and E. G. Moore, 'Intra-urban migration: an actor-oriented framework', *Geografiska Annaler B*, 52, 1970, pp. 1-13.
50 J. Rex and R. Moore, *Race, Community and Conflict*, Oxford University Press, London, 1967.
51 J. Wolpert, A. Mumphrey and J. Seley, *Metropolitan Neighbourhoods: Participation and Conflict over Change*, Association of American Geographers, Resource Paper 6, 1972.
52 D. T. Herbert and D. J. Evans, 'Urban sub-areas as sampling frameworks for social survey', *Town Planning Review*, 45, 1974, pp. 171-88.
53 W. Firey, *Land-use in Central Boston*, Harvard University Press, Cambridge, Mass., 1947.

54 E. Jones, *Social Geography of Belfast*, Oxford University Press, London, 1960.
55 A. Buttimer, 'Grasping the dynamism of the life world', *Annals, Association of American Geographers*, 66, 1976, pp. 277-92.
56 D. Ley and R. Cybriwsky, 'Urban graffiti as territorial markers', *Annals, Association of American Geographers*, 64, 1974, pp. 491-505.
57 K. Boulding, *The Image: Knowledge in Life and Society*, University of Michigan Press, Ann Arbor, Michigan, 1956.
58 R. M. Downs, 'Geographic space perception: past approaches and future prospects', in C. Board *et al.* (eds), *Progress in Geography*, 2, 1970, pp. 65-108.
59 D. T. Herbert and D. M. Smith (eds), *Social Problems and the City: Geographical Perspectives*, Oxford University Press, London, 1979.
60 D. T. Herbert and R. J. Johnston, *Social Areas in Cities*, op. cit., 1978.
61 C. Tiebout, 'A pure theory of local expenditures', *Journal of Political Economy*, 64, 1956, pp. 416-24.
62 K. R. Cox, op. cit., 1973.
63 T. Carlstein, D. Parkes and N. Thrift (eds), *Timing Space and Spacing Time*, Edward Arnold, London, 1978.
64 A. Pred, 'The academic past through a time-geographic looking glass', *Annals*, Association of American Geographers, 69, 1979, pp. 175-80.
65 P. Tranter and D. N. Parkes, 'Time-image in urban space', *Area*, II, 1979, pp. 115-20.
66 J. Eyles, op. cit., 1979.
67 S. Pinch, 'Territorial justice in the city: a case study of social services for the elderly in Greater London', in D. T. Herbert and D. M. Smith, op. cit., 1979, pp. 201-23.
68 B. P. Davies, *Social Needs and Resources in Local Services*, Michael Joseph, London, 1968.
69 G. Rushton, *Optimal Location of Facilities*, Compress Inc., Hanover, New Hampshire, 1979.
70 N. Poulantzas, *Classes in Contemporary Capitalism*, New Left Books, London, 1975.
71 R. Peet, op. cit., 1977.
72 S. T. Roweis and A. J. Scott, 'The urban land question', in K. R. Cox (ed.), *Urbanization and Conflict in Market Societies*, Maaroufa Press, Chicago, 1978, p. 47.
73 D. Harvey, 'Labor, capital, and class struggles around the built environment in advanced capitalist societies', in K. R. Cox (ed.), op. cit., 1978, p. 9.
74 R. A. Walker: 'The Transformation of Urban Structure in the Nineteenth Century and the Beginning of Urbanization', in K. R. Cox (ed.), op. cit., 1978, p. 169.
75 S. T. Roweis and A. J. Scott, op. cit., 1978, p. 73.
76 R. A. Sayer, 'Understanding urban models versus understanding cities', *Environment and Planning*, A, II, 1979, pp. 853-62.
77 B. Hindess, *The Use of Official Statistics in Sociology*, Macmillan, London, 1973.
78 D. Harvey, 'Government policies, financial institutions and neighborhood change in United States cities', in M. Harloe (ed.), *Captive Cities*, John Wiley, London, 1977, p. 126.

79 R. A. Walker, op. cit., 1978, p. 205.
80 F. E. I. Hamilton, 'Multi-national enterprise and the European Econo-mic Community', *Tijdschrift voor Economische en Sociale Geografie*, 67, 1976, pp. 258-78.
81 D. B. Massey and R. A. Meegan, 'Industrial restructuring versus the cities', *Urban Studies*, 15, 1978, pp. 273-97.
82 D. Harvey, op. cit., 1977.
83 P. Williams, 'Urban managerialism: a concept of relevance', *Area*, 10, 1978, pp. 236-40.
84 R. E. Pahl, op. cit., 1975.
85 J. Rex and R. Moore, op. cit., 1967.
86 S. T. Roweis and A. J. Scott, op. cit., 1978.
87 D. Harvey, op. cit., 1977.
88 P. Norman, 'Managerialism: a Review of Recent Work', *Centre for Environmental Studies*, CP 14, London.
89 R. E. Pahl, 'Socio-political Factors in Resource Allocation', in D. T. Herbert and D. M. Smith, op. cit., 1979, p. 43.
90 D. T. Herbert and R. J. Johnston, *Geography and the Urban Environ-ment*, op. cit., 1978.
91 S. N. Eisenstadt and M. Curelaru, op. cit., 1976.
92 I. Taylor, P. Walton and J. Young, *The New Criminology*, Routledge & Kegan Paul, London, 1973.
93 M. Castells, *City, Class and Power*, St Martin's Press, New York, 1978.
94 D. Harvey, *Social Justice and the City*, Edward Arnold, London, 1973; D. Gregory, *Ideology, Science, and Human Geography*, Hutchinson, London, 1978.
95 S. Damer, 'Wine Alley, the sociology of a dreadful enclosure', *Sociologi-cal Review*, 22, 1974, pp. 221-48.
96 J. Rex and R. Moore, op. cit., 1967.
97 R. E. Pahl, *Whose City?*, Penguin, Harmondsworth, 1975.
98 See, for example, G. C. K. Peach, S. W. Winchester and R. I. Woods, 'The distribution of coloured immigrants in Britain', in G. Gappert and H. M. Rose (eds), *The Social Economy of Cities*, Sage, New York, 1975, pp. 395-414.